Rick Simpson

PHOENIX TEARS

THE RICK SIMPSON STORY

Title:
The Rick Simpson Story

Written by:
Rick Simpson

Cover:
Den Beauvais

Editor:
Alexander Xpact

Printing office:
Tiskara Sušak, Rijeka

Publisher:
Alexander Xpact
Self published
Krk, 2014

A CIP catalogue record for this book is available from Rijeka University Library
under the number 130508041

ISBN 978-953-58247-0-1

Rick Simpson would like to thank all who were involved in getting this
book ready for publication

DISCLAIMER
We bear no responsibility if this information is misused and it is provided for educational purposes only.

CONTENTS

PREFACE

To more clearly explain what is going on in our world, and why the cure for so many diseases like cancer has been held back, the easiest way to sum it up would be to understand what follows. Around one hundred years ago, if you had been extremely wealthy and powerful, much like the Rockefellers and Rothschild's for example and yet you desired more power, how could you achieve your goals?

To fulfill your needs it would be helpful if people in political circles and those who work in the legal, medical, and educational systems etc. would go along with your agenda. With politicians, doctors, lawyers, police officers, teachers, and others who have positions of public trust acting on your behalf, success would virtually be guaranteed, but how could this be accomplished?

Since those who are in political power make the laws and control the different systems in each country, the first thing you would have to do, is get the political parties and the governments they form to comply with your plans. If you saw to it that money was funnelled into the right pockets in political circles, or promises were made which they found appealing, it would do much to help them see things your way. After those in powerful positions in politics have accepted your bribes and swayed their parties to work on your behalf, they can do little else but continue to serve you. Then, no matter what political party is in power, you will always have friends in high places.

Once governments are caught up in the corruption they have allowed you and others like you to create, there is no going back, since what governments have already done in the past to please the rich and powerful could be exposed. Rather than face ridicule, governments will then continue to see that your aims are met and they will use all their power, to change the different systems they control to suit your needs. I know how terrible all this sounds but it is more than clear that governments care nothing about those they are supposed to serve. This fact is undeniable when you look at the way they bend over backwards to please their rich friends. Truly, it can be said that as a result of corruption the governments of today are completely enslaved by the money masters who stand in the shadows.

Now that you have the support of the political parties and governments you require to act on your behalf, how were they to coerce people from respected professions into going along with your schemes. When it should be clear to any rational human that what you have in mind is designed to bring harm and has nothing to do with the best interests of the public? This can be accomplished by ensuring that those with the 'correct' mindset fill positions of public trust. We call such people yes-men, because they are more than willing to support anything the government desires, no matter how outrageous it may seem, as long as they are well rewarded. Individuals with these traits have no empathy for others and care only about what is best for themselves. If you or those you care about are suffering, it is of little concern to them. However, they are very good at giving the impression that they are normal caring human beings. Those in professions such as politics, medicine, or law etc. have positions of trust in our society, but sadly it can hardly be said that they deserve our admiration.

It is very hard for most of us to comprehend just how evil and deceptive many so-called humans can often be, especially when they are trying to protect their own best interests. In reality, a large number of those who populate this planet are behaving little differently than psychopaths, who are willing to do anything to maintain their positions and incomes, no matter how many innocent people are harmed by their actions. When those we put our trust in, such as doctors, are confronted about the insane treatments they provide, their standard reply is that they are just following the guidelines which have been put in place or that they are simply "doing their jobs."

Once the roles of individuals in many different professions are examined, the harm they are causing becomes quite clear. Yet, most of those who work in these fields will contend that they are completely innocent and bear no responsibility. In some respects, people who work in professions like medicine do have an excuse, since many years ago those with great wealth took over the institutions in which they received their training. Instead of teaching individuals who were attending medical schools, about harmless effective medicines that can be produced from nature. People who are trained in these institutions are taught to prescribe harmful and dangerous substances that were manufactured from chemicals and poisons, which were produced in factories owned by the rich and powerful who often fund the medical schools they are attending.

This so-called form of medicine is known as the allopathic approach to healing and is not, in reality, designed to heal anyone. This insane method of treating those with medical problems has caused untold suffering throughout the world, but there was certainly no shortage of profit. Any highly trained medical professional, should understand the ineffective and harmful nature of the substances used in the allopathic approach to medicine, which the greed of the rich have inspired. But for the most part, doctors seem more than happy to continue harming their patients and like to pretend that there is no other way in which help can be provided.

What do people who work in the medical profession tell themselves before giving a child with cancer massive doses of poison? No one with any sound medical knowledge or ethics would ever dream of doing such a thing, because common sense itself should be enough to prevent them from doing so. Still, doctors provide these so-called treatments every day and have no trouble sleeping or living with themselves. One would think, since doctors have such a dismal success rate with the use of these absurd treatments, that sooner or later they would awaken to the fact that what they have been doing is simply madness and not medicine.

These deadly chemo and radiation treatments that patients with cancer and other serious conditions are subjected to, have been used despite their destructive effects for decades and, as yet, the medical systems worldwide show no sign of bringing their use to an end. If there really were no rational alternatives that are safe and effective such as hemp oil to treat these patients, then what the medical system has been doing might be forgiven. But unfortunately for those who work in the field of medicine, this is not the case and, sadly, the medical industry we have today could hardly be said to be about easing human suffering. The big money concerns have rejected and restricted the medicinal use of cannabis hemp from those who inhabit this earth, so they could sell us their extremely overpriced chemicals and poisons.

Since hemp has such an extensive history of medicinal use and a safety record that is beyond compare, this in itself should prove just how much we are all being manipulated by our governments and the doctors we have been taught to put our trust in. Extracts produced from medicinal varieties of cannabis hemp are the most medicinally active substances known to man and to even try to practice medicine without their use defies all forms of rational thinking. If we allow these extracts to remain restricted for medical use, then in reality it can only be said that indeed we do not even have a medical system that is designed to reduce human suffering. Under these circumstances, those who develop serious medical problems will continue to suffer and die needlessly, while drug companies and their shareholders reap the profits. I cannot speak for the rest of the human race, but I think most will find what they are doing to be intolerable and will join with me and many others to bring this travesty to an end.

Another prime example of who cannot be trusted, would be most of those who work in law enforcement at the present time. When I was young, I was taught that people who work in this profession, are supposed to be our friends, but sadly the perceptions of my youth no longer ring true. Maybe Marshall Dillon on the old television series Gunsmoke was a fair and just man, but that can hardly be said of many law enforcement officers we have to deal with today. There is little kindness or compassion in the police officers we come in contact with at present; for the most part they are just obnoxious bullies with guns. Of course, this type of behavior suits the government's needs, because they want the public to be living in fear, and so, to help accomplish this, such individuals are hired to police our society. The last police officer I came into contact with, who I considered to be good at his job was in 1962 and I haven't come into contact with anyone of this caliber, who works in law enforcement since that time.

Think about the experiences you have had with the police over the years. Do you believe they handled the role they are playing well and did they earn your respect? I think most of us would answer that question with a resounding 'No', which makes it obvious we should not be at the mercy of such individuals, and to make matters even worse, we are the ones who pay their salaries. As I stated, many in positions of public trust are behaving irrationally and actually help their governments commit crimes against humanity, to further the insane agendas of the rich and powerful. They cannot or will not accept the fact that what they are doing is completely wrong, for this would shatter the glowing image they have of themselves and their professions. Still, it is assumed that we as good citizens, must never question their authority and should have unlimited respect and admiration for the wonderful job they are doing.

If we speak out against the horrible deeds they are responsible for, they then classify us as troublemakers and accuse those who see them for what they really are, as being conspiracy nuts. But those who utter statements like "Conspiracies do not exist," are not doing this because it isn't true. They are simply making such claims to hide their own agendas. How could any rational person look at the world we are living in and say that no one is conspiring against our wellbeing? In reality, if that were true, then why has our world become so toxic? Were we the ones who did this, or was it caused by the profit making policies imposed upon us by the big money concerns? If you happen to be a person who realizes things are not quite right in our world, please read on and I will endeavor to expose the real truth. Once you go through the contents of this book, I am sure most will arrive at the same conclusions that I have. Indeed, we are all trying to exist in a disgusting twisted reality that has been forced upon us by our own fellow-man, so that they might profit from our misfortune.

I have learned a great deal about our world and the people who are running it, but my focus is also elsewhere. Since I stumbled on the truth about the hemp plant, most of my time is now consumed in trying to bring this medical wonder to the attention of the general public. Many seem to think that I should be trying to prove this to doctors but in reality I gave up trying to prove anything to them a long time ago and I could care less what they think. How could I be expected to make those who work in the medical system acknowledge the reality in what I am saying, when obviously it is in their best interests to ignore the truth?

The same holds true for governments and all they control, for I have already been to everyone in authority about this issue and they have done nothing. Since they did not respond in the proper way, their lies and deceptions became more than obvious. Those we are supposed to put our trust in have failed us, so I am bringing what I have learned to the attention of the general public. In the situation we are in, with no one willing to step forward and defend our rights as human beings, I have put my faith in the public to bring about the changes, which are necessary by any means at their disposal.

Most of those employed in the professions I have mentioned, will not enjoy reading what I have to say about their ethics. But the truth must be told, if we are to evolve into a species that is worth saving. In reality, if nothing is done, we are little more than a virus, which is trying to infect the whole universe with our twisted sense of reasoning. In the beginning, my aim was simply to make the medical system accountable for their actions. This led me to discover there is much more wrong with our society than just the doctors stepping out of line. I soon came to the realization that our whole way of life is based on propaganda and lies, which were put in place by those who wish to keep us enslaved. This is not the path, the human race is supposed to be on and, clearly, if we continue, it will bring about our destruction.

After I suffered a head injury in 1997, I went through a very bad time with the medical system and, in the end, it was obvious that I had been treated improperly. Damage from my injury and the pills I was given made it impossible for me to think clearly, while they had me under treatment. One of the major problems I suffered with was high blood pressure. Yet, strangely, not one doctor during that five-year period ever prescribed medication to bring it under control. It seems they were all just sitting around waiting for me to explode and at the time I was in such bad shape mentally I didn't even realize what they were doing. It would have been bad enough if only one doctor had neglected to do something about my condition, but instead none of the doctors I saw even suggested I should take blood pressure medication. I don't consider what they were doing to be the practice of medicine and I am quite convinced they were all just waiting for me to die. After what I had learned, it became clear that most doctors would probably do the same if you or practically anyone else were in my place. Doctors are supposed to be healers, but they made it more than obvious to me that most of us could get better medical advice from an auto mechanic. I found what they were doing in my case to be particularly sinister, because they knew my mental faculties were not functioning properly.

Since we put our lives in the hands of these people, shouldn't we be examining the services they provide more closely? Could what they have been doing be considered mass murder? From my perspective, I feel that this could well be the case and if you had gone through what I experienced, I think you would feel the same. But it is not only the doctors who are working against us, it is all the systems that are under governmental control which pose a threat to our wellbeing. Those in positions we have been taught to respect are by no means trustworthy, but are they really at fault for what they have been programmed to believe? People who work in these professions have definitely been rejecting reality for a very long time, but could the same not be said, about the rest of us as well? I really don't think it would serve any purpose to seek retribution, unless the system continues to ignore the needs of the public. In the end, we all have to recognize ourselves as being the somewhat feeble-minded species we have proven ourselves to be and accept the fact that we are more than susceptible to manipulation.

If we do this in a rational way, there would be no need for bloodshed and we should be able to build a solid foundation that would enable us to make a new beginning. I tend to look at the situation we are in, somewhat in the same way that Gandhi did when he taught the Indian people and the rest of the world, the power of passive resistance. All we have to do is stand as one and let the system know that we the human race, will no longer go along with their insanity. I hope this method achieves success, since it would be better for all concerned, if no harm comes to anyone. If not, then we can expect to see a terrible confrontation, between ourselves and those who think they have the right to guide our destiny.

If those who are in control at present refuse to change their attitudes and intend to carry on with this madness, then the public will be left with no option, other than to use violence to bring what they have been doing, to an end and that is something I hope we can avoid. Surely, by now we have all learned from our own history that violence solves nothing and should only be used, as a last resort to protect ourselves. So, from my point of view, what is to happen in the near future depends on how those who have been giving the human race all this grief react. If those presently in control work with us, then we should be able to build a better world in which we all can live in health and happiness. But if they choose to do otherwise, I'm afraid, then just like the line from one of Clint Eastwood's movies states, "Hell's coming to dinner".

The mega rich have access to deadly technologies that we cannot even dream of and if they feel threatened, these horrors could be turned loose upon us all. Could the wealthy be heartless enough to start a pandemic that would end the lives of vast numbers who populate our earth? Judging by what is going on presently, I think this is a distinct possibility. If anything out of the ordinary should arise, here are the names of some top banking families, which will probably be responsible: Rothschild, Rockefeller, Warburg, Morgan, Hambros, Lazard, Erlanger, Fould, Schroder, Selingman, Speyers, Mallet, Mirabaud, and there are also others. The way I look at it, if they try to bring about our destruction, then, under these circumstances, the least we can do is the same for them.

I do not want to see things end up like this, but if the rich and powerful insist, I certainly think if we choose to do so that we have the numbers to defeat them and put them in their place. If indeed it does go this way, many will probably perish, but we will rid ourselves of these corrupted governments and the control, which the wealthy elite have been exercising over our existence. Many of us are no longer in a stupor over what the mega rich have been doing and we know the individuals against whom our anger should be directed. We can only turn the other cheek for so long, so if it is violence and destruction the rich want, then that is what they will have, but a good portion of it will be directed towards them and their families as well. It is my hope that the start of the new age we are entering will not begin like this, but if the rich want to do it the hard way, it is their choice.

I am sure many will have whatever faith they had in our system shattered, as they are reading this book and for quite some time, there will be those who will find it inconceivable that these events even took place. But everything you are about to read, regarding this medicine and the corruption which stands in the way of its use is the honest truth , and once you look into the facts for yourself, this will give you all the proof you need. I hope what you are learning will help you to avoid the nightmare, which I went through, and I am sure it will be of great benefit to both you and your loved ones. Knowledge is power, so please arm yourself well with the facts you have gathered, then let's get together and make this world a better place for everyone.

DEDICATION

I would like to dedicate this book to three of the most important people who have shaped my life. Unfortunately, two of these wonderful individuals have already passed on, so I will have to dedicate what I have written to their memory. Those I wish to honor are my mother and father and the late great Jack Herer. My parents endowed me with the guidance I needed to become a rational compassionate human being and Jack Herer provided much of the knowledge I required to see how this world could be changed for the benefit of us all.

Rick Simpson, June 2012

POINTS TO PONDER

There are a few basic things that should be understood by anyone reading this book, so please take the time to go over the information below.

1) The oil currently available in health food stores and elsewhere is not hemp oil, it is really hemp seed oil. This has caused a great deal of confusion and although hemp seed oil is very good for you, it does not have the healing abilities of extracts produced from high-grade resinous varieties of the hemp plant itself.

A few years after I started supplying this medication, I began to be contacted by hemp seed oil suppliers that were upset with the name I gave this substance. Some even went so far as to say that I was doing great damage to their industry, but that was not my intent and I cannot imagine why curing cancer with the use of the essential oil of the hemp plant could harm their businesses. Throughout history, farmers who grew this plant called it hemp, so when I produced the essential oil from different varieties of hemp, naturally I called it hemp oil. I really don't see how my use of this term could harm the businesses of those who produce hemp seed oil. If anything, I expect it would bring more sales and attention to what they are manufacturing. The main problem here is that they are mislabeling their oils and I see no reason why they should not be calling the oils they produce what it truly is, hemp seed oil. I do not like to see complaints such as this, coming from those who are producing hemp products, and to me, those who voice these objections are simply trying to waste my time.

Anyone who manufactures goods from this plant should be very proud of what they are doing, since they are working in an industry that is earth-friendly and of great benefit to mankind. From my perspective, I think we all should be standing together supporting the use of this plant in every way possible. The important issue here is that everyone must be given the right to use hemp in whatever way they choose and the faster this occurs, the less mankind will have to suffer. We do not have time for any more nonsense and doubletalk; we must begin to heal both ourselves and this planet, if we are to give all forms of life a future.

2) Within this book, you will find terms like pot, grass, hemp, marijuana, cannabis hemp, industrial hemp, cannabis indica, cannabis sativa etc. These are all terms which can be used to describe the hemp plant or the leaf and bud material which it produces. Even many of the less resinous varieties, which are classified as industrial hemp, have been proven to have some medicinal benefits, although there is little resin present on the plants themselves. In the future if the subject is studied properly, even these low-grade strains might have the ability to provide oils, which are effective in the

treatment of some conditions. But while we are waiting for all the medicinal wonders this plant holds to be exposed, there is no reason that the healing should not begin immediately.

At present, there are hundreds of strong medicinal varieties available and if you look into the subject, I am sure you will be able to find many that will suit your needs. Some medicinal types of hemp have outrageous names but don't let the names of some of these varieties throw you off, look at the information many seed companies make available about the medicinal benefits different varieties can provide. If you are planning to grow your own for medical purposes, now you should be able to select and grow a strain that is right for you with little difficulty. There are a tremendous number of different varieties and their genetics for medicinal use can vary a great deal, so please take your time, and look into the issue carefully. Once you understand the subject, you will come to realize that all the bogus information our governments and others have provided indeed has no basis in fact and was simply designed to keep us all misinformed. You will find dosage instructions in the epilogue and information on how to produce the oil properly at the end of the book and all this information, is also available on our website at www.phoenixtears.ca.

CHAPTER 1
CHILD OF A BYGONE ERA

I definitely was not the most likely person to become a hemp activist, nor was it very probable that I would discover a harmless natural medication that could help to heal mankind. But life is full of unknowns and one often doesn't know what path destiny will take them down.

I was brought into this world on November 30, 1949 at All Saints Hospital in Springhill, Nova Scotia. The Canada of my youth bears little resemblance to the Canada of today or the world in which we live. Even the air we breathed seemed much different than the air we breathe at present. It still had the sweet scent of nature, which seems to be lacking now, and air pollution was practically unknown. At that time, people worked very hard to make a living but, for the most part, they were much more friendly and caring towards each other. To us the future seemed bright. In the 1950s and 1960s, crime was almost unheard of in Nova Scotia. People left their keys right in the ignition of their cars and it was rare for anyone, to even lock their homes. Crimes were something that happened in far-off distant places that we felt little or no connection with and for the most part this gave us a sense of security. I spent my early years in an area called Saltsprings, which is about four miles from the town of Springhill. When I was young, even just going to town was a big event.

In my youth, Springhill was a rough-and-tumble mining town. The miners worked hard and they played hard. If you were looking for trouble, you did not have to look far in Springhill to find someone who would accommodate you. I am not trying to give Springhill a bad reputation, for if your intentions were not good you would be met with the same, in most towns at that time. One must remember that it is a different era, of which I speak, and many things have changed a great deal over the years, but few for the better.

What I remember most about my childhood was the close connection the people who lived around our region had with each other. It seemed that every evening neighbors would drop by or we would go and visit with them. After Dad installed electricity to light our home in the early 1950s, a short time later, TV became all the rage. Around 1954, my father somehow scraped enough money together to purchase the first TV in the rural area where we were living at the time. At first, TV seemed wonderful. We had even more neighbors drop by in the evenings to visit and view the programming that was available on the small black and white television that now occupied a corner of our living room. In a short time, everyone purchased their own televisions and visits from neighbors became much less frequent.

It took me a great many years to realize it but television is probably one of the most misused and destructive devices ever invented. The role which media-induced apathy has played in breaking the connection we once had with each other is undeniable. Unfortunately, this device has also been instrumental in brainwashing the public at large. What we observe on television, we try to mimic in our everyday lives. The way most of us behave can best be described as "Monkey see, monkey wants, monkey do."

When I was a child, I was quite fortunate because my parents were very sensible and caring individuals. They never tried to ram religion down my throat and I was brought up to think freely. My father seemed to have no use for the government and he would often make statements I did not understand at the time. I remember him saying, "The biggest mistake we ever made after returning from World War II was that we didn't get together and go to Ottawa to set things straight." Individuals like my father realized even then that something should have been done, but much like today, people would not stand together to make it happen. At the time, I had little understanding of what my father was talking about and I thought his comments about our government might be somewhat irrational.

After four days of fighting in Normandy, Dad had been wounded by shrapnel from a German hand grenade that left him badly crippled for the rest of his life. Like so many others, he fought bravely for Canada and freedom but had become very disillusioned with those who were running our country. I think it's safe to say it was my father who planted the seed of distrust for government within me. What he taught me has much to do with the man I have become today. Throughout our lives, my father and I were very close but I must also add that I have a very kind and loving mother. Many values that were instilled in me were the result of her nurturing and I love her dearly. Good parents are truly a blessing.

During my childhood in the 1950s, many devastating occurrences rocked the town of Springhill. In 1956, there was a horrible explosion in the No. 4 coalmine, which resulted in many children I knew losing their fathers. In 1957, a fire consumed most of the business district on Main Street, putting many more individuals out of work. At the time, I was traveling every day by bus to attend school in town and, to my young mind, Springhill seemed as if it had been badly ravaged by war. In 1958, disaster struck again when a bump occurred in the No. 2 mine, which took many more lives. A bump or rock burst are terms that are used to describe a seismic event that occurs in a mine, which causes an explosive collapse of a wall or support pillars in the area being mined. If you are unlucky enough to be working in a coal mine when such an event takes place, there is a good chance you will not survive. Again, more children I knew lost their fathers and Springhill was left with few industries to provide employment. It appeared as if the town had become cursed. In no time, many people left the area to seek employment elsewhere and suddenly it seemed every second house was vacant.

In 1950, Springhill had a population close to 7000. By 1960, the population had been reduced to about half that number. It was obvious that if nothing could be done, Springhill would soon become a ghost town. Just when it seemed there was little hope that the town could ever recover, a new federal prison was built on the outskirts of Springhill and slowly the town began to revive.

When I was 12 years old, we lost our home in the country to fire. Dad then took what little insurance he had on the property and bought a home in Springhill. Of course, being a teenager, I was quite happy to be moving into town, but it took a little while for me to fit into my new environment. As always, a few bullies felt it was their duty to try to slap the new kid around. In most cases, this did not work out too well for them because my upbringing in the country had made me very strong for my size. Even at 12 years of age, I could lift just about anything a full-grown man could, so for the most part I was left alone.

Throughout my childhood up until the time when we moved into town and I went into Grade 7, I never opened a book to study the different subjects being taught and I made 100 or A+ on all of my exams. When I was in Grade 4, the teachers talked about advancing me and another student named Eric Hunter into Grade 6, missing the fifth grade altogether. For some reason, this did not take place, so Eric and I spent a year in each grade just like everyone else. It is hard for me to describe what happened to me in Grade 7.

I completely lost interest in school and barely passed into Grade 8. I remember telling myself upon entering the eighth grade that I had better wise up. Still, no matter how hard I tried, I just could not summon the interest required. My mind was always somewhere else. If I were attending school today, many learned doctors would say I was suffering from attention deficit disorder. They would then probably try to fill me full of drugs like Ritalin to treat this imaginary condition. Luckily for me, when I was in school, no one had ever heard of ADHD, but I do feel sorry for the children of today who must suffer the consequences of these so-called medications that are being forced upon them.

From my perspective at present, knowing that hemp oil is harmless, I think a medication like this would be better suited for a child that is overactive or has attention problems than the use of dangerous chemicals that could cause problems later in life. I have the feeling that if such a medication had been available when I was in school, I could have found it much easier to take in what they were trying to teach.

Of course, being a teenager, I had also started to notice all those developing females in my classes and no doubt this did play a role in distracting me. I spent two years in Grade 8 and passed into Grade 9 by the skin of my teeth. At first, I did do a little better in

Grade 9 but again I found maintaining any interest in schoolwork to be almost impossible. The only thing I enjoyed about attending school was our wood-working classes. That year, a new industrial arts teacher was brought in and he was a great instructor. So just before Christmas, I collected enough money from other students to get him 24 pints of beer as a present from the class.

About a month after Christmas, the rest of the teachers found out about the gift our class had given him and deemed it inappropriate. Three teachers walked into our class and started blasting us about the gift we had given him, so I then stood up and told them I was the one responsible, whereupon I was taken out into the hallway. They wanted to know how I had acquired the beer, since I was underage and I could not have purchased it myself. I then refused to tell them what they wished to know. Of course, this made them even more angry and they began to scream and shout at me. It appears their intention was to give me a good dressing down, but I had already heard enough.

I told them the only reason they were upset was because they had not received such a present themselves and if they treated their students a bit better, perhaps they would. At that point, I turned on my heel and walked out the door, leaving this form of academia behind forever. The man who supplied the beer to me is no longer with us, so I feel free to name him. Carmen "Pookie" Legere was the man who bought the beer. Since I refused to identify him, we remained friends right up until the day he died. Pookie was not a criminal for helping me get this present for our instructor and he is one of the most beloved and remembered citizens that Springhill ever produced.

Many people have fond memories of their school years but I was not one of them. To me, most of the time, going to school was a bore. I couldn't wait to see my time spent there come to an end. Possibly if I had been advanced, as they had talked about doing when I was in the fourth grade, I might have been able to maintain an interest, but this never occurred. I really can't put too much blame on the school system for my lack of attention, since it does seem to work for some students. Nevertheless, I do feel our system of education has failed to reach many young minds in the proper way and there must be a better approach. For me, the day I left school was a new beginning and I could not wait to become the proverbial working man.

I had just turned 16 a couple of months before I left school, so I was now at an age that would allow me to join the workforce. A few days after leaving school, I was hired to work with a crew of about 35 men who were clearing the trees off the right-of-way for the Trans-Canada Highway. I was paid the grand total of a dollar and ten cents an hour and most people of today cannot even imagine such work. We would shoulder logs that were often three times our own weight, then carry them through deep snow and tricky terrain to pile them up, sometimes as far as 75 meters from where we had shouldered them. This was bull work in the extreme and only the hardest workers were kept on the payroll. By May 1966, four months after I had started this job, there were only four of us left. Everyone else had either been injured, or they were laid off because they lacked the strength and stamina to do the work that was required.

I decided there was not much of a future in this line of work since at any time I could have been replaced by a yard horse or tractor that could have done a much better and more efficient job. The section of the highway we were to clear was just about done, so I decided it was time to look elsewhere for employment. My cousin David had gone to Toronto, Ontario a couple of years earlier and had been successful in finding work. Dave was three years older than I was. We had grown up together in the country and I thought of him more or less like an older brother. A great number of people from our area traveled to Toronto to find employment in that era. Going to the big city to seek our fortunes was a popular topic of conversation among my friends and often we talked about it for hours.

We all dreamed of buying nice cars and going somewhere that had more to offer, for at the time it seemed there was little to be had in our area. I knew it would be hard to leave because all my friends were here and I enjoyed the local dances and other events that I attended. Still, all things must come to an end and since there was little work available, Toronto seemed as if it could provide the answer. Dave had been doing well in Ontario and I thought the same might hold true for me, so off I went. A city the size of Toronto is quite a shock to someone who comes from a small town. Life there moved at a much quicker pace than it did in Springhill and it seemed there was always something to do or an event to attend.

When I left Springhill, to the best of my knowledge, there was no one smoking pot or doing drugs of any kind except alcohol. Although Springhill was a bit off the beaten track, we had heard about Yorkville, often called The Village, an area in Toronto known to be the heart of the drug scene at that time in Canada. Even though I had nothing to do with drugs, I was curious as to what it was all about. At the time, Yorkville contained many coffee shops and clubs like the Flick 88 and the Myna Bird club, in which I spent quite a bit of time. Yorkville also had the biggest cops I had ever seen in my life walking the streets, and they didn't mind pushing people around.

The police paid no attention to me because I was short-haired and clean-cut, but they were really giving the hippies a bad time. All you had to do was have long hair and you were an instant target for the police. It all seems silly today, for the drug scene at that time would certainly be considered very tame by today's standards. All I remember are a few young people sneaking around smoking a little pot and for some reason, the police were treating them as if they were dangerous criminals. All of this was very strange to me since I did not smoke pot myself, but the scene in Yorkville was lively enough that it kept me entertained for a while.

Then everything changed. I bought my first car and could never seem to make enough money to keep it on the road. Dad had warned me that I should put off buying a car for as long as possible but I paid no heed to his advice. Being young and headstrong, I refused to listen and, as usual, I had to learn everything the hard way. I only stayed in Toronto a little over a year and a half but it was a time I will always remember well.

In 1967, the Vietnam War was raging, so a friend and I were thinking about joining the American army to do our part. To us, it seemed this was our war. Dad had fought his in the 1940s and now I felt it was my turn. If I joined the American army, I could instantly become an American citizen. At the time, I thought America was the greatest country in the world, so joining the American military did sound inviting. If it had not been for the actions of a truly amazing man, I probably would have lost my life in a rice paddy or jungle somewhere in Vietnam.

Both my father and I had always been boxing fans and Muhammad Ali was my hero. I thought he was the greatest heavyweight that ever put on a pair of gloves and I still feel the same to this day. When Ali refused induction into the American military, it really got my attention and put a halt to my plans of joining the American army. I remember many people back then were calling him a coward but I looked at his refusal in a different way. Would a coward step into a boxing ring to take on some of the toughest men on this planet? In addition, if Ali had been willing to enter the military, it is highly unlikely he would have been put into battle anyway.

Ali was the reigning heavyweight champion of the world. The military would probably have put him on tour doing boxing exhibitions, much the same as they did with Joe Louis during World War II. It is very doubtful that the American government would put such a man in harm's way on a battlefield. Ali refused induction not because he was a coward but because he was against this horrible war and he was right. His strength of character changed my mind about Vietnam and this, in turn, may have saved my life. I will always feel indebted to Muhammad Ali for being the man he is. In my eyes, he was not only the greatest heavyweight boxer of all time, he was also someone who knew right from wrong and was obviously, a very wise man.

It was inevitable that sooner or later I would lace on a pair of boxing gloves and this happened a few months before I left Ontario to return home. I was strong as a bull but I led with my face and this caused a great deal of discomfort and swelling. Although I did suffer a bit during my early instruction, after a while I found my timing. Boxing is much like a dance and once you find your rhythm, you can become very good at it and quite dangerous. All of a sudden, you are sliding punches instead of catching them full force with your face. Now it is your opponent's turn to suffer, for you are no longer easy to hit and your reflexes allow you to score effective blows quite easily.

I always had great natural reflexes and a deep sense of rhythm. Now, suddenly, I could knock another man out with either hand. To me, speed bags were all right but I liked working with the heavy bag and that is where I learned to power punch. When you knock another man out with a left hook, you can feel the shudder from the impact of the blow travel down your own legs when the punch connects. It's wonderful to be in good shape and have such great control over what your body can do and to be able to deal with whatever punches your opponent can throw.

Still, at the same time, you have to realize you are no longer like a normal person who has not had such training. It is one thing to get into the ring and do sparring sessions with gloves on but you really have to watch yourself on the street. Without the padded gloves on your hands, someone can suffer a serious injury very easily. When we are young, we are all full of piss and vinegar. In the exuberance of youth, many think they cannot be hurt until they catch a solid punch in the ribs or face, at which time they learn their own limitations very quickly.

Just weeks before I decided to return home to Nova Scotia, a few of us got together and were fooling around with no gloves. Suddenly, this guy I didn't know came at me and I knocked him out with a very light left jab. I didn't even throw the punch hard and had been moving backwards away from him when the punch connected, but down he went. Luckily, as far as I know, he suffered no permanent damage, but this event actually scared me. I thought, "What if I had hit him like I normally would have?" Suddenly I started looking at my hands for what they now were, dangerous weapons that could bring about someone's death and get me in a great deal of trouble. Seeing the eyes of the man I had struck so lightly roll back in his head and watching him collapse was a very sobering experience.

A short time later, I returned to Nova Scotia, just about as mixed up as I had been when I departed for Toronto. Yet, with what I had learned, at least now I knew I could defend myself somewhat better. I also knew, none of us are as tough as we think we are and anyone can catch a punch the wrong way that can do them serious harm. From that time on, if I found myself in a fight, I usually used my strength and agility to best advantage and tried to avoid striking anyone full force, especially in the head. But too often it seems when you are young, no matter what you do, it can be almost impossible to avoid trouble. In such a situation, often a hard punch or two is the only thing that can get you out of harm's way.

While I think it is a good idea for everyone to have some knowledge of self-defense, I believe that it is more important to know when you must use your skills. If harming someone else can be avoided, that is usually the best course of action. Going to jail because you happen to have the ability to strike someone with enough force to do them damage or bring about their death is not a wise thing to do. No matter who you are, we all do stupid things sometimes and the right words are often enough to put such a person back on the right track. If everyone were to practice such restraint, this world would be a much better and safer place to live for us all.

CHAPTER 2
CANCER - RARE BUT DEADLY

Upon returning to Nova Scotia, it took me a few months to get used to the much slower pace of life again. We had a lot of snow in the winter of 1968 and I spent most of my time trying to get my old car to start or shoveling the snow from our driveway. I went out to a dance now and then but most evenings I could be found at Gib's Snack Bar, chewing the fat with my friends.

Within a week after my return to Springhill, I was at Gib's one night when a guy walked in, who had been a bit of a bully in the past, and thought he could still push me around. He was about five years older than I was but it took me only a few seconds to show him I was not the same kid he used to punch whenever he felt the urge. When he shoved me, I exploded and slapped him all over the snack bar. Within seconds, he knew I could hit him at will. He then quickly became very respectful of my new skills and threw his hands in the air. Over the coming weeks, the same thing happened to a couple of other guys who tried to get smart. At that time, my hands were so fast you couldn't even see them coming. Even though I did avoid using the power punches, most people quickly realized it was not a good idea to push my buttons.

During my absence, very little had changed around Springhill. Smoking pot was talked about but very few of us actually knew anyone who had tried the substance. Like most people at the time, we believed the negative propaganda about pot; many of us were afraid we would become addicted and that pot was bad for you. It almost seems funny, when I think back to those times, how innocent and misinformed we all were about the hemp plant.

As the months passed, practically all my friends became pot smokers. Of course, me being "much smarter" than most, I stuck with liquor as my drug of choice. At the time, this may have been a good thing for me, since the police in Nova Scotia began to behave in much the same way as the police in Toronto were acting in regards to pot. Many friends of mine were given a hard time by the police and quite a few wound up with criminal records, which made it very hard for them to find a good job. I could not understand why the police were so gung ho against pot smokers, since they were doing no harm and certainly causing no trouble. In addition, no one was dying or seemed to be addicted to the substance, so why were the police behaving like the Gestapo when it came to pot? At the time, it was a complete mystery to myself and many others.

One of the reasons I stayed away from smoking hemp was all the coughing involved with its use. Back then, I used to think that possibly my friends might be harming their lungs by smoking the substance, but in years to come I would learn the truth. When hemp is inhaled from a joint, it goes into the lungs and causes the person smoking it to cough and gag and if they are also cigarette smokers, it is usually even worse. What is actually taking place is really a benefit to those who enjoy its effects and it is simply making the person cough up toxins such as the tar that accumulates from smoking cigarettes. Studies have shown that the lungs of a pot smoker are every bit as clean as individuals who smoke nothing at all. In addition, those who smoke pot have less chance of getting lung cancer than even people who have never smoked anything in their lives.

Shortly after I returned to Springhill, I started going out with a girl who I often used to dance with before I left for Toronto. We got along well at the time and enjoyed being with each other, so in late 1968 we were married. Looking back now, to be married at such a young age made little sense, but that's what it is to be young and foolish. Many I knew that were around my age at the time were doing the same and it felt like the right thing to do. Still sadly, most of us had no idea what love and marriage was all about. I found work in Halifax and rented a small apartment in Dartmouth. We then began our married life together. Money was hard to come by, but since both of us had jobs and no children at the time, we could manage to make ends meet.

In the summer of 1969, we drove to Toronto to visit my cousin Dave and his wife. At the time, all seemed well and we had a good trip but shortly after returning home, I received word that Dave had cancer. I could not comprehend what I was being told and thought he had been misdiagnosed. How could a 22-year-old man who was the picture of health have cancer? I had heard of cancer but, up until that time, I never knew anyone who had suffered from this disease. Back then, cancer was something you didn't hear much about. I must admit, other than knowing that cancer was not a good thing to have, I knew little else about the condition.

David had noticed a tiny lump on his rib cage about the size of a pea and at first did not pay much attention, thinking that whatever was wrong would simply disappear in a short time. After a few weeks, when it had not gone away, he went to his doctor to have it checked. Dave had weighed about 200 pounds when he discovered the lump. After an extensive operation and treatment, his weight dropped to 120 pounds and his complexion became much darker. It was horrifying to see him in such condition, but the medical system said that they thought they had been successful in removing it all. Indeed, as time went on, he did seem to be making a very slow recovery from his ordeal but everyone could see he was not the man he had been.

While Dave was going through all of this, I was becoming a power engineer. I studied many courses on the subject and when I passed my fourth-class ticket, I was the youngest licensed engineer in Nova Scotia. This made it easier for me to find work but I still was not making much money and times were tight. In 1970, I decided to accept a job up

North, working on an isolation site. The pay was much better and I thought the extra money I would be making could help build a better life. The installation I worked on was a telecommunications site and it was part of the Pine Tree Line that was connected to the Dew Line, which was put in place to provide us with early warning in case of nuclear attack.

My duties included taking care of the boilers and heating system, plus doing whatever maintenance and repair work which was needed to keep their refrigeration systems running smoothly. Often I would go up to the communication center and talk to the men who worked there. One day, I just entered the communication center when the alarms went off and the big display they had lit up red. I asked the person who was working there what all this meant and he said, "We are on red alert. That means they are ready to launch missiles in the US." I replied, "Are you telling me that right now people in missile silos are sitting there with their fingers on the button?" He stated, "That's correct." I then asked him how often these red alerts occurred and his answer was, "All the time." I knew about the Cuban missile crisis and the showdown between the US and Russia but up until that moment in the communication center, I had never thought we were in constant danger of such a thing occurring. All of this came as a surprise that left me with a very uneasy feeling.

The time I spent in the North has left me with some great memories. I have seen how harsh Mother Nature could be in that bare and treeless land, but still there was a beauty to it all. I watched Arctic foxes in their natural environment and even fed one by hand. Then I got a close-up look at a polar bear. That creature looked to be the size of a Volkswagen Beetle and I hope I never encounter one again. After seven months in the North, I returned home to meet the daughter my wife had given birth to in my absence. I then decided I should try to find work in the Springhill area so we could settle down there. In a short time, I found employment as an engineer at All Saints Hospital, the same hospital where I had come into this world. I cannot say that they paid too well but at least I was living in the area where I had grown up and was fortunate enough to find steady employment nearby. Most of the people I had attended school with were long gone, since there was very little work to be found in our region, so I considered myself lucky.

It was around this time that I first experienced smoking bud material from the cannabis hemp plant. I was drinking beer at the old Buffalo Club in Springhill, when a friend asked if I would like to join him in his car to smoke a joint. The beer I had consumed loosened my inhibitions a bit, so I said, "Why not?" By that time, I knew from watching other people smoking pot that its effects were harmless and non-addictive, so what did I have to lose? Within minutes, I was out of the car and throwing up violently in a nearby field. Of course, I blamed the hemp I smoked instead of the beer I had consumed for making me sick and decided that maybe pot smoking did not agree with my system.

All around me, more and more people were smoking pot. The only problem was that more and more of them were going to jail and getting criminal records over their use of this plant. I have to say I was actually angry with the police over the way they treated pot smokers. I didn't use the substance myself, but I still felt that others who enjoyed its effects should not be treated as they were by the police.

In the summer of 1972, my cousin Dave came home on vacation. By this time, he had fought his way back up to 140 pounds and he did look a bit better. Then one day we were talking and he collapsed right in front of me. The first thing I thought was that the cancer had returned but I hoped this wasn't the case. Sure enough, when Dave arrived back in Toronto, the doctors told him he had six months to live and they could do nothing further to help. He had managed to save a bit of money, so he and his wife and young son moved back to Springhill to await his fate. It was very hard on the whole family watching him go downhill, but we knew of nothing we could do to help. Dave had a tremendous will to live and he fought this horrible disease with that will right to the end.

We watched his weight drop to the point that he weighed only about 55 pounds when he passed away on November 18, 1972. His death simply shattered me. I thought, "How could this be?" Dave had a good wife and a young son and had lived a very healthy and sensible lifestyle. How could a strong young man in his prime be struck down by this horrible disease and have to die such a terrible death? Even to the present day, when I think back upon this time, I still have a great deal of trouble coping with what took place. I was twelve days shy of my 23rd birthday when Dave passed away. He was the only person I had ever known at that time who had died from cancer. His death was my first experience with this dreadful disease but unfortunately, it would not be my last.

Two or three years after Dave's death I was pulling out of the hospital service entrance one day with my car. I had just tuned into our local radio station, CKDH in Amherst, when the announcer started to read a report. He stated the findings of a recent cancer study done in the United States had shown that THC, the active ingredient in marijuana, had been found to kill cancer cells. Of course, all during this report the announcer was laughing like a fool. I cannot explain why but when the word marijuana is used, it seems everyone feels obliged to try to turn whatever is being said into a joke.

Because of my cousin's recent death, what the announcer had stated certainly did catch my attention, but still it seemed so outlandish that I thought it must be just someone's sick sense of humor at play. As time went by, there were no other reports and I heard nothing more about THC killing cancer, so I thought what I had heard on the radio was a prank. I didn't know it at the time but the report was real and, as I was to find out later, it concerned the study that was done in the Cancer Center at Virginia Commonwealth University's School of Medicine in 1975. For some reason, this report stuck in my memory bank and I am very thankful it did. In the future, this information would be invaluable in easing people's suffering and saving many lives, including my own, but it would be almost thirty years later, before I put this information to good use.

In the 1970s, I fathered three children, but my wife and I were having more and more trouble putting up with each other. I had fallen into the habit of getting bombed on liquor about once a week, and my wife also had a few little flaws of her own. I was still spending quite a bit of time with my children but whenever possible I would be off to the woods and this did not sit too well with her. It's easy to put the blame on someone else when things go wrong but, in truth, it takes two to tango.

In the mid-1970s, I was studying to become a second-class engineer. It had taken years to get the experience needed to take such an exam and I was trying to prepare myself. I understood it all and could do the work but I lacked the math skills to take this exam and did not know where to turn. Charlie Huzar had recently been hired as an engineer at the hospital and we became friends. One day, I mentioned to him the trouble with math I was having. He just laughed and said, "Come to the boiler room some night when I'm on shift and I will explain it to you."

He made it sound easy but I had never understood the new math that was introduced about the time I left school. Algebra and all the rest made little sense to me and I really did doubt that Charlie could be of much help. The exam was coming up and I had nowhere to turn. So one night when Charlie was on duty, I went to the boiler room, but with low expectations of success. Within three hours, Charlie Huzar educated me in all the new math and then some. It's hard to explain but he just stepped me through it in a way that kept my interest. When I left the boiler room that night, anything they threw at me in the exam would now be a joke.

I spent almost four years in junior high school and learned nothing, then Charlie comes along and takes me right into college-level mathematics in three hours. Now I understood why the school system had not worked for me. It was not that I lacked the brainpower to do the work easily, what I lacked was proper instruction. Charlie Huzar was the greatest teacher I have ever met and he was a power engineer by trade. Perhaps it's safe to say Charlie missed his calling. I can only imagine what a difference it would have made in my life if I had met such a teacher when I was attending school.

When I was young, my father had always wanted me to be a doctor and I would have liked to have been able to fulfill his wishes. But how was I to do that when I was not able to understand the new math and I was unable to even finish junior high school? Meeting Charlie made a great difference in my life and we remained close friends until he died in his early 'seventies from cancer. A good friend and mentor lost to a disease that was curable even back then.

I remember one summer during the mid-'70s that I found particularly hard. About a dozen local people I knew well all died in car accidents. For years around our area, death by car accident had been quite rare but, all of a sudden, in a short span of time it seemed everyone I knew was being killed. Of course it was not pot that was killing them. In most cases, it was good old-fashioned alcohol and driving recklessly that was the culprit. Instead of focusing on the rampant drinking and driving problems on our highways and streets, the police continued to pursue anyone they suspected of being in possession of pot. Somewhere along the line, one would think the police would have realized that pot was not hurting anyone, but this did not occur.

In those days, people were trying more and more illicit drugs, and a good number of these substances could be very harmful. Unfortunately, when most saw someone under the influence of these substances, they usually gave pot the blame. Good old hemp seemed to get the credit for the actions of people on all different types of drugs, when really it was about the only thing that was being used recreationally that actually was not doing any harm. That is what a little well-placed propaganda and corruption can do and they did not hesitate to use such things to convince the public that pot is dangerous and that black is white.

During the 1970s, I had become an avid hunter and I took an interest in all types of shooting with handguns, rifles, shotguns, and just about anything else I could get my hands on. My father and I spent many wonderful afternoons target shooting in a nearby gravel pit and I have very fond memories of those days. Dad had one arm that was practically useless as a result of his war injury but he is the only person I have ever shot against that could often outdo me with a rifle. I was spending so much time in the woods that some friends even began to call me the Mad Trapper. Most years, I could easily shoot my limit of deer or other big game during the hunting season. Of course, the meat was not wasted and my family seemed to enjoy a steak or roast, if my hunt was successful.

At the time, I really felt I was doing nothing wrong. I was raised in the country, I had no fear of the woods and was quite at home even miles from the nearest roads. For me, hunting and roaming the woods was a very natural thing to do but today I often wish I had done it without all the needless killing. It's one thing to kill to survive, but I had a steady job and could have fed my family without killing all those innocent animals. Like many things, it seems, sometimes it takes a while to realize what is right and what is wrong.

In 1978, I left the hospital after seven years of service and found employment at the Maccan power plant. At the time, it seemed like a good move and the pay was much higher but the problem was it did not last. Within three years, the Maccan generating station was slated for closure. By this time, I had become a shift supervisor and was offered other positions at larger generating stations. The pay was much better than I would receive at the hospital, but I would have to move my family to a new location and buy another home. Therefore, I decided to return to work at the hospital if possible. Fortunately for me, a position needed to be filled in the boiler room and I was welcomed back with open arms. For some reason, I had always felt a close connection to this institution, so to me it was like returning home.

Shortly after I started working there again, my first marriage came to an end. After 13 years, it was time to throw in the towel. What I felt worst about was the effect I knew it was going to have on my children. Was it better to stay together when it was obvious that we couldn't get along and our marriage had become a farce? I thought trying to live like this would probably do more harm to my children than good, so we decided to bring our union to an end.

As anyone who has ever experienced the breakup of a marriage can attest, these can be very trying times. Then, just a few weeks after the breakup, along came wife number two. Like my first wife, I had known her for a long time, or thought I did. In the beginning, all was well and during the following summer of, 1982, I was remarried. I don't really know what happened but right after we were married, suddenly our relationship just seemed to fall apart. Up until we were married, we lived together and were very happy. The day after I married her, she seemed withdrawn and distant and suddenly it was like living with a total stranger. Within six months, the marriage ended and I now think it was best for both of us. I don't know if she ever found what she was looking for but it certainly seemed that we were never meant for each other. At that point, I guess you could say I gave up on the sport of marriage. It was very expensive and too hard on the head, so why go through the effort? From my perspective, I thought it would be much better to stay single and have no one to whom you must answer.

With everything that had been going on in my life over the last couple of years, believe me, I was in a pretty mixed-up state and my nerves were completely shot. The main problem was that I couldn't sleep no matter what I did, and I was starting to look like death warmed over. In desperation, I tried to medicate myself with a weak wine called Lonesome Charlie that was available at the time. Although the wine was easy to drink, it did nothing to improve my situation and was of no help in giving me the rest I required. Two young men from the neighborhood dropped in one day and were shocked by the way I looked. One of them pulled two joints from his pocket and put them on the table, telling me to smoke them, and then they left.

From my past experience with pot, I had no use for the substance and wondered why they had left the joints behind. Everyone knew I didn't use this substance, so why would they do such a thing? Back in the mid-1970s, my friend David and I had both eaten a marijuana brownie. It made me feel like I was paralyzed and after I had made my way to bed, I slept for 12 hours. Given the condition I was in, I felt I had nothing to lose, so

I smoked about half a joint and woke up 14 hours later. After what I had been through, this was exactly what I needed and the sleep this substance could provide was truly refreshing.

I smoked a small amount every night for about two weeks. After this time had elapsed, I looked much better and was pretty well back to normal. My opinion about the use of pot had changed radically but I still liked to drink, so I backed off on my use of the substance in favor of drinking liquor again. Other than the two-week bout with Lonesome Charlie, I really can't say I have ever looked at myself as being what could be considered a heavy drinker. I still liked to tie one on once a week but now the liquor was starting to exact a toll on how I felt. By the time I was 35 years old, the hangovers were unbearable and would last for days.

About this time, I bought a V-65 Honda Magna. A powerful motorcycle like this does not go well with booze, so I started eating hash and smoking a little pot instead of drinking. I called this motorcycle Big Thunder, because on some sports programming I had seen a 90-meter ski jump with that same name. I figured when anyone came off that jump, they must get about the same feeling I did when I rode this two-wheeled monster. That bike was like a rocket sled to ride but if I put a small piece of hash in my mouth, in about 45 minutes, the bike would slow down and I would drive this machine much more rationally. Many try to tell you that the effects of pot or hash impair your ability to drive but I would disagree. I rode thousands of miles on that bike under the influence of hash and pot and had absolutely no problems.

It seems when I had the substance in me, it was the only time I rode this bike properly. Without hash or pot in my system, every time I went somewhere on this motorcycle, I was just a blur. Therefore, in my case I am convinced that this substance caused me to operate this powerful machine in a much safer manner. I tried to ride the Magna one evening after four or five beers and almost succeeded in killing myself in my own driveway. That's what "impaired" means and nothing will show you more quickly than a motorcycle if you are in this condition. Once I became used to the effects of hash and pot, I respected the speed limits and no one could tell I had it in my system. Even if someone new to the effects of this substance is driving under its influence, it's doubtful if they will present much of a danger to the public. From what I have seen, those under the effects of this substance tend to drive much more carefully and slowly than those who have ingested pharmaceuticals or liquor, or even many who are taking nothing at all.

Alcohol affects your motor skills, as do many pharmaceuticals that people commonly use every day and still drive their cars. The effects of derivatives from the hemp plant do not necessarily impair your motor skills. If you are driving under the influence of hemp and have built up your tolerance for this medication, you are not impaired. From my experience, if anything, hemp can often improve a person's motor skills. Look at Ross Rebagliati, who won a gold medal at the Olympic games for snowboarding with hemp in his system. Could a person who is impaired even in a slight way win a gold medal? In the sport of snowboarding, you would not do very well if your motor skills were not functioning properly. Or ask any musician who smokes pot if their performance and creativity are not often enhanced by its use.

Again, what the system is trying to tell us about the danger of using hemp with regard to driving is far from the truth. I think if all drivers had a little hemp in their systems, there would be a lot less speeding, and road rage could disappear for the most part, since many drivers would be in a much better mood. Eating a small amount of hash or smoking a little hemp had reduced my consumption of liquor very dramatically. It seemed as time went on that I was turning more and more away from the use of alcohol. The hard liquor I once liked to drink had now become very distasteful and often made me deathly ill with its consumption. As for the substance that caused this to happen, at the time I was really using very little. I didn't indulge myself by using the substance during the working week and would wait for my days off to enjoy its effects. Even though I was buying it, the pot was costing me a whole lot less than the liquor it had replaced. At the time, I was only consuming a gram or two a week, so even though I purchased it, the cost was negligible. I was spending much more than that amount every week on cigarettes, so to me it was certainly not an expensive or harmful habit. Most people had no idea that I even used hemp. I believe others just thought I was simply getting away from my use of liquor and that finally I was becoming more responsible.

Then came the dry spell. From Christmas 1987 until September 1988, you could not buy hemp in our area. A couple of local growers were selling leaves for 15 dollars a gram but they had no strength, so I decided I had to start growing my own, since the supply on the street was so unreliable. I purchased a small device designed for growing hemp and grew six small plants in it. I found this grow unit very hard to work with, so one day, after I had harvested what little it produced, I took it apart and kept what was of any value, sending the rest to the dump. It did not take long for me to figure out better ways to grow a steady supply and then I no longer was at the mercy of those who sold the substance. During the following years, I built a few different little grow units that achieved varying degrees of success. Even though these units were homemade, they were all much nicer to work with and more productive than that plastic device I had thrown in the trash.

CHAPTER 3

THE END OF MY WORKING CAREER

During the 1980s, many things changed in my life. I no longer went hunting and roaming the woods, as I had been doing for years. After killing dozens of deer, the urge to harm such creatures simply vanished. The first few years I hunted, it seemed like sport, but by the mid-'80s, it began to feel much more like outright murder. There was no longer any thrill in the hunt for me. When I came upon a deer in the woods, it was basically a foregone conclusion that the animal would die. By the time I was 36, I was spending more time with my children and friends and had more or less hung up my guns. The Mad Trapper nickname that friends had given me years before no longer applied. I still might be classified as being somewhat mad but it seemed the trapper was gone forever. It appeared that I was finally mellowing out and within a couple of years I started dating Leah, the woman I am still with today. They say everyone needs a rock to cling to and I would have to say we have been just that for each other. We never married but have stood together through very little thick and a great deal of thin, so we must have been doing something right.

About 1990, I had a very strange experience with hemp. Back in the mid-'80s, I had a relationship with a woman who had a 15-year-old son. He was a very intelligent boy and it seemed he had knowledge that was far beyond his years. Once, he asked me what I thought the meaning of life was. I replied, "That's a rather deep question." He said that to him it was simply money and sex. After thinking a few moments about his statement, I could hardly disagree. It seems the world we live in does revolve around such things for the most part, but it was strange to hear it from a person that was still so young. He had already quit school before we met, so I encouraged him to take an electronics course, which he did, and passed with little effort. I then suggested he take the entrance exam to become a teacher. He really didn't think he could qualify but, upon taking the entrance exam, he was accepted.

His mother and I were no longer seeing each other but he had become a constant fixture in my home. My oldest son was living with me at the time and they got along great, so he was treated like one of the family. During his last year in teacher's college, he began to speak and act strangely. He did graduate, but was diagnosed as a schizophrenic and in a short time, I watched this horrible condition destroy one of the smartest young men I ever had the privilege to know. There was nothing I could do to help the situation he was in but stand there and watch it happen. One day, he came to my home, talking very irrationally, and lit up a joint that he had brought with him. He was about halfway through the joint when suddenly his thinking cleared and he started talking about trips we had taken in the past on motorcycles. This totally stunned me. I could not believe the transformation I had witnessed. He seemed to be completely back to normal. I had always enjoyed talking with him, but since this condition had taken over his life, sensible communication had become impossible.

As soon as he left that day, I called his mother and told her what had happened and that I thought the hemp he had smoked had caused this to occur. She had been told by doctors that anyone with this condition should stay away from the use of hemp. Then she proceeded to try to give me a lecture about giving him pot, which I had not; he had brought his own. There was no getting through to this woman. To be honest, I knew what I had seen, but could it really have been the pot, which had caused this to take place? At the time, I accepted the fact that the doctors probably knew more about his condition than I did. I mean, after all, who would believe smoking pot could help someone in his situation?

A few years later, this young man died at the age of 32 and I can only wonder what would have happened if I had known about the oil when he was diagnosed. I now believe there's a good possibility he could have used the oil as a medication and might still be with us, thinking clearly. What a tragedy and what a waste! The medical system filled him full of chemicals, which in the end did him much more harm than good. I am convinced these chemical medications provided by the doctors were partially, if not completely, responsible in bringing about his death at such a young age, while, at the same time, natural medicines that could have really helped him treat his condition were never even taken into consideration.

In 1991, I bought an old camp at 344 Little Forks Road in Athol, about eight miles from Springhill. I had just built a new house in Saltsprings in 1983 but now I was thinking about doing the same in Little Forks. I decided to go ahead and build the new house, thinking my son and I would live there, while my girlfriend could occupy the other house in Saltsprings. Rather than hire someone with a machine to clear the building lot, I bought my own backhoe and did the work myself. I began construction in June 1993 but of course, during this period, I was still working full-time at the hospital. Because of this situation, it took us about six months to finish the house and make it ready to occupy.

I still had many payments to make but at least everyone around me seemed happy. I then turned my attention to the backhoe and the art of operating it properly. The way I looked at it, if I could become proficient in running this machine, it could prove to be a source of income in the future. The backhoe I had purchased was a long way from being new. It was an old workhorse that didn't cost me too much and was cheap to run. I then started renting my services to people for practically nothing; I only charged enough to cover the cost of keeping the machine running properly. When I began doing work for others, I charged 15 dollars an hour for myself, the machine, and the fuel.

As the months went by, I slowly became a decent operator and learned to run this machine in the proper way but it did not come about without a lot of effort on my part. Even after I became quite good with the backhoe, the most I charged was 30 dollars an hour, which was about half the fee most people who owned similar machines charged. Since I was doing the work so cheaply, there was no shortage of people who wanted me to do excavation work for them. I did a wide variety of different tasks with this machine and after a few hundred hours in the seat, I could then do just about anything that was put before me. I think a great number of people, especially men, would love to run a piece of heavy equipment. At heart, many of us are much like children who want to play in the mud and what better way to do it than with a backhoe?

I really enjoyed this type of work and after acquiring enough experience, I could become very creative with a piece of land and still accomplish a great deal. During my upbringing, it seemed everything was done by hand with sweat and hard work but now with my own backhoe I had joined the machine age. I didn't have many years to go before I could retire from the hospital and now that I could run this machine in a more productive manner, I could look forward to having my own small landscaping and excavation business upon retirement. It seemed my future was now laid out.

I continued to produce hemp in my little grow-chambers but I was now beginning to wonder what this plant would do in natural surroundings. It was now time to see how hemp grew in the great outdoors. A few plants were put out in late May down by the river that flowed at the edge of my property and by harvest time in September, there was a nice crop. What a difference from growing inside! I found the plants grew a great deal larger and the bud itself seemed to be more potent. About this time, I started thinking there must be better ways to use hemp than just smoking plant material, so I looked into methods of producing hash and oil.

Producing hash was relatively easy, but making oil was a whole different story. The crop I had planted down by the river produced much more than expected, so I took two pounds of bud and tried to produce oil. What a dismal failure! The instructions I had followed were flawed, but through this experience, I figured out where I had probably gone wrong. After destroying two pounds of prime bud and having the oil I produced prove to be worthless, I had little incentive to try it again. For now, so to speak, producing oil was put on the back burner.

I had been growing my own hemp for about seven years and I acquired a group of friends that were doing the same. Often, we would get together for bull sessions and compare notes about growing in different ways. None of those I knew could be considered big growers. For the most part, we were lucky if we could keep ourselves supplied. The system always tries to portray hemp growers as big-time drug dealers. They give the public the impression these growers are making vast amounts of money and are having an easy life. Judging by the way the growers I knew lived, this was about as far from reality as you can get.

Growing illegally is not easy and there were few growers that I had met who actually made any real money growing back then. Most of the growers I had come in contact with up to this point were just poor people trying to stay alive. They were not driving fancy cars or living in big homes, they were just scraping by in life. If the growers I knew sold any hemp, they were not doing it because they wanted to be so-called drug dealers. Instead, they were doing so because they didn't have a choice in the matter. The area I come from is not exactly booming economically and when you don't have a job, how are you going to feed your children?

Smoking hemp is the least medicinal way to use this plant, but it still has desirable effects for many conditions. Some growers and others I knew did have medical problems that smoking hemp seemed to help them with. Of course, at the time, none of us looked at this substance as a medicine, but unknowingly many were already using hemp as a medication. Despite the fact that it was restricted and those who used and grew hemp could face harsh penalties, quite often people would simply acquire and smoke pot instead of purchasing medication from a drugstore. Hemp smokers are not hurting themselves or anyone else by their use of this substance, but if too many began doing the same, it would have a devastating effect on the profit margins of the drug companies.

This plus the fact that the free growing and use of hemp would decrease liquor sales and the viability of many other industries which are doing harm to our world were the main reasons that hemp was made illegal in the first place. To see that their aims were met, those with vast amounts of money and power saw to it that corrupted laws, acts, and regulations were introduced. They needed to have this plant restricted, or their dream of dominating the human race would surely fail. Therefore, it had nothing to do with this plant presenting any real danger to the public; instead, these restrictions were put in place to please those who wished to control us. If looked at rationally, how could anyone consider individuals who grow and distribute hemp as being criminals? When you look at the damage the pharmaceutical industry and others are doing to our species and planet, it appears that those who are supplying hemp are only doing what is right.

Many growers I knew thought hemp grown indoors was better and more potent. From me, such statements always produced an argument. By that time, I had become a confirmed outdoor growing fan and felt very strongly about the subject. I used to tell other growers that if we had a good growing season, hemp grown outdoors was by far the best. From my point of view, open ground, good drainage, and soil with a proper pH would produce the best crops. All a person had to do was use a good natural fertilizer and give the plants plenty of water. The sun was my main selling point in such lectures, for at the time you could not compare the intensity of indoor lighting systems with the intensity of the light the sun can produce. With the recent advent of plasma lighting that is now becoming available, all this may soon change. Several companies are making some excellent plasma lighting systems, which could change the face of indoor growing completely once the prices of such fixtures are reduced.

Many indoor growers are also having good results with the new compact fluorescents and LED fixtures. They are easy on electricity, create little heat, can reduce water consumption, and most maintain their light intensity for many thousands of hours. Even though growing indoors can produce a decent crop, doing so on a large scale is very costly, when compared with growing the plants outside. One must remember that nature designed these plants to feed off the energy of the sun and not a light bulb. In addition, there are stress factors in nature that can make the plants more healthy and vibrant, so, if possible, I prefer to grow these plants in the great outdoors.

Throughout the years I was employed at the hospital, I had the opportunity to work on many different types of equipment. This had broadened what abilities I possessed a great deal and, for the most part, I enjoyed this type of work. By the mid-1990s, things were changing for the worst, it seemed the institution where I worked was now not doing much to help the public and healing was of little concern. People who were good at their jobs were being replaced by those who could not handle such positions properly. It appeared to me that all they were looking for were yes-men. Instead of having a chief engineer, as had always been the case in the past, we now had a team leader. Therefore, I thought it might be best for me to give up the maintenance work I had been doing at the hospital for years and return to the boiler room. Going back to what I had previously been doing would increase my pension a bit because engineers received a slightly better salary than maintenance staff. In addition, this move would put me back on shift work, which would allow me more free time to take on jobs with the backhoe and I would have little to do with the new team leader. To me, it looked like a win-win situation.

Since 1972, when my cousin had passed away, I had watched the waiting room at the hospital filling more and more with individuals who were seeking help. I didn't have a real understanding of what was going on, but I used to wonder why so many more people appeared to be getting sick. The cancer rates were exploding, as were the rates of many other diseases. Some of these conditions had been so rare in the past that I had no knowledge they even existed. When I first began working at the hospital, it was providing an important function in our area. Now few patients were being helped and the staff was spending a great deal of time going to meetings that accomplished nothing. It was very sad to see an institution that had done so much good in the past turn into something that could be considered little more than a band-aid station. During the years I had been employed there, it was very rare for me to use any sick time. No matter how bad I felt, I would always drag myself to work. A couple of times, I was even asked to go home when they realized how sick I was.

Since I did not abuse sick time and had never used compensation or long-term disability for an injury, I used to think I would be protected if something were to happen. I guess it could be said I had a very strong work ethic and was more than willing to do the job under any circumstances. Funding had been paid for years into workmen's compensation and long-term disability for coverage to protect my income in case of injury. Unfortunately for me, in the near future I was to find out all about our so-called safety net, or lack thereof. By the time I was 48, I was still going through life as if I was bulletproof. All I had in mind was my upcoming retirement at 55, after which I planned to be working the backhoe full-time. I never thought for a second that something could happen and due to an injury, I would be taken out of the picture.

On December 21, 1997, a crew had been called in to repair one of the boilers. They removed the asbestos insulation in one area and had forgotten to seal it off. Asbestos is very harmful to your lungs and I knew the engineer who was to relieve me would not be happy to see the job was done improperly. So I decided to seal the area off myself, since it was part of my duties and I had done the same many times in the past. I took a can of spray adhesive and some duct tape and climbed a ladder on the side of the boiler to cover the asbestos. To get the tape to stick to asbestos, you have to spray the asbestos first with adhesive, then wait about a minute and spray it again. At this point, the duct tape will stick.

I was spraying the area for the second time when everything went black. An hour or so later, I came back to consciousness, hung up in the piping of the small boiler that was next to the large boiler on which I had been working. After struggling for a while, I was able to disengage myself from the piping and get back on the floor, but I couldn't walk. As a matter of a fact, I could not do much of anything. I crawled back to the office on my hands and knees and then tried to call for help but in the condition I was in I couldn't make the phone work. It seemed like forever but finally the engineer who was to relieve me arrived on the scene.

From what he has since told me, I guess I was quite a sight to behold. When he took me into the hospital, apparently I could not even tell them my name at the reception desk. All I remember was that it felt as if my head was going to explode. I was then taken to the trauma room, where I was given oxygen. After a few hours on oxygen, the pressure in my head seemed to subside a bit. I was still very disoriented but I was then told I should go home. By that time, I could walk again, though not very well, and I have no memory at all of driving home that evening. Today, I have to question if I should even have been discharged that night, for certainly I was in no condition to drive.

It's almost as if my car found its own way to my yard that night. The following two days, I was not scheduled to work but I have no memory of them either.

On the morning of December 24, the grogginess I had been experiencing for the past few days eased off. I was scheduled to go to work that night on my regular shift, so, still a bit wobbly, off to work I went. Little did I know this would be the last shift I would ever work. My injury had left me with some scratches and bruises on my arms and shoulder and there was a welt about four inches long on the right side of my head. The swelling ran from my right temple back over my ear and was quite nasty-looking. The first thing I did when I got to work that evening was try to figure out what had happened. I found the can of spray adhesive I had been using and in tiny print on the back that I could only read with a strong magnifying glass, it stated, "Vapor can cause temporary nervous system failure."

Now I knew why I had passed out and fell off the ladder. I then looked at where I had been hung up in the pipes. There before me in the dust was the whole story. I could see how my body had landed and slid down the side of the rounded boiler shell where I became entangled in the piping. On top of the small boiler was a heavy steel loading ring and this is what had caused my head injury. I had fallen about six feet and landed head first on the loading ring. At least now I knew what had taken place. I remember thinking at the time that I was very lucky. If the small boiler had been running when I passed out and fell, I would have been very severely burned.

As the shift went on, my thinking became more clear and I felt a bit better. At about 10 PM, the computer that had been installed to run our systems began to give me some trouble. I had been working on the computer for a few minutes when a ringing noise began in my head. At first, I tried to pay the noise no attention but it kept increasing in volume. Six hours later, at 4 AM, it felt as if a tuning fork had gone mad in my brain. There was also the sensation that a metal band was being tightened around my skull. I was feeling very woozy, so I went over to the hospital and told one of the nurses that I didn't feel well. The nurse took my blood pressure and, after doing so, told me to remain still. She then returned with a pill, telling me to take it and not to move. It seems my blood pressure was so high that she thought I might explode. My injury had left me with this unbearable noise in my head, high blood pressure, balance issues, and other related problems. From that time onward, I was at the mercy of the system. The morning of December 25, 1997, I left the hospital to go home to a very uncertain future. I didn't know it at the time but my working career was now at an end.

CHAPTER 4

DOWN THE CHEMICAL HIGHWAY

I can only term the first neurologist I saw about my injury as being not much of a doctor but he was only the first of many. Even the consultation report I received that was supposed to describe his observations about my medical problems seemed to be written about someone else entirely. My condition continued to degenerate because I could not get any sleep with all this noise that was going on in my head. It seems stupid to me now when I think about it that I did not immediately turn to hemp for relief.

At the time, hemp was the farthest thing from my mind. Possibly, my lack of clear thinking had something to do with my injury and the chemical medications the doctors had given me to take. It was nine months later, in September 1998, before I even got a diagnosis, at which time I was told that I had post-concussion syndrome. When I explained how my injury had occurred to the ear, nose, and throat or ENT specialist who was trying to treat me at the time, he told me I was a very lucky man. In the situation I was in, I certainly didn't look at it that way. With all this racket going on between my ears twenty-four hours a day, it was very hard for me to look at myself as being fortunate.

The day I was injured, I had been wearing a baseball hat, which had a plastic band. When I had fallen, the plastic band had contacted the loading ring first. This band had spread the force of the impact and had apparently saved my life. The doctor said the injury I had sustained would be about the same as if someone had taken a baseball bat and hit a homerun with my head. He told me it was amazing that I had survived. Ironically, it appears I owed my life to a plastic hatband.

The doctor said the prognosis for my condition was not good. There was no operation that could be performed, so the only hope I had of recovering would be the medications they provided and I was told to avoid stress. When I was injured, I should have immediately been put on compensation or at least long-term disability. In my case, the hospital put me off on sick time I had accumulated and six months later, when the sick time ran out, I was left with nothing. I later found out our team leader had manipulated the paperwork and that was part of the reason I was in this predicament. What he had done was completely wrong, but in my present situation, it took me quite some time to understand what had taken place.

It is easy for doctors to say, "Avoid stress," but how do you do that with nothing to live on and no income? I was forced to sell off many things I owned, including the backhoe that I could now no longer operate anyway because of my injury. The Compensation Board and Long Term Disability, it seems, had decided to play the "Let's Starve Rick" game. I feel sorry for anyone who is forced to pay money into organizations like this for coverage, for if something happens to them, they will probably get the run around just as I did. Fortunately for me, my father stepped in and provided the money to keep me alive.

Sadly, many people who suffer serious injuries are not so lucky. In many cases, our system is not designed to help someone who has sustained an injury. Instead, it often bewilders an injured person and helps bring about their demise. I don't know if what these organizations did in my case could be considered attempted murder. But from where I was sitting with no help from them and nothing to live on, it sure felt that way.

In late 1998, I watched an episode of the Nature of Things, hosted by Dr. David Suzuki, called "Reefer Madness 2". They showed many people with different medical problems, who were having great results from just smoking hemp for their conditions. It was as if a light had been turned on. I thought, "Of course, if anything could help me get the rest I required, it would be hemp." I was in no condition to grow the hemp I needed at the time and did not have any in my possession. So I obtained some from a friend, and sure enough, it gave me more rest than anything the medical system had provided.

Upon realizing this, I have to admit I felt very stupid, knowing what I had already learned about this substance from past experience. Why did I not use hemp from the very beginning to help me sleep? I cannot explain this but up until that moment, I had never looked at hemp as medicine. Suddenly before me was something that really did help and I immediately started asking doctors for prescriptions, so I could use this natural medication legally. The doctors I asked all refused to provide it, saying things like "hemp was still under study" and "was bad for the lungs." I could have saved myself a lot of grief and injury if I had simply told the doctors to get lost, but at the time I still believed in the medical system, so I continued to take their chemicals and the damage they caused accumulated.

As time went on, my situation became more and more hopeless. One medication after another, but none of their chemicals helped. By 1999, the effects of these substances on my thinking and the depression I was suffering from caused me to put a shotgun in my mouth. I could not imagine my condition improving, so I simply felt it might be best if I brought my life to an end. The only thing that stopped me was the thought of the mess my children would have to face. This brought me back to a more sensible state of mind and forced me to struggle on. It seemed the medical system was going to provide no help, so I started trying to think of ways in which I could help myself.

I already knew smoking pot was of some benefit to me but even pot seemed to lack the power to give me the proper rest I required. Of all the medications I had tried, hemp had the most beneficial effects, but it still lacked the punch I needed for me to sleep properly. Then I thought about the oil. What would happen if I concentrated the cannabinoids into an essential oil and ate it? If the effects of smoking indica dominant varieties of hemp made me sleepy, the concentrated oil from these plants should knock me out. The next time I was in my doctor's office, I explained to him what I was thinking of doing. He got a very strange look on his face, but he then agreed this would be a much more medicinal way to use this plant but he still would provide no prescription.

I could not understand the behavior of all these doctors. They were supplying me with addictive and dangerous medications, which were doing me nothing but harm, but they refused to give me a prescription for hemp, so I might be able to help control my condition with its medicinal benefits legally. This baffled me but at the time I thought there might be something harmful about the use of hemp, of which I had no knowledge.

Many people try to ignore the side effects of the drugs they are prescribed, but often their effects are worse than what you were originally being treated for. In my case, the effects of these medications were very debilitating. Some just stupefied me, while others gave me horrible dreams and thoughts that were truly unnatural. The medications I was prescribed made me feel dead inside and it was virtually impossible for me to think clearly. They also did nothing to help my balance and sleeping problems. From my perspective, they were simply making my condition worse.

One of the main side effects of an injury like mine is a very bad temper, since you have to try to live with the frustration and endless noise such an injury can cause. For those around me, it was much like trying to deal with a ticking time bomb, for they were never sure when I was going to lose control of my temper. I continued to take their chemical medications but also produced a little oil about this time in case the need should ever arise. I didn't start taking the oil on a steady basis because I must admit I was somewhat afraid of the effects it might have.

I produced the oil because I was losing faith in the medical system's ability to help me and wanted something else I could try in case all else failed. Every medication I was given worsened my condition to the point where I became not much more than a chemical zombie. Then, one day in 2001, I was at my doctor's office, when he told me there was nothing more he could do to help. According to him, they had tried everything at their disposal and nothing improved my situation, so I was now on my own. Again, I asked for a prescription for hemp and was promptly refused.

Even in the chemically induced state I was in, I thought, "What is this? They couldn't do anything to help me, but these people seemed to believe they had the right to deny something natural, which they already knew was of benefit for my condition?" On top of all that, if I was caught with hemp, even though it was for medicinal use, I would be charged and prosecuted as a criminal. As might be expected, all this did nothing to reinforce any faith I had in the system. Given no other choice, I went home and started ingesting hemp oil as my only medication.

I had used the oil a few times in the past between medications, taking tiny doses that did not seem to affect me too much. To me, the effects of these small doses were somewhat similar to smoking hemp. The main difference between smoking and ingesting this substance was that it took about an hour to act on my system, instead of feeling the effect immediately. I was quite wary of the oil at first and was concerned about what other effects it might have on my body. But for me, after being let down by the medical system, there was nowhere else to turn.

When I started taking the oil steadily and stepped up the dosage, sleeping was no longer an issue. This stuff could knock an elephant off its feet. I started getting anywhere from eight to twelve hours of solid sleep every night and my condition began to improve. When the medical system had cut me loose, their medications had left me in a chemical daze. My thinking processes were not functioning properly and I couldn't seem to remember anything. Suddenly, after only a short time on the oil, my memory and thinking processes were exhibiting a marked improvement. I started to lose weight and noticed I no longer needed to take Glucosamine for the arthritis I had been suffering from in my knees.

In the beginning, I really had no idea what medicinal benefits this oil could produce other than its sedative qualities. In some ways, its effects were even a bit scary and I began to wonder about all this weight I was losing. Could the oil I had produced be doing me harm? I had no idea at the time that the oil was simply detoxifying my body and bringing me back to a healthy weight. Who would think the essential oil of the hemp plant could even do such a thing?

It was great to see my condition improving after all this time, but I still had the ringing in my head. Using the oil was definitely helping me in many ways, but it did not take the noise away. Without the use of the oil, the noise takes over my life and my blood pressure can become extremely high. When I took the oil, it seemed to free my mind from most of the effects of the noise, but it was still there. Although I was now able to cope with its presence much better, I still required the use of this medication to keep my condition under control. I don't know what doctors would say about all this, but they are not the ones who are suffering. From my experience with this substance, I can honestly say the oil is by far the most effective medication that I have ever found.

After only using this substance for a short time, my weight dropped from about 185 pounds down to 160. Then it leveled off and I remained that way for years to come. There was also a marked improvement in my balance and suddenly I was no longer falling down all the time. Of course, a lot of this might be credited to the rest I was now getting and the lack of chemicals in my system. The oil was doing a great job controlling my blood pressure and to me so far there was no downside. I was not addicted and it seemed to be helping me in every way when nothing else could.

I will always remember the effects of the first big dose of oil after I had ingested it. I had worked my way up to taking fairly large doses, but one night I decided to see what would happen if I took more. I put about half a gram on my finger and popped it into my mouth. About an hour later, I went to bed. Within a few minutes, I started to feel as if I was about to become sick and it seemed that whatever was in my stomach would not be there for long. Rather than make a mess, I decided that I should go to the bathroom. It was at this point that I suddenly realized I couldn't move. It felt as if I was paralyzed; I could not even lift a finger.

I thought, "There now, look what you have done to yourself." I have to admit, for about 45 seconds, there were some very panicked thoughts going through my mind. Then the aggressive side of my nature came forward and I said to myself, "Get out of this bed!" Suddenly, I could move again but I did have some trouble making my way to the bathroom. I stayed in the toilet for about a half an hour but never became sick. A few minutes later, I went back to bed and had a good night's sleep. About ten hours afterwards, I awoke well rested, but still exhibiting the effects of the oil. After about an hour that heavy tired feeling, which the oil can give a person, faded away and I felt great. So, in my case, when I needed to do something, all I had to do was use "mind over matter" to overcome the oil's sedative effects, which then allowed me to at least function.

Taking oil internally does not affect you like ingesting alcohol. When we consume too much booze, most of us still want to drive our cars. If you take too much oil, all you are looking for is a bed. Judging by the effects of the oil I have witnessed upon myself and others, driving a car is the last thing a person who has taken too much would want to do. So the chances of someone taking a large quantity of this substance and then becoming a menace to the public on our highways are very remote.

From the time I took my first large dose to this day, I will still take such doses once or twice a month, if the oil is available. It doesn't give me that sick feeling in the stomach any longer and I have come to enjoy the effects and extra sleep such a large dose can bring. After all, I am just going to bed and the oil is good for you even if you do take too much, so what was the harm?

During the 1990s, some unhealthy areas had appeared on my body, which refused to heal. When asked about them, I would try to brush such questions off by saying they were just barnacles. But I strongly suspected that these lesions were skin cancer. The problem was I simply did not want to admit to myself that I probably had cancer. No one wants to go to a doctor and be given that dreadful diagnosis, even if they only have skin cancer. Individuals such as myself who worked in hospitals have witnessed people die a gruesome death in the past from this form of cancer also, so I was not looking forward to hearing my doctor's opinion. When the doctor examined these areas in late 2002, he said it looked like skin cancer, but he could not be sure until he got the pathology report he would receive after the operation.

One of the areas which was giving me discomfort was on the side of my nose and he seemed very concerned, since it was so close to my right eye. He told me they would operate on this area first, because of its proximity to my eye. They would then take care of the other two areas that were giving me problems at a later date. Around the end of January 2003, the operation was performed and I have to say, it was not a pleasant experience. About a week after the operation, I was examining the area where they had removed the lesion on the side of my nose. It was now infected and a gruesome sight indeed, but this was hardly unusual, since many who have gone through operations at the Amherst hospital often get infection.

That's when the report I had heard on the radio almost 30 years before popped back into my mind. At this time, I had been taking oil for quite a while and thought by now my body must be full of THC. If THC kills cancer, why had it not cured my skin cancers? I did not understand it all at the time, but the largest organ we have is our skin. Even if a person takes the oil internally, they would need to rapidly ingest quite a large quantity to have the desired effect on skin cancer. In most cases, the oil should be applied directly on the affected area externally, or topically, as this form of treatment is commonly known, to achieve results quickly. I have to admit that because of the lingering faith I still had in the medical system, I almost did not even bother applying the substance. I knew the oil I produced was full of THC, but to me, curing skin cancer could not be this simple.

If what I had heard on the radio were true, surely the medical system would be using THC to treat cancer? I still had doubts, so I decided to find out for myself. I applied a small amount of oil to bandages and placed them on the other two areas I suspected were cancerous. I left them in place for four days and did not feel a thing, so I assumed the oil had done nothing. Even though the irritation that the cancer had been causing disappeared shortly after I applied the oil, at that point I did not know what was taking place.

When I removed the bandages and found only healthy pink skin, I was astonished. This could not be true! The two areas I had treated were completely healed. When I started telling friends I had cured my cancer in this manner, they simply blew it off as if it meant nothing. It may have seemed unimportant to them, since they were not the ones afflicted with the condition. But it does mean something to people suffering from skin cancer, who must endure multiple surgeries and often die horrible deaths in the end, no matter what the medical system does.

Again, I was going through another very mixed-up period. Was it the oil that had truly worked the magic? After all, at the time I had only seen it work on myself. I have always been quite a serious person and if I said something, most of those I knew tended to at least give what I was saying some consideration. But when I told people about this, even close friends would laugh and say, "Come on, Rick, pot cures cancer? Yeah, right." I was starting to wonder if quite possibly they were correct, when the cancer close to my eye, which had been surgically removed, returned. I watched it develop for a few days and it gave me the same feeling it had before the operation, as if I had splinters in the affected area. It was also swelled up and bleeding now and then, like it had in the past.

I applied the oil to a bandage and put it in place on the side of my nose close to my eye. Four days later, when I removed the bandage, the cancer was completely healed. There was only one question now left to be answered: had it really been cancer that I cured with the use of this oil? A short time later, I went to my doctor's office to get a copy of my pathology report. The report confirmed that indeed it was basal cell carcinoma that had been removed during the operation they had performed. I told the receptionist, who happened to be the doctor's wife, that I would like to come back in the evening and discuss something I had been working on with the doctor. She asked me what this was about and I told her the cancer they had removed that was close to my eye had returned. I explained that I had applied hemp oil to this area and the other two areas, which had been affected, and cured all three with the hemp oil. I can't say I have ever seen anyone's demeanor change so rapidly. From her reaction, it was clear that both she and her husband, the doctor, wanted nothing to do with this topic.

She started yelling, "The doctor will not go there, the doctor will not prescribe this." I was standing in my doctor's waiting room with five or six other patients present and his receptionist was shouting at me as if she were some kind of nutcase. I found the whole incident very unnerving. What was with these people? I cured my cancer with hemp oil and wanted to discuss it with my doctor, but all the receptionist wanted to do was shut me up and get me out of his office. Certainly, I was less than thrilled with her behavior and that little seed of distrust I had within me grew some more. I could think of no rational reason why any doctor would not be interested in how I cured my cancer unless they knew something I did not. Also about this time, I started connecting the dots. Just look what this oil had done for me. My thinking processes were pretty much back to normal, my blood pressure and balance issues were under control. I no longer had arthritis in my knees, I was back to a healthy weight, and now my cancer was cured.

I then thought about something else that this oil must have played a role in healing. When I first began to produce oil, I got a little careless and set myself on fire. I really don't know if one could call it carelessness or the fact that I was full of these mind-altering medications the medical system had provided, but I ended up with severe third-degree burns to my right hand. When I say severe, I mean severe. It was as though three-quarters of my hand had melted and was now hanging in big gobs.

A few hours after I had sustained this injury, my girlfriend arrived on the scene. After looking at the burn, Leah took a pair of scissors and proceeded to cut off all the dead flesh. I know this sounds horrible, but the flesh she cut off was dead and I hardly felt a thing. When I had burned myself so badly, I thought I was going to be scarred for life and that my hand would probably never be able to function properly again. I knew other people who had endured severe burns such as this and I had seen the scars and other damage a serious burn leaves behind. Eleven days after I had burned myself so badly, my right hand was completely healed, leaving no scarring. Even the hair follicles on my hand, which had been completely destroyed, grew back. At the time, my thinking processes were so bad that I just brushed it all off by telling myself I was simply a good healer. But now, thinking of this burn and all the other miracles the oil had worked for me, I thought, "What have I stumbled onto?"

In late 2002, my oldest son Mike went to the province of Alberta to live with his younger brother Mitch in the hope that they could get a business started. They were both looking to get into something, so we decided to put up a website dedicated to the medicinal use of hash and oil. By this time, I was retired. Workmen's Compensation and Canada Pension had finally sent me the back money that was owed and I was put on pension. My working career was over, but my sons still had to make a living and distributing information about this subject seemed as if it might provide them with an income. At first, I wanted to put up all the information on the Internet free of charge, but my sons disagreed. As far as they were concerned, this information was worth a great deal and they intended to sell it as a course for $80 a copy. I can't say I cared much for the idea, but I could see their point, so we put all the information for the website together.

I was sent a copy of what they intended to put up on their website, but there was no mention of curing cancer. I called them up and complained, "What's all this? You haven't put the most important statements in the course." Their reply was, "Dad, you can't say hemp oil cures cancer. That would get us all in a lot of trouble." I completely disagreed, but told them to do as they liked. In the spring of 2003, the course was put up on the Internet as it was and we advertised that it was available in *Cannabis Culture* Magazine. In the end, www.HashishAndHoneyOil.com made nothing. I spent tens of thousands of dollars trying to support the efforts of my sons, but to no avail. The website was a complete failure.

I have a lot of respect for the talents of my children and heaven knows we all make mistakes. I have certainly made a good number of them myself, but in many cases, you have to learn by doing. For me, the only positive thing that came out of all this was that afterwards my sons seldom disagreed with what I had in mind. They may not have liked it, but they usually went along with my way of thinking after the failure of their website. I really felt they should have added all the information about the oil's ability to cure cancer, but I understood the reasoning behind their decision not to.

In some countries, you can be sent to jail for up to 40 years for even claiming to have found a cure. Supposedly, this nonsense was put in place to protect the public from charlatans, but in reality it was done to keep the public away from harmless natural treatments, which truly can be beneficial. If the public were to find out the truth and turn back to nature for their medications, big drug companies could no longer sell their chemicals and poisons and would cease to exist. Anyone who has cured their own cancer or any other disease using natural means should openly discuss what they used as a treatment, so it might benefit everyone.

In February 2012, it had been nine years since I cured my cancer with hemp oil and I have the pathology report that proves I did indeed have cancer. Since I have gone well beyond their five-year limit and the cancer has never returned, I think I have every right to tell the public that yes, hemp oil cured my cancer. In addition, I have supplied this substance to so many people, there are now thousands of others who should speak freely about what the oil has done for their conditions. The longer we remain silent, the more guilt we ourselves must bear for what is currently taking place.

CHAPTER 5
THE FIRST RCMP RAID

A few days after the strange experience I had in my doctor's office, I paid a visit to my mother. She had been suffering for quite some time with weeping psoriasis on her lower leg and foot. I suggested she might try using the oil as a topical treatment. As usual, the oil worked its magic and her condition improved rapidly. I started to wonder if there was anything this oil could not do to improve our wellbeing, because the healing power I had already witnessed was mind-blowing. Even at that time, I was still telling myself, "All this could not be true, for if it was, how could a medicine like this have been overlooked?"

As the weeks passed, I started to supply the oil to people I knew, who were suffering from skin cancer and other conditions like infections or burns, which could be treated topically. Word about what I was doing spread rapidly and more people started coming to me for help. Since I knew little about the topic, I decided it was time to start doing some serious research on hemp, especially the medical aspects of the plant. I had little or no experience with the Internet and newer computers, so I asked my neighbors Ruby and Larry Bjarnason if they would mind doing some research for me on the Internet. Ruby and Larry are very intelligent people who had a deep interest in what I was doing, and since they were retired, I could think of no one better to take on this task.

When I started providing oil to others, I knew that if something went wrong that I could be in a great deal of trouble. People were always saying things to me such as, "You know, one of these days they're going to charge you with practicing medicine without a license." Statements like this from those I was trying to help did nothing to reassure me but at least now we were starting to get some real research done. I had found the effects of the oil to be harmless even when ingested but if someone's condition got worse and the oil was blamed, I knew I could be facing criminal charges. The prospect of this occurring did give me a great deal to worry about in the beginning.

In the summer of 2003, I planted about 140 plants in an area next to my land, which was close to the river, so they would be easy to water. I was supplying oil to people for nothing, so to continue what I was doing, I had to grow the plants myself. The crop grew very well that year, producing large buds, from which I could manufacture the medicine, but that was not to be. On September 13, 2003, about a week before harvest time, the RCMP landed a chopper down by the river in my back yard. From the patio door, I watched them scrambling from the helicopter in a big rush with their guns and flak jackets. I then walked down towards where they had landed, at which time a cop approached, yelling they had spotted a marijuana grow and that I was under arrest.

I told the cop the crop they had found was not on my property and they had no right to even land their helicopter in my backyard. The helicopter was still running and making a great deal of noise, so I am not sure if the cop understood what I had said or not. After I had made this statement, I turned around and he followed me back to the house. They then proceeded to do a search of my home with no search warrant. I had 30 small clones about four inches high in my basement and of course, these were found. The way the police behaved, you would have thought they had found a dead body. Their tone turned nasty and then I got mad. I exclaimed, "Listen, you people have broken every law in the book here today. I am a medicinal user of hemp and I have the medical history to back up what I'm saying." To prove what I had said, I then showed them the large box that contained my medical records. One of the cops then asked, "So, where's your license that allows you to have marijuana in your possession?" After all I had been through with the medical system refusing to give me a prescription, his statement had angered me even further.

In my frustration, I informed them "You would be much more likely to win the lottery than to get a prescription to possess hemp from your doctor." The cop just sneered at me, so I told him, "If you think it's so easy to get a prescription, you should try to get one yourself. I had asked dozens of doctors to give me a prescription and none would comply." I could see my statements were having no effect and this led to even more anger on my part. Finally, I unloaded on them and asked if they knew that they were uprooting the cure for cancer. This statement brought a stunned look to the faces of all the officers present.

To prove what I was saying, I proceeded to show them my pathology report which indicated that indeed I had suffered from cancer in the past. I then sat down with them and told the whole story. Afterwards, at least they did start behaving more properly. Judging by their actions, I have to wonder just how much these cops really know about what they are doing. Strangely, before they left my home, three of them came over and shook my hand. Cops don't do that. It was as if they were trying to show remorse for their actions. Everything that went on that day had a bad smell about it. Did these guys really know more than they were pretending? When they left my property, the crop was gone and many things from my home were taken, but I was never charged. I don't know what most people would call the occurrences that transpired at my home during their raid, but I call it government-sanctioned robbery.

I no longer had a crop to work with, so I purchased some hemp from local growers and continued to supply the oil to patients free of charge. As far as I was concerned, those who thought they had the right to deny this medicine's use had just picked a fight with the wrong guy. Now, come hell or high water, I was going to prove the medicinal value of this plant to those who had restricted its growing and use, by whatever means that were necessary.

A few days after the RCMP raid on my property, Larry Bjarnason dropped over for a visit and he had a very strange look on his face. He had dug up a report called "The Case for Hemp." It is a chronological history of man's use of hemp over the last few thousand years and is quite lengthy. It also contained information about some of the medical research that had been done in the past. That's where I came upon the 1975 Virginia Commonwealth University's School of Medicine study. As soon as I looked it over, I realized this had to be the same study I had heard about on the radio 30 years before. The truth was all there in black and white and to me it backed up everything I had found out about the medicinal use of this plant.

Larry was still acting oddly, so I asked him what was wrong. "Rick, they knew this plant was effective in the treatment of cancer thirty years ago." I replied, "Yes, apparently that's more than obvious." He then stated, "I lost my brother to cancer ten years ago." Now I knew why this report had affected him so much. Through his research, Larry discovered the truth and it shattered whatever faith he ever had in the system.

In September 2003, I sent "The Case for Hemp" and other information about my findings to Dr. David Suzuki. It was due to his television show "The Nature of Things" that I began using hemp as a medicine in the first place. I had thought there could be no one better to bring this information forward. David Suzuki was one of the most respected and prominent researchers in Canada. I knew the public would probably never take my word for it, since I am not a doctor, but I felt they would respect the opinion of Dr. Suzuki. About a month later, I received a reply that stated Dr. Suzuki was currently out of the country on a speaking tour, but he was greatly interested in the information I had provided and would discuss it with his colleagues.

I then wrote another letter to the Suzuki Foundation, offering oil so they might do their own assessment. I told them all they had to do was find someone with skin cancer, apply the oil and a bandage, then change it every three days and watch what happens. Shortly afterwards, I received their reply, which stated, "We are a foundation, not a research facility." I was stunned when I read this. It seemed they must lack the funding to buy the bandages needed to do the assessment. Or could this foundation be a fraud, since they seemed to have no interest in curing cancer? After their last reply, I heard nothing more from Dr. Suzuki or the foundation, which bears his name.

A few years later, I was to find out that the American government had put their medicinal patents concerning this plant in place during the same time period. I can't say with any certainty that Dr. Suzuki had something to do with what the U.S. government did, but it certainly gave me reason to speculate. I had been a fan of his show for many decades, but due to their behavior over this issue, I gave up watching "The Nature of Things" since I had lost all trust in the information this show provided.

Then, in November 2003, I sent massive amounts of information and a proposal to the government in all directions by registered mail. I sent all this information including "The Case for Hemp" along with the proposal I had drawn up to the Government of Canada by contacting the following people; Anne McLellan, who was at that time the Federal Minister of Health for the Liberal government that was then in power, Jack Layton, federal leader of the New Democratic Party, Murray Scott, the provincial Conservative MLA for our region, Darrell Dexter, provincial leader of the New Democratic Party in Nova Scotia, and Marc Emery, the owner of *Cannabis Culture* Magazine, who I thought should at least take an interest.

The only one that even replied was Jack Layton, but all he sent was a form letter, which stated "Vote for the NDP." There was no mention in his reply about the information I had sent and it seemed that the New Democratic Party had no interest in the issue. I arranged a meeting with Murray Scott who sent me along to Bill Casey, our local Conservative MP, stating he did not want to see marijuana legalized and that this was a federal issue. I told him this was not about legalizing marijuana; it was about the medicinal aspects and use of this plant. I then informed him that curing cancer should be an issue to everyone.

From 2003 onward, many people went to the office of Murray Scott about this issue. He knew people like Ed Dwyer, who had used it personally and was well aware of what the oil had done for Ed and many others. But he did nothing to help bring the use of this medication forward, so it could help the people who had elected him. To my way of thinking, Murray Scott is a shining example of what a politician should not be. In Canadian politics, it seems people like Murray are the ones who currently occupy the driver's seat. Fortunately for us, I expect that in the near future we will no longer have any need for people of this caliber to speak on our behalf. In addition, Darrell Dexter was approached by quite a few people about this issue as well, but refused to take an interest. Darrell Dexter is now the Premier of Nova Scotia, but I do not expect too many people will be happy about him playing this role once the truth is known.

About two months later, I had a meeting with Bill Casey at his office in Amherst. I then informed him about what I had been doing. I gave him all the information and "The Case for Hemp" along with the proposal I had sent to the Canadian government in November 2003. I started naming people he knew who had used the oil as a treatment, but he pretended he did not know the people of whom I was speaking, so I replied, "Get in the car with me and we'll go to the Amherst hospital and find someone with skin cancer and I'll prove it to you." "Oh no, we can't do that," he replied. Instead, he said he would go to the Parliamentary Library and get the lowdown on all of this. I just looked at him and stated, "You're going to get the lowdown from Ottawa and the very people who are supporting this propaganda against hemp's medicinal use? Is that what you're saying?" By this time, you could see Mr. Casey was becoming a bit flustered, but he said he would look into it and let me know. In the coming months, I heard nothing more from Mr. Casey and people continued to die needlessly.

After this very unsatisfactory meeting with my local MP, I contacted the Canadian Cancer Society. I thought that surely they would do something about this situation. The reply I received set me straight. Their website informs us that the first mission of the Canadian Cancer Society is to eradicate cancer, but when they are contacted about a possible cure, you receive a stupid reply back from them, like I did: "The society does not endorse medical or dietary supplements." What they left out is the fact that the Canadian Cancer Society does not want a cure. If one were found, this would put them all out of work. The Canadian people have been donating funds to this organization for decades and this is what they get for their support. In the past, I myself have given money to the Cancer Society, but never again.

Over the years, the public has donated billions of dollars to organizations like this and what have they received in return? On top of all that, when they call us on the phone, looking to raise more funding, their representatives are experts at making us feel as if we are not good citizens unless we donate to their cause. My father only gave money to the Salvation Army. He said the rest were just a pack of thieves and, by all appearances, again he was correct. In the near future, I was to find the majority of medical associations, foundations, and societies are not for real. They were just very good at instilling the belief that such organizations should be supported by the public.

In the early 1990s, the administrator of All Saints Hospital, William "Bill" Gilbert, had to leave his position because of a medical condition he was suffering from. Through the job he had performed, Bill had made many contacts in the medical system and I thought he might know someone that could help. I went to Bill's home one night and told him what I had discovered and he invited me in to explain. He had known me for a long time and he knew if I was making statements like this, there had to be something to it. He stated, "You're telling me you have found a cure for cancer?" I answered, "That's correct." He then asked if I had known that he was suffering from cancer. I told him I didn't have any idea he had been suffering from this condition. When Bill left work, it had nothing to do with cancer, so what he told me came as a surprise.

Bill then explained that some of the medications they used to treat his condition had given him stomach cancer. I then asked him what they were doing to treat it. He stated that he was taking chemotherapy. I asked, "What does the chemo do?" He told me he had a tumor in his stomach about the size of his fist. Every so often, he would go in for chemo and the tumor would shrink but when it came back, it got bigger every time. I pointed out to him that it didn't sound as if the chemo was doing him much good and that he should give the oil a try.

There was no question Bill had taken what I was saying about the oil quite seriously. He stated, "Rick, I'm going to give my son, who is a chemist, a call and see what he thinks of this and I'll get back to you." About a week later, Bill invited me to come to his house and showed me a stack of e-mails from his son. The first one read, "Stay away from this guy, Dad. He's a nut." I looked at Bill and stated that everyone is entitled to their opinion, but he asked me to read on. The next one said, "Dad, this guy might be onto something." The rest of the e-mails were more and more in support of using the oil to treat his father. Bill told me he would be interested in trying the oil as a treatment, but right at that moment, I had nothing to give him. At that time of the year, it can be quite hard to lay your hands on the proper material to produce the oil. Just a few days previously, I had given the last oil I had to another patient. I told Bill that I would have some to give him in a few days, but in the meantime, we would have to wait until the grower harvested his crop.

About a week later, I received word that Bill had died after he had gone in for another chemotherapy treatment. It seems this time the chemo had succeeded in doing much more than just shrinking Bill's tumor. Within two days of Bill's death, I received a call from the grower, telling me the material I was looking for was ready. At this point, I was just starting to become aware of how deadly and dangerous chemotherapy and radiation treatments really are. It's a great shame that a man like Bill Gilbert, who was a well-respected administrator in the hospital system, should become a victim of the very system for which he had worked.

On April 18, 2004, my father passed away at the age of 81. He was a wonderful man who had taught me a great deal about life. Three years previously, Dad had endured several heart attacks and was not expected to live, but he fooled the doctors and survived. After going through all of this, he was not in very good shape and required a lot of care. My family worked together to do what we could for him, but it was very hard on everyone. I wasn't exactly in great shape myself at the time, but I did what I could to help.

Just a few months before his death, Dad had moved into a nursing home in Amherst. Every day, I would go see him and usually take him out for a drive. He did not seem to be happy in Amherst, so we decided that he would come and stay with me at my home in Little Forks. I was just getting the house organized for his arrival when he passed away. Dad and I had always been very close and he was well aware of what the oil had done for my condition. Dad's wish for me to become a doctor was never fulfilled, but he knew the oil I produced was a wonderful medicine, so in some ways it seemed his dream had been realized.

He used to talk to the staff at the nursing home about the healing power of this medicine but at the time, many people did not believe what he was telling them. If I had only known then what I know now, I would have filled him full of oil and he still might be with us today, but, as they say, hindsight is 20/20. If nothing else, at least I did use the oil to help him successfully treat a skin condition that had been giving him problems.

Up until Dad's death, I did not have the time to help that many others. Going to see him every day had kept me quite tied up, but I don't regret a second of the time we spent together. Now he was gone, and to fill the hole that was left in my life, I felt I should spend my time helping more people. After Dad passed away, I then turned my full attention to producing as much medicine as possible.

It was about this time that I first supplied oil to treat a dog that was dying from cancer. I had been contacted by a man from Parrsboro who owned a seven-year-old dog, to which he had become very attached. He had taken the dog to veterinarians, but all they offered was expensive chemo treatments and little hope that the dog would survive. He had heard about what I was doing through a relative of his who had used the oil, so he called and asked me if I thought it could help his dog as well. I asked him to come to my home, so I could give him a small amount of oil to get the dog under treatment.

He explained that all the dog could now eat was little tiny pieces of dog treats. I told him to put the oil right on the dog treat and feed it to his pet. About a week later, I received a call from him, telling me the dog was now eating properly again and seemed to be back to normal. A few weeks afterwards, he brought the dog to my home and, by all appearances, his much loved companion was now in good health again. He had taken the dog back to the vet, but now they could find no cancer present.

He was very happy to have his pet back, but you could tell he was quite disturbed about what he had just learned. He exclaimed in disbelief, "Rick, they have been lying to us, haven't they?" I stated, "That's right, and the proof is standing next to you, wagging his tail." In truth, vets do not treat animals any better than most doctors do humans and this dog would probably have died from the effects of the chemo they were offering to provide. There is big money in treating animals, but a great deal of it would disappear if the oil was freely available. So, at present, not only are we in peril because of hemp's medicinal restriction, but also our pets are as well.

By the late spring of 2004, I was very disillusioned with the system. Did they enjoy watching their own loved ones suffer and die? The way they were all behaving towards this medicine's use, this did indeed seem to be the case. At the end of May, I planted a large crop in the valley behind my home, which was quite well hidden. When the plants matured, some very nice prime bud was harvested, which I turned into medicine as quickly as possible, and it was given out to those in need.

That same summer, I supplied oil to Cecil Hoeg from Maccan, who had melanoma skin cancer on his face. The medical system had tried to remove it five times, but it kept coming back and was getting worse. The cancer had created a hole in his left cheek that you could have put the tip of your finger in and the area was very inflamed and sore to the touch. Within three weeks, the oil had done its job and the cancer was completely gone. Cecil and those around him were greatly impressed and amazed that the oil had been able to heal the cancer so quickly.

He then informed me he also had glaucoma and arthritis in his knees. I told him there was no better treatment for glaucoma than hemp and it should also take care of his arthritis. To convince him, I then went home and picked up the books I had accumulated on the subject and showed him the information. He was doubtful at first, but the oil had just cured his cancer and since he knew I was already ingesting it myself, he replied, "Why not?" I told him taking the oil in the same manner I did would be the best way to use this medication. Before starting to use the oil, Cecil needed to put a pillow between his knees to ease the pain from the arthritis so he could get some sleep. Within a month, his arthritis was gone and there was no further need for the use of a pillow.

When he started taking the oil, his ocular pressure was 31 in one eye and 32 in the other, and he was on the verge of losing his driver's license, because of his vision problems. As time went on, there was a marked improvement in his vision and his overall health improved dramatically. The last I heard, his ocular pressure was 13 in one eye and 14 in the other. This man is doing very well today and is in no danger of losing the right to drive his own car. In addition, he can now read and see many things that were impossible for him to see before he started taking the oil.

As a matter of fact, many including myself have witnessed substantial improvements in their vision with the use of this medication. Glaucoma is one of the leading causes of blindness and many who suffer from this condition lose their vision entirely and are declared legally blind. Since the 1800s, it has been a well-known fact that hemp is very effective in the treatment of this condition. But most eye doctors of today choose to ignore it and instead use lasers and eye drops to treat their patients. In the end, through improper or ineffective treatment, many of their patients become legally blind. It seems unbelievable, but most eye doctors will watch patients slowly lose their sight and refuse to use hemp to help them. As horrible as all this may sound, sadly that is exactly what the vast majority of them have been doing.

Shortly after treating Cecil, I supplied oil to a lady in Maccan who had been diagnosed with Bowen's disease. This is a condition, involving what they call precancerous cells she had on her privates. A couple of weeks before she heard about what I was doing, an operation had been performed and when I first met her, she was in a very agitated state. She examined what they had done after the operation and found they had removed everything except the area with the precancerous cells. At first, I found this hard to believe, but she then showed me a copy of her pathology report. Sure enough, there were no precancerous cells found in the tissue they had removed. The doctor had operated on this woman and mutilated her, leaving the area that should have been removed untouched. To add to all of this, she now had a lump up inside and the poor woman was frantic. She started ingesting the oil and applying it topically. In a short time, all was well and she was once again back in good health.

I did quite a few experiments at that time, using the healing power of the oil in different ways. Often, I would mix it with skin creams and salves and I achieved great results. One day, I added about fifteen grams of oil to a large jar of skin cream and gave myself a facial. I washed my face, then applied the skin cream/oil mix, rubbed it in and then went to bed. The next morning, my face was as smooth as a baby's behind. The wrinkles I had acquired over the years were much diminished and all the little lumps and bumps had disappeared overnight.

I really liked what this had done for my complexion but being a man, I paid it little attention. A few hours later, I was over at Larry's having a cup of coffee and Ruby, his wife, kept looking at me strangely. After a while, she walked over to me and said, "Rick, did you have a facelift?" I told them what I had done and we had a good laugh about it. Still, she said that she was amazed at the difference in my appearance.

Women spend vast amounts of money on the way they look and, for the most part, what they purchase is of little or no value. If women only knew what this substance could do for their complexions, I have little doubt it would be legalized once more tomorrow. One day, when I was at my mother's, I asked her to apply it to the age spots she had on the back of her hands. In no time, they just disappeared, leaving healthy pink skin. Was there anything this oil couldn't do? I was really starting to wonder.

No one seemed to be willing to do anything to bring the truth about the medicinal value of this substance out, so I decided to go to the newspapers. I contacted Chris Gooding at the Springhill Record in the late summer of 2004 and explained to him what this medicine was all about. Gooding did a full-page article in the Springhill Record, describing what I was doing with the oil, but he did twist the truth a bit. In the article, he stated that the oil had healed some sores on a local man's face. I was there when the interview he did with Cecil Hoeg had taken place. Gooding had been told it was cancer that had been healed and not sores. When I approached him about this, he said he was playing the devil's advocate. I told him he was lying and that he was in league with the devil, for why else would he do such a thing? Possibly, I should not have been so upset with this reporter. After all, he did not own the paper he was writing for. Big money concerns own the papers and in the end, they are the ones that determine what is being fed to the public.

Just after this edition of the Record came out in September 2004. I sent a copy of it, along with all the other information I had acquired and another proposal, to Ujjal Dosanjh, the new federal Minister of Health. I figured that eventually I would have to come in contact with someone that is at least half honest. Again, nothing happened, but about six months later, I did receive a letter from the Minister of Health, telling me that I was breaking the law.

People were suffering and dying everywhere around me and our federal Minister of Health has the nerve to inform me that I'm breaking the law for the act of healing them? I hate to be the one to tell you this, Mr. Dosanjh, but you are the one breaking the law, because you did not do the job, for which you were elected. As Minister of Health, you should have looked into this issue and done something to help the Canadian people. Instead, you sat behind your desk and did nothing.

Over the years, many people have asked me where I came up with the name "Phoenix Tears" to describe the oil I produced. To satisfy the wishes of all those who are interested in mythology, I am sorry to tell you I did not exactly choose this name for that reason. The name came straight out of my head one day, when I was watching a Harry Potter movie. A huge serpent had sunk his fangs into Harry and things did not look too good for our hero. Then a Phoenix flew in, shed tears on Harry's wound, and he was saved. At that moment, I said the words "Phoenix Tears," and just seconds later, Harry said the same, and I felt it suited the golden drops of oil I was using to heal everyone.

At first, I don't think most people even liked the name. But as time went on, the name stuck and of course, when we put up our website, we called it www.PhoenixTears.ca. Now there are dozens of sites that use the word Phoenix but there were very few, if any, when we put up our site. It appears I may have had a hand in making the use of this word more popular. Or to be more correct, perhaps, the credit should go to the author of the Harry Potter series, J. K. Rowling.

One day, a woman who I had supplied oil to in the past was at my home and she was talking about the holy anointing oil. After discussing the subject for a while, she asked me, "Rick, why do you do this?" I immediately replied, "To prevent myself from becoming an asshole." She just looked at me and said, "Now, what does that mean?" I answered, "If you have cancer and I know how to cure it and don't tell you, what would I be?" She admitted, "In a case like that, you would be an asshole," and we both laughed.

I then inquired, "What about Jesus?" To that statement, I received a blank look. I went on to tell her that long before the time of Jesus, hemp medicine was already in widespread use. If there really was a man named Jesus healing people 2000 years ago, what do you suppose he was using to perform all those medical miracles? Do you think there is a good possibility that he could have been using hemp to perform these deeds? If so, why does the Bible not mention the substance he was using? Or are we simply supposed to believe that it was the power of God?" I explained that in all likelihood, I expect Jesus did not keep anything hidden from those he helped. But in years to come, individuals who were powerful in religious circles, when the Bible was printed hundreds of years later, may have felt it might be best to hide the truth, so they could control the masses more easily. The implication of what I had stated slowly sunk into her mind.

I explained further by saying, "Dear, religion is one of the main stumbling blocks that has stood in the way of the free use of hemp medicine." If you simply look into what I am saying with an open mind, it's very hard to dispute the facts, which I have given you. She absorbed everything I had said and became very quiet. I think it's safe to say, she was a very disillusioned Christian when she left my home that day, but I believe she was somewhat more in tune about the truth of the matter.

Blind belief in something does not make it right. When the truth is staring you in the face, how can you deny its presence? Around our area, we often hear the statement "God will get you." If God wants to punish me for healing the sick with hemp, then go ahead, I'm waiting. Was it not God or some facsimile thereof, which put this plant on Earth to help and heal the human race? If this is so, then I think I have little to worry about.

Word was spreading rapidly about the healing power of this substance and many new faces appeared at my door. Obviously, I cannot name all the cases here, but it's true to say there was no shortage of patients who required my assistance. A circle of people was now starting to form around me and the cause I was fighting for. Many of them were just as convinced about the healing power of this plant as I was, for they had also seen what this natural medicine could do with their own eyes and seeing is believing. Even the research we had done up to this point indicated everything this medication did was beneficial to the patient. It seemed this plant could do no wrong, but what else could I do to get the public's attention? For the time being, I would continue to produce this medicine and help as many as possible, thinking sometime in the near future all would change with regard to its use.

CHAPTER 6

MEETING MY FRIEND RICK DWYER

Pat Gouchie, a lady to whom I had previously supplied oil to treat her cancer successfully, contacted me and said Rick Dwyer, the bartender at our local Royal Canadian Legion branch in Maccan, would like to meet with me and find out more about what I was doing. When I met Rick Dwyer, I instantly liked this man. He was very open and honest and wanted to know all about the oil. He then asked if I would mind taking him along when I called on people who were using the oil as a medication. I told him I would enjoy the company and I would be happy to have him travel with me to visit patients.

The first time Rick went with me he was convinced, here were the real people who were using this substance for medicinal purposes and he seen for himself what the oil was doing to help their medical conditions. At that time, I carried a movie camera with me on these visits to chronicle the patient's progress and to provide proof to anyone who wished to view the footage, so I had no shortage of evidence. Rick and I talked it over and decided this issue should be of concern to the Legion. After all, I am the son of a war veteran and the Royal Canadian Legion as a veterans association is supposed to stand for the rights of veterans and their families. What more basic right could there be than to have the freedom to heal yourself with a natural herb? To stop the wrong that was being done against us all, Rick and I scheduled a public meeting at the Royal Canadian Legion Branch 134 in Maccan to discuss the issue.

The meeting was held in April 2005. About a dozen patients made themselves available to tell the audience what the oil had done for their conditions. Around 45 people attended the meeting that day and we had set up a movie camera, so the whole event could be videotaped. During the meeting, I openly stated I intended to grow hemp that summer right in my own back yard, so I could produce the medicine from it and, as usual, I hid nothing from the public. I produced copies of the video we had taken at the meeting and they were sent to W5, The Fifth Estate, and The Nature of Things, which were very popular information shows in Canada.

A couple of weeks later, on May 6, 2005, I took a copy of the same video into the Amherst detachment of the Royal Canadian Mounted Police, telling them that local politicians should be charged with criminal negligence causing death. I also asked the RCMP if they would supply me with what they confiscated during their raids, so I could produce more medicine. Due to my distrust for the RCMP, I had Rick Dwyer come with me and film everything while I was giving the information and video to them. The woman behind the counter at the RCMP detachment that day seemed more than just a little shocked when we walked in with the camera in hand. By filming it all, I knew the RCMP couldn't deny they had been given the information and that I had provided this evidence to them. Three months went by and I never heard a thing from the RCMP. Then, on August 3, 2005, this same detachment staged a raid on my home.

A friend of mine had just dropped in that day and I left him on the sun deck, while I went to make some coffee. Suddenly I heard a knock at the door and when I opened it, there stood an officer from the RCMP. When the cop stepped through my door, I asked him if he was there to do a count. He just looked at me stupidly and said they were there to confiscate the crop. I asked him about the evidence and video I had given his detachment three months before. He stated that he knew nothing about any videotape or evidence, which I had provided. I then stepped further into my kitchen, from there I could see out the patio door and I could clearly view what was taking place. There were three or four cops standing on my deck and one was holding a gun right to my friend's head. If there had been weapons present, this type of behavior might have been excused. Instead, it was later proven that there were no restricted weapons present in my home. All they discovered was a perfectly legal pellet gun, which even a child is allowed to purchase at local hardware stores. The pellet gun was standing in the corner of my living room behind the television and due to its low muzzle velocity is not classified as a restricted weapon.

I thought this was beginning to look much the same as the Wild West and to me these so-called police officers were acting like nothing more than a pack of drunken cowboys. When we stepped out on the deck and the officer that had come to my door could see all the hemp, he stated, "Four of our fellow officers just lost their lives over that stuff out West!" I knew of the case he was referring to and asked if he expected me to believe that nonsense. The RCMP had already made press releases, admitting that these officers had not been killed over marijuana, but instead had supposedly died in the line of duty, trying to repossess a pickup truck. The RCMP are not accustomed to having the truth thrown back in their face and the officer who had made the statement just looked at me with a blank expression. But at least after a while, they did allow my friend to go on his way, since he had nothing to do with the crop that was present in my back yard.

As soon as you came down off my deck, there was the hemp, no more than twelve feet from my house, growing on an open hillside. About eight cops were milling around my deck, but none had walked into the hemp. One of them walked over and asked me if there was anything in the hemp garden they should know about. Seeing that these heavily armed public servants were quite nervous, I couldn't resist the opportunity, so I told him there were just a few claymores. The look on his face was precious and you could tell he had been shocked by my statement.

I let what I had said hang in the air for a few seconds, then laughed and informed him patients had helped me plant this crop and some of them even bring their grandchildren over to walk through the garden. Would a person install land mines under such circumstances even if they had them at their disposal? He nodded his head and started to walk away. He then turned to me again and asked, if there was anyone with guns in the woods surrounding my property. Here they were, armed to the teeth, and yet they were afraid someone might take a shot at them for what they were doing. I told him, "Of course there are people with guns; the woods are full of them, especially in hunting season." I could not help but think, "Where did the RCMP ever find a pack of winners like this?"

Six or seven of them went down to the back of the garden and began to cut the crop down. I was left alone on the deck with a female officer and I definitely was not in a good mood. I was going on about what they were doing when she stated, "I want you to know I believe every word you are saying." That one was right out of left field. I looked at her and said, "You're telling me you believe everything I'm saying about the healing power of this plant? To this she nodded yes, so I inquired, "Well, where are your morals then? How can you just sit there and watch them destroy this crop, knowing that it's for medicinal use and cures cancer?" She then just dropped her head and remained silent.

During the raid, they had confiscated the boiler I had been using to boil off and reclaim the solvent. When the cop that was carrying it to their van walked by me, there was a big smirk on his face, which I expect was intended to get under my skin. I just laughed at him and said, "If need be I can produce the oil in a used beer can and taking my boiler would not put a stop to what I was doing. Then I was taken to Amherst to be charged and fingerprinted. Later that day, when I returned, the house was all torn to pieces. Not only was my home a mess, but evidence I had on videotape of patients being healed with this medication was now missing. It must be great to have a job that allows them to destroy other people's property and steal whatever they like in the name of the Canadian government. It was certainly now clear to me that the RCMP were not working in the public's best interests and couldn't be trusted.

At the time, I had many people under treatment, so how was I now to produce the medicine they required, without my boiler and a crop to work with? When I first began producing the oil, I tried to boil the solvent off using a crock-pot, but the oil had been ruined when it overheated. Obviously, this method would be of little use to me or anyone else and the oil could not be produced in a reliable manner, using these devices. Still, there had to be a simple way it could be accomplished, without harming the medicinal potency of the medication that was being produced. By confiscating the boiler I used to distill the solvent off and taking the crop, they had really thrown a monkey wrench into my activities, but where there's a will, there's a way.

About two days after the RCMP raid, I was in our local Canadian tire store in Amherst, walking through the appliance section, seeking something that could replace my boiler. After looking at different appliances, I picked up a rice cooker and read about how it worked in the instructions. Rice can burn very easily, so a rice cooker has two different heat settings, high (cook) and low (warm). When the temperature within one of these cookers becomes too high, it automatically switches itself back to the low-heat setting. I thought if this device can protect rice from overheating and burning, it might do the same for the oil and, sure enough, it did. I have never ruined any medication with the use of a rice cooker. If the lid is not used, these devices do the job perfectly with no danger of overheating the remaining oil.

As far as I'm concerned, using a boiler, often called a still, to reclaim the solvent and eliminate any danger of fire or explosion is one of the best ways to accomplish this task. But unfortunately most people do not have access to a still, which can boil the solvent off safely, at their disposal. Such devices are illegal to own in many countries, including Canada, unless they are simply used to distill water. In most distillers, which are designed to distill water, the element is immersed right in the water, much the same as an electric hot water heater. Only a fool would try to use such a device to boil solvent off, since the whole thing could blow up right in their face.

If you intend to boil solvent off, the distiller must be well designed and heavily built, with no internal elements, which could come into direct contact with the solvent. In addition, even though the process is quite simple, few have the knowledge to do this properly, since most individuals never had the opportunity to work with such devices. In a situation like this, a rice cooker can be of great value to anyone trying to produce the oil and many people already own one. If not, these devices can usually be purchased for about $30. The use of a rice cooker solved my problems involved with boiling the solvent off and has allowed countless people to produce their own medication with ease.

Three days after the raid, I was sitting on my deck in a very depressed state, when I noticed a small hemp leaf blowing in the wind. Suddenly, I realized there were quite a large number of these leaves on the small hill behind my house. There had been 1620 plants in my back yard that summer and I expect those who helped me plant them can verify this number, if need be. When questioned, this was the figure I had given them, although the police later claimed there had been less than 1200. So it seems that after the raid there were well over 400 plants missing and I have no idea what the RCMP did with them. I found all this to be very unusual, because the RCMP in most cases are noted for claiming more and not less than what was really there. Perhaps those who were involved in the raid decided to borrow the missing plants for purposes of their own; other than that I have no explanation as to where the plants could have gone.

They sheared the plants off very close to the ground and then had taken a spade and driven it through the middle of each plant's root system. As they had worked their way up the hill toward my house, they must have tired. Up closer to my home, some of the plants had been cut off about 4 inches above ground level, leaving enough for these amazingly hardy plants to make a comeback. What was left of these plants was still trying to survive and had put on the small leaves, which I had noticed. In the hope that they might still be able to produce a small amount of bud, I rounded up a water hose that the RCMP had neglected to take and did what I could to help the remaining plants revive.

The Springhill Record did an article about the raid and Chris Gooding took a look at where the hemp had been planted. All he went on about in the piece he wrote was what the RCMP had left behind. It seems the devil's advocate had missed the point again as to what he should have reported. Why had he not written about the RCMP confiscating the plants that could cure cancer and relieve the suffering of millions from other conditions? At least the Chronicle Herald, our provincial newspaper, did do a slightly less biased piece about what had transpired. Still, I felt these papers could have done much better articles and should have investigated and interviewed people who had used the oil for their medical conditions. Of course, this they did not do. Instead, they fed the public their version, ignoring the real issue as usual. Many local people were upset about the raid, since they knew I was not a drug dealer and was supplying the medicine to people free of charge, when I had it available.

The disgust local people displayed brought about another public meeting at the Maccan Legion. We all knew what the RCMP had done was a crime, but we felt helpless to do anything to rectify the situation. The meeting was well attended, but I had already been everywhere there was to go about this issue. Knowing no one in authority would step up to represent the public's best interests, none of us knew where to turn. Rick Dwyer and I talked it over and decided to let the Legion's Maritime Command know what was happening. Rick had been the past President of our local Legion branch, so he contacted the Head of Maritime Command, whose name was George Aucoin, on two or three separate occasions. We even sent him a copy of the video from the meeting that had taken place in April. But just like all the rest, Maritime Command refused to become involved with this issue and would not lift a finger.

Right in the Legion's own handbook, it states that the Royal Canadian Legion is to have no political affiliations. If this is true, why had they not acted? The Royal Canadian Legion is supposed to be a watchdog that protects us from corruption on our government's part and those who represent their interests, like the RCMP. By this time, I was starting to wonder if there were any organizations in Canada that were not controlled by corruption and government manipulation. For if there were, why would they not step forward and defend the rights of the Canadian people?

Many growers I knew were coming to me to have oil produced for themselves and friends who were suffering from medical problems. A few growers were even giving the oil away the same as I was and they liked the quality of the oil I produced. One day, I was in Amherst and a grower I had produced oil for about three months before walked up to me and said, "Rick that oil really does work." When I had produced the oil for him, I had not been aware that he himself was having medical difficulties, so I asked him what had happened. He then told me he had been diagnosed as a bipolar borderline schizophrenic. Instantly, I thought back to the young man with schizophrenia, who had shown such a marked improvement in his condition, when he had smoked the joint in front of me years before.

The grower told me that when he went home that day, after getting the oil, he had thrown all of his chemical medications in the trash. He then went on the oil and now he was back to work and feeling great. His reply had just tipped me off to another miracle about this medication's use, which could not be ignored. Now I knew we had a harmless medicine that could help many schizophrenics as well as others who were suffering from mental disturbances of a different nature.

In September 2005, I entered the hallowed halls of the Canadian legal system. When I appeared in court, I gave the Crown prosecutor a videotape of the meeting, which was held at our local Legion branch that past April. This videotape also showed me taking the information and video into the RCMP in May, months before I was ever charged. It also included a segment directed at the Crown prosecutor himself, telling him that none of this belonged in a court of law. A copy of this same video was also given to the Chronicle Herald reporter, who was present in the court that day. I thought they just might watch this video and come to their senses. Of course, by that time I should have known better. If memory doesn't fail me, I believe this was the day the judge put a publication ban in place, stopping reporters from doing articles in connection with my case.

Even though it appeared the legal system was going to play games with this issue, at least the plants that were left in my back yard had made a strong comeback. When I started watering them again after the raid, I hoped that by the end of September, I might be able to harvest a few ounces of good bud. After harvesting what had regrown and drying the crop out, there was 22 pounds of prime bud, which was instantly turned into medicine. Given the fact that I would not have to purchase as much from other local growers, I was really grateful to have even this small amount to work with. I was still giving the medicine away and buying the starting material from local suppliers was draining what little money I had left very quickly. When I started down this path back in 2001, the $125,000, which I received from Canada Pension and Workman's Compensation in back payments, had provided me with the money to make this happen. But now the well was running dry and I had to be very careful how I spent what little remained.

In the fall of 2005, I was approached by a man who wanted me to produce oil for the biker gangs. I told him I would not become involved in such nonsense. If they wanted to sell oil on the street, they would have to produce it themselves. He told me they would give me 45 dollars a gram, if I would produce it for them. If I had to buy the starting material, on average it cost me about 40 dollars a gram to produce this substance. That amount does not include the price of the solvent being used, or the power that is being consumed, so to me what he was offering did not sound like much of a business opportunity.

In addition, if I were to become involved with groups like this, in a short time I would probably end up in jail. Again, I told him I was not interested. He then informed me that he was connected with a gang out of Montreal and they could make my life quite difficult, if I did not comply. I just laughed and told him to send them down and I would leave a trail of crushed motorcycles all the way back to Montreal. To make matters clear, I informed him that I drive a 6500-pound diesel truck and if they wanted to mess with that, I wished them all the luck in the world. It appears what I had said must have been taken seriously, because I heard nothing more from anyone involved with this group again. Believe me, in the line of work I was now in, there was no shortage of strange characters to deal with.

The next time I attended court in the fall of 2005, it was suggested that I should mount a Charter challenge. The judge told me to gather as many affidavits from people as possible and to make them available to the court system by early March 2006. He stated, "In cases like this, it usually takes about two weeks to render a decision." For some unknown reason, in my case, he said it would take about five weeks and I would then have my decision from him in April.

I put out 120 affidavits and this is when I started to figure out what most of the human race is really about. In the end, I could only collect 48 affidavits and even gathering that number presented quite a few difficulties. In many cases, even individuals who had cured their cancer with the oil refused to become involved. These were times when I really had to stop and ask myself why I was fighting for the public's right to have free use of this medicine, when so many of them didn't seem to care one way or another if it was available to anyone else but themselves.

It was great that the oil had helped with their medical conditions, but it was not their problem that other people were being denied the use of this medication and were suffering and dying needlessly. Apparently, this is the way that the vast majority of people think and it is thinking like this that has put us in the situation we are in today. If something is causing some to suffer, then we are all suffering. This self-centered thinking many people exhibit is destroying us and exposing what a sad species we have truly become. If such people refuse to stand up for what is right, then what purpose do they possibly serve on this Earth and what right do they have to even call themselves rational caring human beings?

In the beginning, the lawyer I had hired to do the Charter challenge bumped heads with me. The first few meetings I attended were very stormy in nature and there were many arguments. One day during one of these meetings, he looked at me and stated, "Rick, I owe you an apology. From the time you hired me, I have been trying to treat you like a criminal and it is now more than obvious to me that you are not." It seemed he had finally realized that my intentions were pure in nature, but at the time I don't think he completely believed what I had told him about the healing power of this medication.

I shot back, "Finally, you're starting to get the real picture." He then went on and told me that he had discussed my case with some of his other lawyer friends. "My associates and I want you to know, Rick, we think what you're doing is wonderful." I answered, "If it's so wonderful, what am I doing tied up in your legal system?" To this, he did not reply. I asked him if I would be wrong in thinking that possibly half the lawyers in Canada are making a living off hemp cases, when they must be aware that these laws should not even exist. He looked at me and admitted, "You know, Rick, most lawyers are crooks."

By that time, such information was no surprise to me. I then asked him if the statement he had just made was supposed to be some kind of excuse. Again, he made no attempt to answer my question. I then expressed my dissatisfaction with his statement by saying, "What is wrong with you people, have you no common decency? Where are your morals?" He just looked at me and shrugged his shoulders. Statements like this from the lawyer I had hired to defend me did nothing to instill any confidence that myself and this issue would be treated fairly by the legal system. From the position I was in, you would have to be brain dead not to see what these people and their legal system were really about.

When patients started coming to my lawyer's office to have their affidavits sworn before him, he was very impressed by the number of people who came forward and what they had to say about their experiences with the oil. I had supplied this medication to a lady named Shirley O'Brien from River Hebert to treat a nasty condition involving her ears. The doctors had been seeing her for about two years, but all their treatments had been unsuccessful. Her condition continued to worsen and the doctors could not even provide her with a diagnosis. One of her ears was completely broken out in sores and the other was not much better. She told me her ears were giving her so much discomfort she could not get any sleep, and it was easy to see that the poor woman was exhausted. After discussing her problems I gave her some oil and explained that she should apply it to her ears and then cover them with plastic wrap, so it would not get on the bedding. I told her if she did this, she would be able to sleep and her ears should heal quickly.

Two days later, Shirley again came to my home, but this time she told me she was there to apologize. I asked, "Whatever for?" She then laughed and explained what had happened. "The other day when I got the oil from you, on the way home I thought this guy has got to be some kind of nut. He wants me to go home and put what looks like axle grease on my ears and he's telling me I will get a good night's sleep." Since she had nothing to lose, she applied the oil as I had instructed and slept like a baby. Within a week, both of her ears were completely healed and she was one very happy patient with the results.

I was present on the day when Shirley brought her affidavit into my lawyer's office. She looked at him, then pointed her finger at me and stated, "That man is worth his weight in gold." My lawyer just smiled and replied, "Apparently so." You could tell he was quite mystified by what was unfolding before him. I was disgusted that only 48 affidavits had been submitted as evidence from the 120 I had put out, but my lawyer was amazed. He explained, "In a case like this, a person such as yourself would be considered lucky if he they can collect six or eight statements from patients. Look at the number of affidavits you have; this is truly unbelievable."

The next time we were in court, my lawyer made it very clear to the judge that this case was no joke. He told the judge I really did have the evidence to back up what I had been saying. The judge did not seem to be impressed and appeared to be quite indifferent as to what he was being told. In early March 2006, the affidavits were placed in the hands of the legal system. Now all I could do was wait and see what happened. At the time, I still thought I was going to get his decision in April, but I was soon to find out otherwise.

CHAPTER 7
THE RCMP STRIKE AGAIN

Throughout the fall of 2005 and the winter of 2006, the number of people coming to me for help continued to increase. The articles that had been written in the newspapers had received the attention of a great number of people who had thought their conditions to be hopeless until they started using the oil. The success rate of this amazing medication was crashing through all the barriers and breaking all the rules. It seemed to be able to cure or control practically any medical condition for just about anyone. But here I was tied up in the court system with eight Canadians dying every hour from cancer and who knows how many others worldwide.

I wondered at the time how many people would have to die before this natural medication was recognized once more for its healing abilities. It seemed impossible to me that this could go on much longer. I knew there were a large number of people who were standing against what I was doing, but with all the evidence I had, how long could that continue? Those among them with a brain that still functioned had to realize what I was bringing out could save their lives, too. What really sickened me most was the simple fact that if many of those who were restricting this plant's medicinal use had cancer themselves, guess who would be searching for hemp oil? By all appearances, it seemed there were a great number of people who were more than willing to do anything for a paycheck. Even with all the harm they had already caused, whenever possible they continued to relish the opportunity to exercise their misguided authority over the public.

In late April 2006, I called my lawyer and asked what was going on with my decision. He told me it had been put off, because the Crown could not present their case in time. "What kind of nonsense is this?" I stated. "The Crown had since last fall to prepare their case. People are suffering and dying everywhere and I consider what is taking place here to be inexcusable." I could not help but think there is no question now that the Canadian legal system is just as bad as the rest of them. About a month later, my lawyer called me and said the Crown wanted to offer me a deal. He told me if I was willing to drop the Charter challenge, then go back into the regular court system and plead guilty to cultivation, I would be granted an absolute discharge, which meant I would not be given a criminal record. I could then just walk away from the whole thing, if I was willing to comply.

I clarified their offer by saying, "The Crown wants me to plead guilty and pretend I have done something wrong, so they can carry on with this charade. Lawyers will then be able to continue filling their pockets, prosecuting and defending individuals who are facing charges regarding hemp. The Crown does not care that people are dying and that their actions are responsible for this occurring. It's all about the money." I told my lawyer I would have nothing to do with any deals offered to me by these criminals. He stated, he had already told them he did not think I would agree to go along with their plans. He then informed me my Charter challenge was to be held the following December, eight months in the future. It seems the court system's excuse was that they were so tied up with other cases it was impossible for them to hear my case before that date, or at least that was the story I was given. People worldwide were in desperate need of this medication, but the Canadian legal system was just too busy to deal with my case until the following December. Anyone who would believe the excuses I was being given by the legal system in a situation like this does not have too much on the ball.

Right around that time, we had another amazing recovery, which focused the attention of the local population on the use of this medicine once again. Rick Dwyer's father Ed was a well-known and respected man in Amherst and the surrounding region. He ran a store for years in Maccan and he had many business dealings around our local area. It seemed everyone knew and liked Ed Dwyer. He was an 82-year-old veteran and his health had been going downhill for quite some time. Ed had been a diabetic for over 30 years, and he had a multitude of other medical problems. One day, his doctor changed one of the prescriptions he was taking and Ed's kidneys ceased to function. He was taken to the hospital to see what could be done, whereupon they discovered he also had lung cancer.

By that time, Ed's son Rick was totally against chemotherapy. Not knowing the ugly truth about the effects of chemo, Rick's sister took Ed to Moncton and he was given his first injection. After just one dose of chemo, Ed came home and swelled up like a balloon. His lungs filled with fluid and the swelling was so bad, even his legs split open. He was taken to the Amherst hospital and doctors there gave him 48 hours to live. Things did not look good, but he was able to get through the first day. The next morning, the doctors gave him 24 hours. Rick Dwyer was beside himself. His father was laying in the Amherst hospital, dying in agony with his lungs full of fluid and no one at the hospital seemed to be able to provide him with any relief. Rick already knew a great deal about the oil, so he came and asked me if I thought it could help his Dad.

I told Rick, "At this stage of the game, what could he possibly have to lose? If nothing else, the oil should help to ease his way out, so at least he might die with dignity." Rick went to the hospital and spoke with the doctor about giving his father oil. The doctor refused and told Rick he would not be responsible. Rick's father was on his deathbed and needed help desperately, but his doctor refused to comply. This left Rick with only one course of action. He walked into his father's room, put a large dose of oil on a small piece of cracker, and fed it to his Dad. Rick then left the hospital, leaving his two brothers on the overnight deathwatch. He put in a sleepless night, then the following morning he told his mother what he had done and she was afraid the police would come to arrest him.

As Rick informed me later, upon arriving at the hospital the next morning, I guess it was quite a scene to behold. His father was sleeping like a log and Rick's brothers told him, Ed's breathing had returned to normal shortly after he had left last night. His vital signs had been dropping steadily. Then all of a sudden, during the night, they stabilized. The doctors tried to tell Rick this often happens just before they pass away. Rick was not having any of that, so he looked at his mother and told her, "Dad still has a chance to survive, but we have to get him out of this hospital." The doctors didn't think much of it, but Ed's family signed him out and he went home. Rick then started giving the oil to his father on a steady basis. They had installed a catheter while Ed was in the hospital and after a couple of days at home, Ed was having a lot of discomfort and wanted the device removed. Rick talked to the home care nurse, but was told that if it were taken out, they would only have to take him back to the hospital to have another one put in its place. He asked his father if he could urinate and his father replied, "Yes." Rick then instructed the nurse to remove the catheter. When that was done, Ed was able to pass 800 ml of urine with little effort and from then on, his urinary tract functioned perfectly.

Along with insulin, Ed had been taking about two dozen pills a day. Rick, then set about getting his father off all those chemicals. It took a few weeks, but Rick succeeded. All of a sudden, after only about six weeks on the oil, his Dad no longer even required insulin to control his diabetes. Ed was now like a kid in a candy store. After 30 years of insulin and needles, he no longer required them and he could now eat whatever he liked again. For someone his age, Ed had an amazing capacity for this medication. At one point during his treatment, he was taking two grams of high-grade oil every twenty-four hours and was still going to Amherst every day to talk to all his friends.

Another thing that should be mentioned about Ed's recovery was that his bald spot grew in during treatment with the oil. For years, Ed always had a bald spot and when they gave him the dose of chemo, most of the rest of his hair fell out. While he was taking the oil, his hair grew back in and even his bald spot showed signs of re-growth, so yet again, the oil had just showed me another of its many virtues.

Everyone witnessed Ed's miraculous recovery. He soon became the talk of the town and so was the oil that had taken him off his deathbed. Ed lived on for another fifteen months before he died from a heart condition he had suffered from for years. Ed passed away in his sleep and did not die in pain; so again the oil had fulfilled its purpose.

The extra months of life this medication had given him were not wasted. He became very vocal about the oil and joined with us in trying to bring the wonderful healing effects of this medication to the public's attention. He had been a devoted Conservative

Party member and had belonged to the Royal Canadian Legion for most of his life. By the time Ed passed away, he had seen for himself what these organizations were doing and he died having no use for either one of them.

In the spring of 2006, we contacted Stephen Lewis, who was with the United Nations. Like all the others we had approached about this issue, the United Nations also hid under a rock and did nothing. I cannot say I have ever had any use for the United Nations anyway, since I had always looked at this organization as nothing more than criminals in suits. Their only aim was to do the bidding of the rich and powerful that were really running the show behind the scenes. When something happened in this world that the UN should have acted upon, often they would respond very slowly or simply remain silent.

The UN had also gone along with Harry J. Anslinger, the first head of the U.S. Federal Narcotics Bureau (later renamed the Drug Enforcement Administration), a rabid propagandist against hemp. In the 1950s, Anslinger had the UN declare cannabis hemp to be non-medicinal. Then in 1961, they had put the Single Convention Treaty in place, which denied citizens of member countries the use of hemp. After the UN did nothing to look into this, judging by their past performance concerning other issues of importance, it did not come as much of a shock to me.

It was now May 2006 and it was time to plant another crop. I had taken 1100 cuttings, also known as clones, off good female plants from eight different strains. In two to three weeks, they were rooted and, after being acclimatized, were then ready to go into the ground. I knew I could be raided again, but demand for the oil had become so great that I really didn't have a choice. I could only hope the RCMP and the government that controls their actions had grown up enough about this subject to leave this crop alone.

The summer went well and the plants were thriving. Then on September 6, 2006, in came the RCMP again. I thought, "This can't be real, how much longer are these officers of the law willing to carry on in this manner?" Of course, once again, they did not have a search warrant, but they did have a new way of justifying their actions. This time I was told they were with the Marijuana Eradication Program and had come to take the crop.

The Marijuana Eradication Program is just another important-sounding title they use, which allows them to conduct crimes and terrorize the citizens of Canada in the name of their so-called law. It's too bad that in reality they were simply there to steal the cure from the public once again. There was absolutely no question this time that they were acting against the wishes of the people in our area. Rick Dwyer tried to show the RCMP a letter from our local Legion branch while they were performing the raid that was in support of what I was doing. They ignored him and refused to look at the letter, saying they were just doing their jobs.

My home was not searched this time and I was neither charged nor arrested. They were simply there to steal the hemp from which I was making the medicine. As a result of the raids the RCMP conducted in 2003, 2005, and 2006, thousands of Canadians did not get the medicine they required. Patients with low incomes, who could not afford to buy the material they needed that I had been providing for free, would now have to pay for the actions of the RCMP with their lives. Since our national police force is behaving in this manner towards the very people they are supposed to be serving, perhaps it's time that we had a Corruption Eradication Program put in place to rid ourselves of those who mean us harm.

Many people can afford to buy a pound of good hemp from a dealer to produce the medicine they require. Yet the vast majority of patients I had dealt with were poor and lacked the funding to give drug dealers thousands of dollars for the bud material they needed. In many cases, such people did not even have enough income to survive properly, so at least when I could provide the oil free, they did have access to the medication, which could help them. The actions of the RCMP were making it more and more difficult for me to help those who required this substance for their medicinal needs. It's too bad it was not these RCMP officers who were suffering themselves, for then I'm sure they would have felt very differently about what they were taking part in.

When the news spread that I had been raided once again, our local Legion and many citizens in the surrounding area were outraged. This time we came up with something that might bring what was going on to an end. The president and executive of Branch 134 released a letter to the local papers. In this letter, they were calling for an open and honest review of this medicine. We invited politicians, representatives of the medical system, the Cumberland Health Authority, the RCMP, and doctors to attend a public meeting that was to be held at our local Legion.

I also had a good number of patients who were ready to attend the meeting and explain to those present what this medicine had done for their conditions. Everything was set. Then, on the morning of the day we were to have this meeting, Maritime Command, with the aid of the RCMP, came to Maccan and closed our local Legion branch. About a month after our Legion was shut down; a general meeting was called by Maritime Command. We all went to the Legion that night, thinking that finally they were going to do something. When we were seated, we were told by four members of Maritime Command that politics and this medicine could not be discussed. Here we were sitting in the house that freedom built, a Royal Canadian Legion, and representatives from this organization were trying to tell us we could not exercise our right to freedom of speech.

What they were attempting to do was almost beyond comprehension. Especially, since Les Nash, one of the people with Maritime Command who were making these statements, had used the oil for a condition he had himself and he knew the oil worked. Still, he was more than willing to go along with the government and Maritime Command in trying to keep the truth from the Canadian people. In my book, what he did is nothing short of treason against his own friends and countrymen. After listening to their doubletalk and uncaring attitude for a few minutes, I got up and told those present, "Look, we have eight Canadians dying every hour from cancer and we all know this medication can help them to survive, something must be done about this."

Their reply was, "People have been dying forever." Eventually, the Legion would get around to looking into the matter, but that would happen sometime in the future. If the men and women who had fought and died for this country knew what the Canadian government and the Royal Canadian Legion were now doing, they would probably roll over in their graves. This, so to speak, was the straw that broke the camel's back. I had heard enough. I got up and stood in front of Maritime Command's representatives and told them, they were nothing but a pack of murdering freaks. I stated it was too bad it was not them who were the ones suffering from cancer, for perhaps then they would do something about this. Seeing there was no progress to be made here, I then left the building, as did Rick Dwyer and others. We had heard enough from the Royal Canadian Legion.

Before all this took place, I was told that Branch 134 had about 130 members. As I understand it today, this Legion branch is down to 30 members or less and is facing permanent closure. The community would no longer support the Legion, once they found out this organization was not working in the public's best interest. I strongly suspect some government money was funneled into Branch 134 to keep the doors open for a while to try to make it appear as if everything was normal, but with no public support to generate funds, this Legion's closure was inevitable. Just before this book was published, I received word that Branch 134 has been closed permanently. Now since Dominion Command and none of the other legion branches across Canada acted to protect our rights. I wonder how long it will take the Canadian people to close the rest of them, so the deeds of this pathetic organization can be erased from our memories.

It sickens me that the Royal Canadian Legion continues to pretend to honor the memory of real men like my father and many others who suffered and died in the name of freedom. As far as I and a good number of others are concerned, the Royal Canadian Legion is a fraud and should be disbanded. I will not even buy a poppy from them now to honor those who fought for our country because I know the money goes into their coffers. Throughout his life, my father himself would have nothing to do with the Legion. He said they were just assholes that stood for nothing more than a bottle of beer. Again, it appears, he was correct.

Just a short time ago, I got word that Les Nash is now the new head of Maritime Command. He admitted to Rick Dwyer that in 2006 orders to shut down Branch 134 had come straight from Dominion Command. It appears that for his complicity Dominion Command saw to it that Mr. Nash was rewarded. I think it should now be more than clear what a disgrace the Royal Canadian Legion really is and why I refuse even to buy a poppy from this traitorous organization.

In the fall of 2006, the Legion's closure did bring some attention to this issue. Papers again wrote more biased articles, but finally, the TV news became involved. Global news, CTV News, and CBC News were all at my home on the same day. We explained to them what was going on and they did interviews with people, who had used the oil as a medicine. The Global News reporter Ross Lord said, "Rick, this is unbelievable." To this, I replied, "You have to believe it when the real patients are standing in front of you." The people they interviewed that day were not a bunch of kids looking to get high. Most were senior citizens that had been suffering badly, before using this amazing medicine.

All three networks did a news report the following day and Global even put it on their national news broadcast a couple of days later. Of course, they did not show viewers the interviews with patients, as they should have. Instead, it was all about the Legion's closure and whether marijuana is medicine or menace. From my point of view, it was just sensationalist nonsense, but at least the issue we were fighting for had received some national attention.

People were now coming in droves for the medicine and I thought, "Finally, this is over. With the coverage we had received, surely someone out there would do something about this situation." A month after the news broadcast, we received an e-mail from the TV show W5. It simply stated, "Where's the proof? We e-mailed them back and told them to watch the videotape we had sent them a year and a half before. If this did not satisfy them, they could send a reporter down and I would take them directly to the patients. I have never heard another word from W5.

Global News came back just before Christmas 2006 to do another story about this subject. When the reporter was there, I asked him if they hit many walls of resistance, when they tried to report on a story such as this. He looked at me as if he didn't know what I meant. A few hours later, I received a call from him, telling me he had found that wall I was talking about. He stated he had done a great story, but it was rejected by those in higher positions. He was quite apologetic about it and told me he had done his best. I could tell by the way he spoke after being told the article he had written was not to be published that he was very disillusioned with the news agency which employed him.

In the fall of 2006, a federal election was called in Canada. I thought if I ran in the coming election on this issue, it could do much to awaken the public. I got all the paperwork done and delivered it to the proper authorities. Now, I was an independent candidate running on the issue of curing cancer and other conditions with the use of hemp oil. Even though the platform I was running on concerned the health and day-to-day lives of all Canadians, the news media tried to brand me as a one-issue candidate, whose only motive was to have pot made legal.

On the few occasions during the election that I was permitted to speak, the public just seemed to sit there in disbelief. Nothing I was saying was really disputed, but I could not seem to reach the people. All candidates are supposed to have equal time and be treated fairly during an election campaign, but I found otherwise. I was not even invited to speak at some venues during the election campaign and if I showed up, I was ignored. It appeared as if those who were putting on these events felt independent candidates did not deserve the same rights as those who represented a party. Therefore, the behavior of individuals who were staging some of these so-called political debates made it impossible for me to present my platform to the voting public.

I cannot say I did well in this election, since I only received 524 votes, but my presence had caused a ripple. Bill Casey, whom I had run against, said to some of my supporters, "Do you really expect me to believe a cure for cancer has been found in Maccan?" During his election campaign, Mr. Casey displayed a mixture of corruption and ignorance about this issue that I found to be unparalleled. Unfortunately, the others I ran against in this election were no better for the most part and refused to see the importance in what I was trying to bring forward. Politicians will try to do anything to please the parties, which they represent and during the campaign, I saw the levels of deception to which they would stoop.

While speaking to the public, many times Mr. Casey went on about the made-up evils of marijuana. At two places we spoke, he told the listening audience he had been to the homes of 40 people or more, whose children were addicted to marijuana. He then went on like Dr. Doolittle about the destructive nature of this plant. All this, if it were true, might not have been so bad in itself, but the government themselves had finally admitted quite a few years previously that marijuana is not addictive. So how could Mr. Casey have interviewed people whose children were addicted to marijuana, when his own government had said this is not the case? It appears he may have been stretching the truth a bit on that one so he could look good to those in the audience, which were brainwashed enough to believe that cannabis hemp was harmful. In addition, by this time, Casey knew first hand that the oil worked, since I had treated an old friend of his successfully. To add insult to injury, the public, in all their wisdom, reelected Casey with a landslide to another term in office.

While I was dealing with the election campaign, my Charter challenge had taken place. Just before Christmas 2006, my case was finally heard. In Canada, we have what's known as the Marijuana Access Program. But in reality, this program is just a feeble attempt on the governments part in trying to convince the public that they are actually doing something, but unfortunately it is little more than just a farce. A small number of individuals who have serious conditions like cancer, MS and a few other medical problems were granted licenses so they could grow and use the hemp plant legally to help with their conditions. Still, there is no provision under Canadian law, which allows patients to collect the resins or to produce the oil, since these are considered to be controlled substances. All patients are allowed to do is smoke the plant material, or break it up and put it in such things as cookies. Of course, governments are already aware of the fact that these methods will do most who suffer with serious conditions little good and that is why they prevent patients from producing the oil legally.

During my Charter Challenge, Monica McQueen, the prosecutor from the Justice Department and Doug Shatford, the Crown prosecutor, called people who represent the Marijuana Access Program in to testify. In their testimony, they stated my condition is not covered by their program and even if I applied, I would be rejected. This proved to me that their so-called program, which is supposed to help those who are suffering, is little more than a bad joke. None of the doctors I had seen would provide a prescription or the needed paperwork, which would allow me to even apply, so I had turned to the Chronic Pain Center in Halifax. I was told by others who had acquired the right to use this plant medicinally that the pain center had helped them through this process. I wished to use hemp legally, so I contacted them but was told that I would have to wait 21 months for an appointment.

Can you imagine someone in my condition waiting this length of time for their medication? And since then, I have been told that the waiting list has grown even longer. All this had transpired shortly after the medical system told me there was nothing more they could do to help in 2001. Therefore, as you can see, it's not that I didn't try to stay within the law, instead I became what they call a criminal because I was left with no other option if I wished to survive. This is how they treat patients with serious health issues in Canada and that is why today I would not even consider applying for such a license. They can save their song and dance routine for someone else and I think that anyone who has a license should send it back to the government and tell them that they are no longer interested in playing their stupid games.

When my Charter Challenge took place, there were only about 800 registered medicinal users in Canada out of a population of well over 30 million. Just these numbers alone should be more than enough to convince anyone that the Marijuana Access Program is simply a smoke screen. The Canadian government had put this program in place to try to make themselves and their policies look good in the eyes of an uninformed public.

Yet, the sad reality is they are doing little to help anyone but themselves and their policies are simply protecting the interests of the big drug companies.

Another topic the public should be aware of is the low quality of the marijuana that is supplied to the patients by the Canadian government. If they so choose, registered patients can get their pot right from the government for 150 dollars an ounce plus tax. This works out to 172.50 per ounce or 2760.00 dollars per pound. Many patients who tried what the government is supplying could not even use the substance and refused to make payment.

The last I heard, the government of Canada was stating that they were owed hundreds of thousands of dollars because patients who had received hemp from them would not pay. In reality, who can blame them, since much better quality cannabis hemp can be purchased from local growers at far less cost? Even in rural Nova Scotia, I could purchase a pound of high-grade medicinal hemp for 2400 dollars and I have been told that at the time in British Columbia the same could be purchased for 1500. Put simply, the Canadian government has been trying to supply low-grade trash to medicinal users at a very big price. This shows, they have no compassion for those they are supplying and since they are charging these outrageous prices, it begs the question, "Who are the real drug dealers?"

During my Charter Challenge, much of this was discussed and they went through a great deal of legal hocus-pocus, but in the end the judge dismissed the affidavits I had provided, saying they were anecdotal. He also stated I had not proved to have a life-threatening condition. Imagine a plant that has been used in medicine for 5000 years and sworn affidavits attesting to its effectiveness from people who had used it are "anecdotal." In addition, according to this judge, cancer and post-concussion syndrome are apparently not life-threatening conditions. I guess he was just not aware that a good number of the 200 people who die every day from cancer in Canada are dying from skin cancer. Or that post-concussion syndrome, which affects my blood pressure badly, could very easily pose a danger to my continued existence.

I really don't know where this judge got the nerve to think he has the right to make such a determination, for he is not a doctor and even if he did have a medical background, how could he arrive at such a conclusion? The statements he made during his ruling were so off-base that I went to the courthouse to get a transcription. They said they would provide it on audiocassettes for $60. When I listened to it, what the judge had stated during his ruling was not present. I went back to the courthouse and demanded the full transcription I had paid for. They refused to provide it to me. It seemed someone was covering up for the judge and did not want me playing what he had said to the public.

I had often heard the term that best describes this situation as having the deck stacked against you. Now I was living it and it was not stacked against just me, but everyone. In Canada, we have what is known as the Charter of Rights and Freedoms. Under the Charter, we, as Canadians, are all supposed have the right to life. Hemp oil is a natural, harmless, non-addictive medication that comes from a plant. Yet, surprisingly, the Canadian government seems to think it is within their jurisdiction to deny its medicinal use to people such as myself. I really should not have needed to even go through a Charter challenge to allow me the use of this medicine, since our right to life is clearly stated in the Charter.

Nevertheless, to further the agenda of the rich elite, governments, lawyers, medical professionals and drug companies etc., people like myself are forced to go through the legal system to see our rights are upheld. Of course, all this takes place for very profitable reasons and lawyers are more than happy to charge clients for services, which in truth should not even be required. After going through my Charter Challenge, it was obvious that the legal system is acting in complicity with the government and in most cases will abide by their wishes. When you are dealing with corruption on this level, what hope can we ever have of getting justice? Before we even enter the courtroom, it is a done deal and we haven't got the chance of a snowball in hell of winning. Put simply, either these people who work in our justice system are all criminals with decidedly evil intentions towards the public, or the Canadian Charter of Rights and Freedoms is not worth the paper it is written on.

During the winter of 2007, I made my next court appearance. They told me that if I liked, I could appeal the Charter challenge decision. I replied, "What's the point? I already know you people are trying to prevent the truth about the medicinal value of this plant from reaching the public." They did not seem to care much for this statement, even though it was more than obvious that what I was saying was a fact. I told them I had decided to proceed in the Supreme Court of Nova Scotia and that I wanted this case to be heard by a jury. I also requested that another judge be appointed to preside over my trial, since I had no trust in the one I had been dealing with. From the judge's reaction, it was clear he had taken my statement as a direct insult and it was no more than he deserved. Hearing the truth really seemed to aggravate his worship and he became quite flustered. In the end, it made no difference, anyway. When my case was finally heard, he was the presiding judge and I had the same prosecutors.

In May 2007, a local supporter Steve Ridgway asked a friend of his from Amherst named Christian Laurette if he was interested in doing a documentary and Steve then told Christian all about me and what I had been doing. On May 15, 2007, he came to my house with Steve and spent several hours with me to see what was happening, so he could get the whole story. Christian just sat there quietly with a doubtful expression and listened while taking notes as I was talking about the oil with my friends and patients.

Several times while he was there, Christian would move in his chair and I could see pain in his face. After everyone had left, Christian looked at me and stated he did not find this to be believable. Just as he was making this statement, he moved and it was plain by the look on his face that there was something wrong. So I asked what was causing him all the discomfort. He told me he had scoliosis and asked if I knew what this condition was. I told him I understood his problem and inquired what the medical system had done to help.

He stated that he had spent several years in agony caused by back problems from an injury he had sustained after taking a fall several years ago when he was a teenager. Christian wanted them to do an operation but the doctors would only give him a 50/50 chance of walking again. With odds like this and a shortage of qualified surgeons to perform the operation, he felt there was little that could be done, so he had decided to try to live with the pain and discomfort his condition was giving him. He had tried prescription drugs and received little or no relief from anything he had tried; in fact, he said these medications made him feel horrible, and the pain would never go away anyway.

About that time, Christian asked me what this medication could do to help his medical difficulties, to which I replied the oil is the only thing I know of which could ease his condition and give him a much better quality of life. After my statement, I could see the same look of disbelief on Christian's face that I had observed on the faces of so many others who had been suffering. I then went and got a syringe of oil and gave it to him, explaining that he should begin by taking very small amounts about every eight hours. The next day, Christian called me quite excited about what the oil had done for his back condition and it was then he told me that the documentary would indeed be made. He informed me that after taking the first dose the pain in his back had disappeared within 5 hours. He could not have been more pleased.

A few days later, Christian showed up at my door to discuss some details about documenting the story on video. In what seemed like an agitated state, he exclaimed, "Are you telling me you can cure scoliosis?" I just laughed and asked him to sit down so I could discuss it with him and I would fill in the blanks. I explained to him that the condition he was suffering from would not allow him to get the exercise he needed to build up his back muscles. Therefore, he lacked the muscle structure in his back that he should have and this is what was causing most of his problems. I explained that taking the oil would do some healing and kill the pain but, most importantly, it would allow him to build up the muscle mass he lacked. He informed me about the inflammation he was told his back was riddled with, but I explained to him that hemp oil is the greatest natural anti-inflammatory in existence.

I instructed him to stay on the oil and the day should soon come when he would be able to go for extended periods without using the oil at all. That's exactly what took place and Christian is very grateful to this medication for making him a healthy useful person once more. For years, Christian had been collapsing on the floor in agony from his back condition and lived in extreme pain most of the time. Now, with the use of the oil, he could live a normal life again. This is how I met the man who would produce "Run from the Cure" and I am very happy I did, because I don't think anyone could have done it better. Christian has met and interviewed many people who have used this substance. Now he has complete confidence in this amazing medicine just as I do.

In the summer of 2007, I went back to the woods. I was sick of watching cops tear up crops from my back yard, so I put some plants out where they should not be found and hoped for the best. Growing under such circumstances, it is very hard to produce a crop of any size and since I was now so busy dealing with the public, I could spend little time caring for the plants. If you had to grow your vegetables in well-hidden gardens in the woods, you would find that you could grow very little, so I knew I would also need other sources to supply the material I required. Luckily, from my exploits, I had come to know many growers who were more than happy to help supply the hemp I needed. Many of these suppliers have little money and are poor, so they had to be paid for their efforts. Still, I am very grateful to these growers, for the hemp they supplied eased the suffering of a great number of people.

I continued to supply the oil for free as long as I could grow and harvest the material needed for its production, but demand had become so great that I could not continue unless most patients were willing to purchase or grow the hemp that was required. In many cases, people would arrive at my door with bud material they had grown quietly on their own. It was always a joy for me to work with those who were willing to help themselves and I gave away tens of thousands of seeds so that patients could then grow their own.

When patients came to me with their own hemp, they paid nothing for my time, the solvent, or the power to produce the medicine they needed. If I was buying the hemp from local growers, it usually cost about 2400 dollars on average for enough material to produce a full cancer treatment. When you look at the way drug companies charge for supplying their so-called medications and treatments, paying 2400 dollars for the material needed to produce a full 60-gram high-grade oil treatment that does work could only be considered a very good deal, especially when your life is at stake.

By this time, I had become fully aware of the role drug companies were playing in all of this. After looking into what they used to produce in the past and their business practices extensively, in my opinion, the actions of such companies can best be described as crimes against humanity. Back in the 1800s and early 1900s, many of the big drug firms, which are still around today, were producing hemp-based medicines. As I understand it, up until about 1900, a great number of the medicines, which were produced worldwide, came from the hemp plant. Drug companies used cannabis hemp as an ingredient in a large number of the medicines they produced. Companies like Eli Lilly, Parke Davis, Squibb, and many others produced hemp-based medicines for decades.

Back in this era, it was common practice for drug companies to produce the essential oil from many different medicinal herbs and plants. Throughout history, hemp had always been known to have amazing medical qualities and was one of the most widely used medicinal plants on Earth. This fact was made very clear, simply by looking at the pharmacopoeia of this era, since it was practically wall-to-wall hemp and it was listed as an effective medication for hundreds of different medical conditions. So of course these companies would produce the essential oil of the hemp plant, but this is where the truth is exposed. The minute these companies produced such an oil, they would be making the same substance I had been having so much success with in healing the public.

Are we really supposed to believe that these drug companies with all their resources, researchers, and laboratories never discovered the true medicinal values of this plant, like I did? Strangely, I have been unable to find any record of these companies ever supplying the real essential oil of the hemp plant to the public. What they supplied were watered-down forms of hemp medicine. They were in control of the potency of such medications and always made sure that what was available to the public had limited medicinal value. Why would the drug companies of that era do such a horrible thing? There were three main reasons.

1. They could not patent cannabis hemp because it's a plant. No patent, means no money, therefore no interest.

2. At the time, farmers everywhere were freely growing hemp. Now what would happen to all those drug companies if farmers found out they could produce this natural miracle medicine from a plant they were already growing themselves? Everyone would be producing their own medications, drug companies would be out of business and this is a fact of which these companies must have been aware.

3. Consider the profits such companies were generating. If they provided a medicine to the public that healed them, there would be no return business. Therefore, it would be out of the question for them to provide high-grade hemp medicines, because their profit margins would suffer.

Certainly, even at that time, the technology was available to allow the production of such a medication, so they have absolutely no excuse. There is no question in my mind that the drug companies knew exactly what they were doing. If it were not for their manipulation of this medicine, we could have had the cure for cancer and a cure or control for practically all other diseases 150 years ago. If drug companies want to try to claim that they had no knowledge of hemp's healing abilities, I suppose it is their right. Still, for them to have overlooked the truth about this substance during all the years which they produced it would have required a PhD in stupid. These drug companies and those who control them have a great deal to do with the medicinal restrictions on hemp and it's high time the public became aware of the role they played.

Today, these same drug companies produce allopathic medicines, which are manufactured from chemicals and poisons and many of the products they sell are liver-toxic, which means they poison our livers. Even though it is more than obvious that such drugs are designed to do harm, these companies try to put the public's mind at ease with the use of pharmaceutical terms and gibberish. Often, we are told how the drugs they sell us are extensively tested with the use of double blind studies and they go on about such things as placebo effects.

What they are telling the public is little more than nonsense that was designed to make those who purchase their products believe that the so-called medications they supply are effective and safe. In reality, though, quite the opposite is true, but the public continues to use these harmful substances and treatments in the blind belief that they might help. If the FDA was not working in collusion with the drug companies, many of the products they produce would not even be allowed on the market. Now you know the truth about the drug industry and why they want hemp to remain prohibited.

It is a well-known fact that many of the greatest thinkers and statesmen in history were growers and users of cannabis hemp. Look at George Washington, Thomas Jefferson, Abraham Lincoln, and many of the other founding fathers that grew hemp and partook in the relaxation and creativity, hemp can provide when smoked. These great statesmen, who would be called potheads today, also produced documents like the Declaration of Independence and the Constitution, which was first written on hemp paper. Judging by these documents, it seems their exposure to hemp did nothing to harm them in any way or impair their thinking abilities. When those who were trying to eradicate the use of hemp for personal gain began using the word marijuana, farmers and the general public did not even know what marijuana was at the time. The words marijuana and high were used to discredit the hemp plant and make the public at large afraid of its use for medicinal reasons and recreational purposes.

The propaganda and scare tactics the system used said marijuana was a dangerous and deadly new menace. Marijuana is simply potent strains of hemp and the word marijuana is just one of over 400 slang terms used worldwide to describe the hemp and/or cannabis hemp plant. Marijuana is not a drug, it is just different forms of the hemp plant's genetics, which can produce large quantities of medicinal resins with a very high content of cannabinoids that do the healing. The system's misuse of the word marijuana certainly did baffle the public in those days and made it easy for those who wished to see its growing and use restricted to achieve their aim.

At that time, they also succeeded in scaring the masses about the dreaded high some forms of this plant can produce when smoked. For the most part, the public had no idea what getting high even was. According to newspaper articles put out by the Hearst publications, getting high was about the most self-destructive thing a person could do. All of this was a pack of lies, which were simply designed to deceive the public, but the people of that era had no way to find out the facts for themselves.

To date, the lies and deceptions of those who wanted the use of this wonderful plant restricted have caused untold suffering and hundreds of millions, if not billions of needless deaths. Now here is the real truth. Getting high on hemp presents no danger to the public or to a patient who is using it for medical purposes. If this had not been true, throughout history there would have been countless real reports about this plant's destructive nature. It is aspects of the high this plant can produce that causes the patient to rest and sleep a great deal when they begin using this medication. Sleep and rest are important factors in the healing process and it is the so-called high that kills pain and gives the patient a whole array of other wonderful healing effects.

History tells us that hemp is the oldest and safest medication known to man. It also tells us that hemp is non-addictive. In reality, this plant never presented a danger to the public, but it was a huge threat to many big money interests. That is why they will stop at nothing to keep hemp restricted for medicinal use and other purposes. Hemp is not harmful and addictive, unlike pharmaceuticals or other potent street drugs including alcohol. There is no resemblance between such dangerous drugs and hemp. Indeed, hemp can even be used to help break serious addictions that many people who use these substances suffer from.

To even try to compare the effects of this harmless plant with those produced from other substances which are commonly in use would be the same as trying to say fresh water is no different than deadly poisons. A great number of substances people use today to get high are poisonous, addictive, and destructive to their bodies.

All you have to do is look at those who are hooked on pharmaceuticals, alcohol, and many other street drugs. These are all prime examples of a poison high. How could anyone say the high that hemp can cause is comparable to the poison high produced from such dangerous substances? The average person can usually build up a tolerance for hemp oil very quickly. Therefore, it is quite rare for someone like me, who is used to ingesting the oil, to even get what they call high any more. Now, if I smoke hemp, my eyes usually do not become bloodshot, unless I have not been using the substance for quite some time, and I do not feel impaired in any way.

Even if I were to take a very large amount of oil, its effects would only put me in bed for a few hours and I would wake up unharmed. The only way I can tell that the oil is even in my system when I am taking proper doses is by the beneficial effects it has on my condition and body. In addition, with the use of the oil, I am usually somewhat more at peace with myself and those around me. The high from hemp medicines produced from strong indica strains is needed to aid in the healing process. Therefore, using the essential oil of the hemp plant as a medication is not about getting high, it's about getting healed. Once a person becomes used to ingesting the oil, others do not even know they are using this harmless substance as a medication.

The medical system has been telling us for decades about the need for preventive medicine. Well, here is a medicine that can fulfill this role and its use is safe for all age groups. Even children can benefit from the use of this medication with no risk of danger. The system has been telling us for years that hemp must be kept away from our children, but it's okay for doctors to fill them full of chemical poisons. The reality is, according to a study conducted by Melanie Dreher in the 1980s, it was proven that the healthiest babies on this planet are born to mothers in Jamaica who use hemp a great deal.

If hemp does not harm a baby in the womb and indeed obviously aids in the baby's development, why would medications produced from the hemp plant not be beneficial to children of all ages? If this medication was used properly, diseases like cancer, diabetes and many others could be prevented from ever occurring. If you have a loved one who is suffering from an illness, what would you sooner see them take as a medication? Poisonous, addictive chemical trash or a harmless non-addictive natural medication, which can cure or control their condition? Not only can hemp do what I have described, it can also reconnect children with their parents, if those with children go about it in the right way.

Today, many parents are totally out of touch with their children and they are very frustrated, because they do not seem to be able to communicate with them. When you were a teenager, you probably went through something similar with your parents and to you it may have seemed that they had no understanding of the way you thought about things. Parents have a great deal to worry about during this stage of their children's development, since peer pressure provided by those they consider to be their friends can often put your child in harm's way. With all the dangerous substances like hard drugs and pharmaceuticals that are flooding our streets today, anything might happen. So what can be done to protect them?

The first thing you will need to do is re-establish a connection with them and you cannot do this by being what they perceive to be the enemy; this will only serve to make them rebel even more. Somehow, you must change their attitude towards the role you are playing, so they will look at you as not only a parent but also a friend, which they can openly talk with about their problems and concerns. Since hemp is harmless and does not lead to the use of hard drugs, I consider it a wonderful way for some parents to get back in touch with their children.

Simply smoking a joint or eating a small dose of the oil with them can radically change the way a troubled teenager looks at their parents. Now, all of a sudden, you are someone they can openly speak with and put their trust in. This can do much to allow parents the opportunity to give them the guidance they require. Discussions about drug abuse and other dangers they may face can now be openly dealt with in a more rational way without all the screaming and shouting. Open conversations about topics like the use of hemp, which our society has lied to them about with the use of their demented propaganda, would do a great deal to make teenagers realize their parents are there to help and they are not the enemy.

Even to this day, we still hear foolishness like, "The marijuana you smoked when you were young is not the same substance that is available today, it is a great deal stronger and much more dangerous." Statements like this that we are constantly being fed are totally ridiculous and I can only ask the question, "Who writes this stuff?"

What I am suggesting may not work in every case, but certainly, it can only be said that it has worked for many parents in this situation. Now that the truth is finally being exposed and we are moving into a new age of reason, I think what I am saying should be given some serious consideration. You no longer have to beat and abuse your children into seeing things your way. Now, with the use of this amazing plant, many parents have the option to do something sensible to see that the right values are instilled in those they love.

The average person, for the most part, has little understanding of what medicine is really about. To most, medicine is some deep dark science that only highly trained doctors can understand. When you begin working with this substance, you will find nothing could be further from the truth and that practically anyone can grow hemp and produce this wonderful medicine. Once the public sees what this substance can do, there is very little mystery left in medicine. If we work together to get rid of these absurd laws restricting the medicinal use of hemp, the cost of acquiring good bud for medical purposes would drop dramatically.

The only reason high-quality medicinal strains are so expensive at present can be blamed on the fact that most of us have to purchase the material we need from illegal dealers and growers. If good hemp strains were grown properly and without interference from the system, this medicine could be produced for almost nothing. It is the laws, which governments have put in place, that keep the prices high. So why do we allow such laws to exist? In reality, no one has the right to control the medicinal use of hemp and if anyone continues to try to do such a thing, they are simply trying to control us, so they can turn a big profit.

Hemp is just old-fashioned herbal medicine and it is the same medicine that our ancestors used freely. We must take back our rights, which will allow us the freedom to grow this plant everywhere again and use it in every possible way. Whatever laws restricting the free use of hemp which are currently in place are based in corruption anyway, so why do we allow them to enforce such nonsense? There is no other rational way for us to proceed. The idiotic laws against the free medical use of this plant must go and those who have forced their agendas upon us must do the same.

CHAPTER 8
A COURT FULL OF KANGAROOS

Since my Charter Challenge had eaten up what little funding I had available, I could not afford to hire a lawyer to defend me, so my only option was to try to defend myself. All the court paperwork was delivered personally to me by the RCMP during the spring and summer of 2007. The police, it seemed, had gone through a real change of attitude and all of a sudden they were very pleasant and supportive. For months before my case could be heard, there was often RCMP cruisers in my yard. Every officer which came to my door with paperwork told me that they hoped I would win the case. This was certainly a radical change from the way they had behaved in the past, but it was a change for the better and was welcomed.

One day, an officer came with some paperwork and we struck up a conversation. He stated, "Rick, I don't know exactly how you have been treating people but if I were sick, I would go to the medical system." I laughed at what he had said and asked him, "Do you think the people that come to me haven't already been to the medical system? In many cases, it's the damage the medical system has caused that brought the patients my way in the first place." I asked him, "If you had stage 4 cancer and the medical system could do nothing to help, where would you turn?"

I think our talk did much to make this young officer realize what was really happening. When he left my home that day, he was very friendly towards me and now seemed to support what I was doing. By all appearances, it looked as if the police were beginning to wise up and that quite possibly many of them had finally seen the light. Maybe they were starting to think about sick and dying loved ones in their own families and what this medicine I was producing could do to help them.

Less than a week before my court case started, I saw my first unidentified flying objects. My neighbor and supporter Mark Allen had talked about seeing something strange in the sky a few months before, but I had not paid too much attention. It wasn't because I didn't think they existed. Millions of people have seen some very strange things in the sky. I just thought, since I was now 57 years old and had not witnessed such occurrences myself, that it would be very unlikely I would ever see something of this nature.

On that particular night, Mark was at my home and we had been talking about my upcoming case. I was getting tired, so we went out into my yard to get in the truck and I was going to drive him home. I had just stepped out of my door, when something above the power pole that was close to my house caught my eye. In the sky was an object that had a glowing hexagon shape on its bottom. Then, out of nowhere, it seemed, another one joined it and then a third object flew into formation, forming a triangular shape. They did not look to be that high, but yet we could hear no audible noise coming from them. I went to get my movie camera, but when I returned, they were flying off. I then tried to get some footage but could not.

Mark and I, got into my truck and drove to a nearby hill, in the hope of spotting them again. We could still see them way off in the distance flying in formation. They looked to be about 2000 feet up in the air and it appeared they were doing some sort of survey. We watched them for quite a while and finally called it a night, after trying to signal them with a spotlight and getting no response. I do not think these objects were piloted by anyone human, since no human being could withstand the G-forces of some of the maneuvers we witnessed.

I thought, "Isn't this great? I'm trying to get ready to defend myself in an insane court case and now I'm seeing UFOs." At least, Mark was with me that night and we both saw the same thing, so either these objects were really there, or Mark and I were seeing things at the same time. I think there's a lot about UFOs that is being hidden from the public, but why? Someone out there has the answers.

Since I lacked the time and ability to do it myself, my neighbors Larry and Ruby Bjarnason had done a great job preparing for the trial. My Supreme Court case began in September 2007. When asked if I was pleading guilty or innocent, I answered I can make no plea to any charges stemming from a law that is based on corruption. The court then automatically entered a plea of not guilty on my behalf.

I had been charged with cultivation, trafficking, and possession. As for the cultivation charge, if I didn't grow the hemp, how could I supply the medicine free to patients in need? Trafficking, according to the dictionary definition, means the exchange of goods for monetary gain. Obviously, the real definition of this word does not apply in legal circles. I consider this and other terms they misuse to be proof our legal systems have a language of their own of which we have no understanding. Do you not find it strange that courts do not use the same definitions for words as we do? But I suppose if they did, it would be much harder to hide what they are really doing.

I gave this medicine to patients at no cost, and for doing so, the legal system charged me with trafficking. As for possession, how could I supply suffering people with the oil if I did not possess the substance it was produced from? All these charges were just legal nonsense. I had not broken any real law or harmed anyone. I knew it and so did the legal system. Yet, being the vermin they are, they just had to go on with their vicious games.

If they did not know the suffering they were causing, all might be excused. Sadly, when I entered the courtroom, there was no possible way that the judge and the prosecuting attorneys did not know the truth. I do not know as yet who was giving the orders, but I strongly suspect they were coming straight from Ottawa. If any of these legal types had a shred of common decency, they would have done the right thing and thrown this case right back in the government's face. Of course, because of the corruption of those just mentioned, this did not occur.

When the jury had been picked for my case, I asked the judge if I was supposed to have the right to an unbiased jury. We have all been brainwashed from decades of propaganda about hemp. How could this jury be considered unbiased when they too had been exposed to the same propaganda that I had been subjected to? I asked that the jury be allowed to watch a videotape about the true history of hemp and man's use of this plant. My request was promptly denied. This made it impossible to have my case heard before an informed jury of my peers, but that was only the beginning of the tricks the Canadian legal system had up their sleeves.

I brought ten patients and six doctors in to testify on my behalf, and we gathered a mountain of scientific studies I had planned to introduce into evidence. About six RCMP officers testified during the first phase of my trial. First, the prosecution presented their case and officer after officer told the jury of their brave exploits in my back yard. Then, when I cross-examined them, they all wound up testifying on my behalf. During the cross-examination, in each case, I held up the article which had been published by the Springhill Record in 2004, a year before I was raided and charged. I asked each officer in turn if a criminal would have a newspaper do a full-page article detailing his or her activities. Of course, the officers all had to admit a criminal would not behave in such a manner. I then asked each officer about the videotape and information I had provided them with on May 6, 2005, three months prior to their raid. They all admitted they knew of this video and information, but had never viewed its contents. I asked if it was common practice for the RCMP not to examine such evidence. I do not remember any officer answering this question. They all just sat there with a blank look on their faces. Of course, the judge should have ordered them to answer, but this did not take place.

While giving testimony, the female officer who had been on the deck with me during the raid was asked if she recalled telling me that she believed everything I was saying to her about the healing power of this plant. She told the jury she remembered our conversation very well and had believed everything I was telling her that day. When the officer, who had held a gun to my friend's head on the day of the raid was cross-examined, I asked him why he had done such a thing. He tried to convince the court that he thought he had seen a gun on the deck when he came around the corner of my house. My deck is closed in with corrugated carbon fiber panels that go about four feet up the sides and the floor of the deck is three feet off the ground. Even if there had been a gun, which there was not, from where he was standing, he would have to be twelve feet tall to even see what was on my deck. Once he had climbed the steps, it would be obvious that there were no guns present, so why had he threatened my friend in such a manner? I told the court there had been a perfectly legal pellet gun in the corner of my living room, but there had been no weapons present on my deck or in my home, other than the guns the RCMP were waving around, and the gun this officer had put to my friend's head. By the time this gun-happy cowboy was done testifying, he was looking rather sickly.

Why do we put up with actions of this nature from such people, when cowards like this man obviously should not be allowed to have a gun in their possession? I hate to think what could have happened if something had startled this young gung-ho cop. My innocent friend would probably have wound up with a bullet in his brain. If that had transpired, this shining example of what a police officer should not be would probably somehow have gotten away with his outright murder. After witnessing what had transpired on my deck, I could not help but wonder how many other innocent people have been harmed or killed in the same manner?

Next, the prosecution put the RCMP's marijuana expert on the stand and he did put on quite a show. During the cross-examination, I opened with, "Sir, you are here as a marijuana expert for the RCMP, is that correct?" "Yes," he replied. I then asked this so-called expert what he knew about hemp. He stated he knew nothing about hemp. I then inquired, "You are considered to be a marijuana expert and you don't know marijuana is hemp?" I could not believe it, but he actually tried to argue the point. He asserted, "No, no, marijuana is one thing, but hemp is something entirely different." Anyone who is familiar with this subject is aware of the fact that, in reality, marijuana is simply cannabis hemp. I quickly realized that if this man could be considered to be an expert in anything, it certainly was not in this field. I then reached down and picked up a copy of the corrupted law, which was put in place in 1923. I explained to the jury what this document was and pointed out that strangely the word marijuana was not present, but the words "Indian hemp" were.

This law had been put in place before the system started using the dreaded M-word. Therefore, the Crown's witness was left in a somewhat bewildered state after my explanation of what he as an expert should have already known. It was obvious the RCMP were spending a great deal of taxpayers' money trying to eradicate this plant. You do not put all those police officers in helicopters and cruisers for nothing. On top of that, the government even had the Canadian military involved in this witch-hunt. I asked him, if he knew how much of the money the RCMP were allotted was spent trying to eradicate hemp. He answered, "Over 60%." I went on by stating, "The RCMP are spending over 60% of the public's money they are provided with, pursuing the eradication of a plant that never hurt anyone?" My next question was if he felt all this money and effort could not be put to better use pursuing criminals who were committing real crimes. He mumbled something to the effect that he did not make the laws, he just enforced them.

I then went on to ask this so-called expert if he thought marijuana was addictive. He stated that as far as he was concerned it was. I then asked him if he had ever smoked marijuana himself and he admitted that in the past he had. I asked if he had become addicted. He answered, "No." This expert did not even know his own government had admitted years before that marijuana was not addictive. I had warned the prosecution that if they put their expert on the stand, I would shred him during the cross-examination. By the time he was done testifying, that's exactly what took place, because, unlike him, I did know my subject.

After these officers were done testifying, the prosecution's case was looking pretty shaky. Their aim had been to try to convince the jury that what I was doing in some way could be considered a criminal act. All the officers that testified had said a criminal would not behave in the open manner, which I displayed, and I had not gone about this in a criminal fashion. If you had been chosen to be on my jury after hearing all of this, what would you be thinking?

The prosecution phase of my trial was now supposed to be over. The following day, I was to begin presenting the case for my defense. After the jury had retired for the day, the judge asked me how I intended to proceed. I told the judge I first planned to obtain testimony from the patients who had used the oil themselves. They could then tell the jury what the oil had done for their conditions. Next, when each patient was done explaining what they had experienced, I intended to put their doctors on the stand. That way, the doctors could not twist the facts, because the jury had already heard the testimony from the patients.

I already had a sworn affidavit from an oncologist, concerning one of the patients who was to testify and it was completely bogus. According to the affidavit he provided, this oncologist who was treating Jim LeBlanc denied the fact that Jim even had terminal cancer. Furthermore, the family doctor of another patient who had been dying of terminal lung cancer supplied this person's medical records in a very distorted way. What he had provided ignored the fact that this terminal lung cancer patient was now cured, and he had neglected to supply the X-rays proving this to be true. You see, unlike the patients, doctors would not attend court willingly, for they were well aware of the threat the use of this oil presented to their profession. They did not want to help prove to the public how effective this medication really was because it was not in their best interests.

By this time, a great number of doctors in Nova Scotia and other parts of Canada had already seen what this natural oil had done for the well-being of their own patients. Many who had been suffering from terminal cancer were now cancer-free thanks to their use of this oil. But, for the most part, doctors would go out of their way to keep the truth about this medication hidden from the public. To me and the patients to whom I had supplied the oil, there was no question that these doctors were willing to lie to avoid doing what was right and in the best interests of the Canadian people. Our current medical system is truly a sad thing to behold. Doctors walk around playing God, while filling their pockets. Consequently, we get to suffer and die, because most doctors refuse to do their job properly. Anyone willing to put their trust and their very lives in the hands of people such as these have been badly misinformed. I am not telling you every doctor will behave in this manner, but I am saying that real doctors who you can put your faith in are few and far between.

When I had finished telling the judge what I intended to do, he stated that the patients and doctors I called in to testify had nothing to do with the charges I was facing. He stated that their testimony had no bearing on this case. I was stunned. Who was he to say their testimony had no bearing? To me, such a statement was completely illogical and defied all forms of reason. What these people were going to tell the court had everything to do with my case. They were the patients I had supplied the oil with to treat their conditions and some had even been cured of terminal cancer. Just where did this judge get off saying they had no bearing upon my case? To prevent an ugly confrontation, he then said he would think about allowing their testimony and we could discuss it the following day when court resumed.

The next morning, he informed me he had given it a great deal of thought, but could see no possible way to allow their testimony. I was dumbfounded. Was there anything these so-called public servants would not do to keep the truth from the public, whose best interests they were supposed to be protecting? Now I understood why they had put a publication ban in place when I had first entered the court system. Of course, I really don't think it would have made much difference, since the news media of today are not noted for bringing us the truth anyway.

At least, I knew the prosecution had not done a bang-up job during their phase of the trial. Since I had all this scientific evidence at my disposal, even without the testimony of the patients I still thought I had plenty of evidence to justify my actions. Guess again. According to this judge, "You cannot introduce scientific evidence unless you have the person who published it present in the courtroom." I fired back, "If this is truly the case, then these proceedings cannot be legal, because those responsible for writing and putting these laws in force are not present either." As expected, my argument was ignored and they continued on with their little inquisition. It seemed they had some absurd excuse for everything I was denied and just being in the presence of such people made my skin crawl.

I remember telling the judge during the proceedings, "Before this is over, you will be the one going to jail." I don't think it could be stated that I was making such remarks for no good reason and, at one point, the judge said, "Mr. Simpson, you can't take this personally." I came out of my chair and shouted in anger, "Take it personally? Everything that is going on here is a crime! As a result of the raids the RCMP conducted on my property, a great many people have suffered and died. Do I take this personally? You're damn right I do!" The judge never replied, he just dropped his head. This was truly our legal system at its best. People dressed up in penguin suits, pretending to be administering justice. If the public were actually aware of what these corrupted public servants were doing to them, they would probably string them up from the nearest tree with a hemp rope.

In the end, it all came down to me. I was the only one that was allowed to testify in my own defense. I spent about two hours on the stand, explaining the whole story to the jury and I didn't pull any punches. By the time I was done, it should have been more than clear to the jury what was going on here. This jury had listened to the testimony of everyone concerned except those the court did not allow to testify. I felt it would be impossible for any of them to find fault in what I had done. I explained very carefully what this wonderful natural medication could do for the human race. After I had been cross-examined, all I had to do was leave the stand and take my seat. In a few minutes, I could then make my closing argument and the outcome of the case would be in the jury's hands.

Then in comes another monkey wrench. All of a sudden, the prosecution felt there was a great need to hear testimony from a representative of the Marijuana Access Program. The Crown had already presented their segment of the case before I began my defense, so what they were now proposing was highly unusual. In legal terms, what they were trying to do is called splitting the case. Doing such a thing is frowned upon in legal circles and it should not have been allowed. Instead of refusing their request, the judge went along with the prosecution and allowed the testimony. I did not understand what was taking place other than the fact that I knew what they were intending to do made no sense, but now I would have to wait until this person testified before I could make my closing arguments.

The individual the prosecution so desperately needed testimony from was not present, so it would be the following Monday before they would be available. I already knew whatever testimony this representative from the Marijuana Access Program was going to give would be useless to the prosecution. The same person had testified at my Charter challenge, so I was aware of what to expect and I knew it was a waste of time. On

Monday, the testimony was given and, sure enough, it had no impact on my case whatsoever. It appeared the Crown had used the ploy of splitting the case to stall for time or some other sinister purpose that had not as yet become evident. Unfortunately, since the judge refused to do his job properly, there was nothing I could do to prevent the prosecution from having their way.

After we had heard the testimony from this person, I was finally allowed to make my closing argument. I asked the jury what they would do if they found a cure for cancer and who they would have gone to with their information that I had not already contacted. I tried to put the jury in my position, so they could see what the system is doing to us all. I told them about the great number of people this oil had already helped and I expect they must have known the patients and the doctors I had brought in were not allowed to testify. When I was done, I felt the case was won and my supporters that made up the audience felt the same.

The jury retired and within three hours they had reached a decision. We were then all called back to the courtroom to await their verdict. Monica McQueen, the prosecutor from the Justice Department, who had done all of the talking during my Charter challenge and in this court case was present in the courtroom. Yet, strangely, Doug Shatford, the Crown prosecutor was nowhere to be found. A short time later, Shatford came in and seated himself beside McQueen. About three minutes afterwards, the jury entered the room. I stood and waited for their verdict. "Guilty, guilty, guilty." I couldn't believe my ears. This jury had an excellent opportunity to change everything and bring this life saving medicine to the attention of the public. With 70,000 people dying every year in Canada from cancer, not to mention the countless deaths from other conditions this medication is an effective treatment for, and they find me guilty.

To anyone who sat on that jury and took part in all this, I hope you realize how much blood you have on your hands. I had supplied oil to relatives of people who sat on that jury and it had healed them and they find me guilty. Guilty of what? Healing? If just one of them had said, "Not guilty," it would have been a hung jury. Something certainly did not smell right here. I was mystified. This could not be happening.

When the jury left the courtroom, their heads were so low their chins were almost dragging on the floor. I looked at the judge and said, "Well, you might as well lock me up right now, because I am going to continue supplying the oil to whoever needs it until I am sentenced." At every court appearance I had made, it was perfectly clear I was still supplying the oil. Yet, not once did this judge ever tell me to stop. If he had thought I was really committing a crime, would he not have called a halt to my activities? I must say I have never been able to figure out what was going on with this judge. One moment, he would seem almost decent, the next, he would be a monster. I never knew what to expect from him.

The day after my verdict had been given, I got a call from Rick Dwyer. His wife Margaret claimed she had seen Doug Shatford exit the jury room just before they came in with my verdict. Now it all made sense. After witnessing the behavior of these people throughout this case, would they stoop to jury tampering? They had already made it clear to me that they were capable of anything, so jury tampering was certainly not out of the question. I asked Margaret why she had not spoken out at the time. She said, "Rick, I don't know about court procedures. When I had seen him leave the jury room, I didn't pay too much attention, but later when I thought about it, something didn't seem right." I stated, "Look, Margaret, jury tampering is a very serious charge, we have to be certain. I want you to go back to the courtroom and go right back to the same seat you were sitting in and make sure which doorway he exited from."

Margaret went back to the courthouse and did exactly what I asked her to do. Afterwards, Margaret and Rick came straight to my home and told me that from where she had been sitting, only one door in the hall was visible to her, and it had been the jury room door. Immediately, we contacted the judge with this information and a couple of weeks later, we were summoned back to the courthouse. I thought we were going to have some type of meeting about this, but when we entered the courtroom, Judge Cacchione was sitting behind the bench. McQueen and Shatford were also present with some pasty-faced lawyer from Halifax who was representing them.

The judge said, "Mrs. Dwyer, I hope you realize you could face fourteen years in prison, if we find what you are saying to be untrue." The judge's threat had no effect. Margaret said, "I'm here to tell the truth about what I witnessed," and she took the stand. The pasty-faced lawyer did his best to punch a hole in Margaret's testimony, but he could not. He asked her about her use of the oil and insinuated, she was doing this so she could continue to get the oil from me. Margaret paid what he was saying no mind. She just laughed at him and said, "Look, I can get the oil anywhere. There are plenty of growers around." This woman was a rock and I should have expected no less. Margaret Dwyer is one of the most truthful people I have ever met.

After a while, they realized there were no flaws in what Margaret had testified to and she was excused. It was then my turn, so I called Doug Shatford to the stand. A couple of dealers I had come to know through my activities said they had both sold cannabis hemp to Mr. Shatford, so I asked him if he used hemp. Shatford looked as if his head would explode. He went all red in the face and started to stammer. The judge then stepped in and took his side stating, "Mr. Simpson, that line of questioning will not be allowed." I replied, "The lawyer defending the prosecution asked Margaret about her use of hemp, so why can't I ask him the same?" It seemed no matter what I asked, I couldn't get a straight answer, and it was perfectly clear who this judge was supporting.

A couple of flunkies that worked in the courthouse were also questioned. Of course, with their jobs on the line, they testified Shatford had not been in the jury room. This was a first-class kangaroo court, if ever there was one. In the end, the judge stated he thought this was just something Mrs. Dwyer and I had cooked up to derail my sentencing. How could he even make such a statement? Nothing Margaret had testified to had been disproved. If she had lied, then why was this judge not sending her to jail, as he had threatened? I don't know a great deal about the law, especially their brand of it, but in reality, in such a case I think the RCMP should have done an extensive investigation. In addition, why had they not called the jury back in to be questioned during this hearing? Sadly, it was more than obvious they were out to hang me and would stop at nothing.

My sentencing was still slated to occur on November 30, 2007, my 58th birthday. These legal buffoons do not know how lucky they are because I was really getting into a rage over what was taking place. If it were not for the fact I was using the oil to keep me calm, I have little doubt the old Mad Trapper could have returned. If this had taken place, these criminals would have no place to hide and would probably have met a very violent end. I have since reconciled myself to the fact that I now know why such people exhibit these traits and would not choose such a path today. Still, at the time, I was thinking, "If they are going to put me in jail anyway, I might as well give them a real reason," and many others around me felt no differently. It was more or less just sheer luck that this whole thing did not turn into a bloodbath. Somewhere in the back of my mind, I knew this is how my father would have probably handled such a situation, but with the oil's help, I kept my cool.

CHAPTER 9

OFF TO JAIL FOR A FEW DAYS

During the summer of 2007, I supplied a tube of oil to a young woman from Amherst who was off work on stress leave and was also having a problem with back pain. She had great results and was back to work in no time and became one of my supporters. I had not heard from her in a while and tried to call but could not reach her, so about November 20, 2007 I went to her home to provide her with another tube of oil.

At the time, she wasn't there, so I gave the tube to her mother and requested that it be passed on to her. There was no exchange of money, nor was there any need, since I had been supplying her treatment at no cost. I did not know it at the time, but her mother immediately called the Amherst police and gave them the oil I had left with her. The medicine had helped her daughter a great deal but this woman called the police, so I guess that's gratitude for you.

For some unknown reason, it was decided my sentencing should be postponed until early in the coming new year, but on November 30th, I still had to make an appearance in court. When I arrived in the courtroom to have my sentencing postponed, two Amherst cops were waiting to arrest and charge me with trafficking again. All this occurred on a Friday, which meant I would spend the weekend in jail, since my case could not be heard in court until the following week. When Judge Cacchione found out what was going on that day, oddly, it seemed he was not pleased about what the Amherst police were doing. My sentencing was rescheduled and off to the Amherst police station I went in the company of two cops. I had known the parents of the officer that questioned me that day since I was a child. Knowing he came from a good family, I thought he was probably a half-decent human being, but in the coming months, my impression of Tim Hunter would change radically.

After the usual time-consuming mumbo-jumbo at the police station, I was finally taken to the county jail in Amherst. Upon my arrival, they put me in a holding cell, where I was to be held until I could be processed and taken to maximum security. While I was waiting, another prisoner was brought in and put in an adjoining cell. The guard then said to me, "We will be right with you, Mr. Simpson." The prisoner they had brought in got a funny look on his face and asked if I was Rick Simpson. I informed him that indeed I was. "You're a healer, what are you doing here?" he stated. I told him I had been asking myself the same question. About that time, the guard came back and escorted me to maximum security, where I was then locked in a small room with four other inmates.

A couple of minutes later, someone down the hall from where I was being held called my name to get my attention. I went to the small barred opening in the steel door and answered. He gave me his name but I had no idea to whom I was speaking. Then, in trying to clarify his identity to me, he gave me the name of his mother, whereupon I realized who he was. "You're the one that has brain cancer," I replied. His mother had come to get the treatment and I had never met him face-to-face. That's the reason, I didn't know who he was when we were in the holding cells together. I asked what he was doing here and he answered that he was serving time on weekends.

"How's your cancer doing?" I inquired. "Just great," he replied and we talked on about his treatment for a few minutes. I then turned away from the small opening and the other four inmates were right there. They had crowded in behind me, while I was at the door and had listened in to our conversation. "What do they think they are doing, locking someone like you up?" one asked. I just shrugged and said, "Who knows?" The truth was I had no illusions. I knew why I was there. Corruption at the highest levels had put me here.

There was plenty of time to waste, so all five of us got to know each other and I have to say I liked them all. After a few hours had passed, someone came to the little opening in the steel door and yelled, "Meds!", whereupon all four of them rushed over to the door. When they returned, I asked them, "What's all this meds business about?" They appeared to be healthy-looking, so I could not imagine why they would require medications. They informed me that if I remained in jail, I would be able to see the doctor next week, and I could then get anything I wanted. Sleeping pills, painkillers, whatever I liked. I just shook my head.

When they called lights out, we entered five little individual cells off the small main room we had been in and steel doors closed behind us. Ever since I had arrived in maximum security, it seemed to be very warm, but in the little cell I was supposed to sleep in, the heat was extreme. I had never been able to rest well if it was too hot and in here I was locked up without my oil to help me sleep. Finally, the heat became unbearable, so I took the thin mattress off the small bunk in my cell and put it on the floor. When I got down on the mattress, I then realized all the heat was coming from the cement floor. Needless to say, I received very little rest that night.

The next day it was the same thing. "Meds!" and I watched them all hurry over to the little opening in the steel door to get their pills. A few minutes later, I said to them, "Do you realize that none of you should be here and that you are just products of your environment?" Amazingly they all replied that no, they had done things which were wrong and probably deserved what was happening to them. I prodded them with, "Drugs have something to do with every one of you being here, is that right?" They then all admitted that this was indeed the case.

I looked at the oldest one, who was 42, and stated, "You grew up with the hard drug generation. When you were a teenager back in the early '80s, the hard drugs and pharmaceuticals really started to hit the streets around here about that time. Is this what brought trouble with the law your way the first time you landed in jail?" He replied, "That's right." "How do you think these drugs became so readily available?" I asked. "And do you really believe nothing could have been done to keep them off the street? If you or I went to a strange area, how long would it take us to find out, who the people are that deal in hard drugs? If we made it our business, do you think it would be safe to say we could find out within a month?" They all agreed, "Yes, that would probably be quite possible." I told them, "If we can do something like that, why do you suppose the police, with all the resources they have at their disposal, seem to be having so much trouble figuring out who's doing what? The system wants you to have access to these harmful drugs, so they can easily control you. It's all about money and jobs to them. You are simply make-work projects."

To clarify what I was saying, I added, "Sometimes, when people are using these substances, their behavior frightens other citizens. The public is then led to believe that, for their own safety, more jails have to be built and more police officers must be hired to control this menace. Instead of the police doing the job they are paid to do, which would entail taking these harmful substances off the street, they turn a blind eye to what is going on and allow people easy access to pharmaceuticals and other hard drugs, so they then become addicted and must commit crimes to support their habit.

"Sooner or later, those who use these substances are then caught and put in jail, where once again, the doctor provides easy access to harmful, dangerous, and addictive pharmaceutical trash. After you have done your time and have been reformed according to the legal system, you are then again turned loose in society. Tell me, what is going to happen? Are you going to go straight? Now that you are supposedly free? In no time, most will find themselves in jail again, because they must commit crimes to get the money they need to feed their addictions. Then, after those who abuse these substances have been apprehended once more, the public can rest easy, because you have been incarcerated and no longer pose a danger. In truth, you are behaving precisely the way they have programmed you. For the system to continue to grow, they need more so-called crime to keep the public afraid. The system wants you addicted and committing crimes to feed that addiction, so they can make what they are doing look good in the eyes of the public."

In some ways, medicine is really not much different, since the vast majority of doctors are, in reality, simply drug dealers for the pharmaceutical industry and most seem to care nothing about the harm they are doing to their patients. That's why I've been locked up. They do not want people like me telling the public it's all a lie and their so-called medical system is just a sham. The way medicine is practiced today, healing is often of little concern, it's really much more about keeping you sick, so they can sell you as many harmful chemicals as possible before you die. That way, they are able to maintain their positions and keep their precious jobs, while generating vast amounts of money for the drug companies. The problem is most people do not have the time or, in some cases, lack the brain power to stop and think about what is really going on around them. They have been using our own self-destructive nature against us and this is all being done by the so-called powers that be known to us as the system. This planet has been run for a very long time by none other than the filthy rich and power-hungry at the very top. They bear the responsibility for bringing the human race all of this grief and it will never change, unless we stand together to bring it about."

You might say my little lecture got their motors running and we had many lengthy discussions about this subject. In the meantime, my situation was not improving. By Sunday, I was going downhill fast. I had been denied access to my medication, since the previous Thursday night. Because of this and all the heat, I was unable to get the rest I required. I could feel that steel band tightening around my skull, indicating that my blood pressure was very high. All in all, I was not doing well in the Amherst jail and I consider this institution to be little more than a torture chamber for those who are locked up there. It was Monday afternoon before I was taken over to the courthouse in chains and put in a holding cell to await my turn in the courtroom.

Two of my supporters, Bruce and Val Stailing, put up over $20,000 so that I might be represented by legal counsel at my sentencing and this hearing. Bruce and Val are truly stand-up people and I was very touched that they would step forward and do such a deed. They both knew from personal experience that what I was saying about this medicine was true, so it seems they felt it was their duty to support me in my hour of need. I owe these good people a great deal for what they have done and they will always have my undying gratitude. Unfortunately, in the end, all the money they spent would make little difference, because corruption in the legal system seems to have no limits.

When Duncan R. Beveridge, the lawyer they had hired came to talk to me in the holding cell, he seemed very enthusiastic about my case. He told me he had gone over some of my paperwork and was amazed at the amount of evidence I had gathered. He said, "Don't worry, all I have to do is fill in a few holes and we will get this whole thing straightened out." I was not in a good state at the time, but to me it sounded as if he might be able to have my case dismissed. After talking with him, I was left with the impression that there might be some sanity in the legal system after all and perhaps there was something simple that could be done to resolve this issue.

When I entered the courtroom, I was a sorry sight. My blood pressure was extremely high and I did not feel well. Carol Beaton was the judge that day and, of course, Monica McQueen, the prosecutor from the Justice Department was besieging her to keep me in jail. I have to say that Monica McQueen is one of the most evil and insidious people I have ever had the misfortune of encountering. Judging by the pathetic smile on her face, it was not hard to tell she enjoyed the role she was playing. When Duncan Beveridge pointed out the ridiculous nature of my so-called crime, I was finally released until my case could be heard. Still, I found the performance McQueen and this judge put on that day to be truly disgusting. It proved to me that these two women were on nothing more than a power trip and neither of them gave a hoot about those who were suffering, but at least, in the end, I was set free.

After my four-day ordeal in Amherst, I went home, took a large dose of oil, and went straight to bed. After four days with hardly any rest, I went out like a light. Early the next morning, I awoke to the sound of someone knocking at my door, who was of course looking for help with their medical problems. I was always more than willing to help anyone with their medical conditions, but look how I was being treated by the legal system. I never had a drug charge brought against me in my life until 2005. Because I had helped those who were in distress, the system had bent over backwards trying to make the public believe that what I was doing was some kind of crime. Unfortunately for all of us, many people were just dumb or uncaring enough to swallow what they were saying.

About this time, I got word from a prison guard in Springhill who told me I did not have much to worry about if I should go to jail. He informed me that the inmates had been following my story and to them I had become a hero. Since I had spent most of my life around the Springhill area, I knew many of the guards who worked at the prison. In private conversations with them over the years, guards had told me they were in favor of the inmates having access to pot because it kept them calm. Guards who were going on shift knew they would have a good day if the smell of pot was in the air, so I was aware that many of those who worked at the prison did not look down on my activities.

I can't say I had any real fear of going to jail anyway. I have always been the type of character who could function well in most situations. If I were to be sent to prison, the main problem that concerned me would be the lack of medicine I required. Prisons are full of drugs and there is always someone willing to bring them in, but still I knew it would be very difficult to get the oil if I was locked away.

The medical system had already proven that they could do nothing to help, so the chemical trash the prison doctor was dishing out would be of little use to someone in my situation. The way I looked at it, medicated or not, if I was locked up, I would have a captive audience, so to speak, and I would have preached this medicine to all of them. The Springhill penitentiary had about 500 inmates at the time, so as each inmate was released back into society, the system would have to deal with someone else who was producing oil.

Everything I had seen about the system thus far had sickened me, but it was about to get even worse. Duncan Beveridge called me and asked if I could come to Halifax so that we could have a meeting. After what he had said in the holding cell, I thought that perhaps he had made a breakthrough. When I entered his office that day, I noticed from the certificates on his wall that he had attended Acadia University. I asked him if he knew of a man by the name of Scott Sheffield, since I knew Scott had been employed there, so I thought Duncan might have known him. He seemed surprised at my question and said, "Scott Sheffield was my father-in-law." He then asked me how I had come to know Scott.

I told him Scott and my father had been lifelong friends. He asked, "What's your father's name?" and I told him Logan Simpson. He replied, "Now there's a name I've heard before." When Scott had been a young teacher, he taught in Saltsprings and he and my father had become good friends. Later in life, Scott had written a book entitled "Musings of a Country Boy," wherein he described his friendship with my Dad. In his book, he had stated, "If Logan Simpson had been born under different circumstances, he could have been a Rhodes Scholar." This extra connection we now had made me feel even more at ease with the lawyer Bruce and Val had hired. I knew Scott had been an honest and honorable man and thought his son-in-law might be the same. Scott had died a few years previously from cancer, so I felt Duncan might have a vested interest in helping me bring this medicine forward.

When our meeting got under way, I quickly realized Duncan was not behaving toward this issue the way he had when we talked in the holding cell. He now appeared to be very negative and uttered things like, "Rick, you talk about all this as if it's some big conspiracy." I answered, "It is a conspiracy and anyone with a brain in their head should have little trouble seeing this fact." He then switched tactics. Now it was, "You know, Rick, if you were a doctor or if you had a PhD, what you're saying about this oil would be more convincing. Rick, the bottom line is you don't have much formal education, so who is going to take you seriously?" I came up out of my chair and fired back, "Did Henry Ford have a PhD when he invented the automobile? Or did the Wright brothers, who were simple bicycle mechanics, have a PhD when they showed the world man can fly?"

I told him it would please me greatly if he made no further stupid comments like that, since everything I had stated about the oil was the truth. I don't know who had got to this guy, but he was not talking like the same lawyer Bruce and Val had hired. After our first meeting in Halifax, I cannot say that I had any further trust in this man. The statements he had uttered and the way they were delivered made it clear to me he was not working in my best interests or for the greater good of the Canadian people.

Just before my sentencing, Duncan's partner in their law firm was made a judge in the Supreme Court of Nova Scotia. Then, right after I was sentenced, the same honor was bestowed on Duncan himself. Don't you find it a bit odd that both the lawyers from a small two-man law firm would be appointed Supreme Court judges at practically the same time? Nova Scotia has a great many law firms and Supreme Court judges are appointed very seldom, so everything that went on here did not seem quite right to me. But maybe that's just my distrustful nature.

A few years previously, we had put the Phoenix Tears website up on the Internet. Larry Bjarnason set it all up and did a great job operating the site. In the beginning, only a few dozen people a week contacted us and many of the e-mails were little more than aggravations. Every second e-mail we received, there would be questions like, "Can I take the oil with my chemo?" or "Where's the scientific evidence?" All those who contacted us obviously had access to computers and by that time, most were using high-speed Internet connections. Larry put up the site and ran it all on a dial-up connection, which is about the slowest form of Internet access in existence. If Larry could dig up all of this information on dial-up, why could these people not do the same with their high-speed setups?

In many cases, it seemed they just wanted to be led by the hand. Then when we showed them the facts, they would look for other ways to reject them, because for some the real truth was just too horrible to comprehend. Still, we were able to help many people and the numbers coming to my door for treatment were escalating all the time. There's no question our website had attracted a fair bit of attention, but still it was a very slow process.

Then along came Christian Laurette, who produced the documentary that would change everything and make our site explode. Fortunately for me, Christian had been working his fingers to the bone trying to get our documentary together and I must say I admire the end result that he achieved. When Christian produced "Run from the Cure," he had nothing to work with except a camcorder and a broken-down computer that crashed every fifteen minutes. Unfortunately, I had no money to buy any new equipment, so Christian was forced to work with what he had at his disposal. I have no idea exactly how much time Christian spent working on this documentary, but I do know he spent hundreds of hours putting it together. He did all this work free of charge, so I think the public and I owe him a great deal of gratitude for all the effort he put into this project.

We had to get the documentary out before my sentencing and, as always, Christian came through. The first time I saw the documentary he produced from beginning to end, I was amazed by the way he had been able to weave it all together. I told him, "You have probably just produced the most important documentary you will ever make." Anyone interested in producing a movie of any kind should be paying attention to the talents of this man. I feel, if he were given the chance, he could have a very impressive future in the movie industry.

We brought out "Run from the Cure" about two weeks before, I was to be sentenced, and I think Christian's hard work had a lot to do with me not being sent to jail. We made sure that it was distributed far and wide to make everyone aware of its contents. Copies of the DVD were sent to W5, the Fifth Estate, David Suzuki, Market Place, politicians, lawyers, etc. Everywhere we thought it would have an impact. I even gave one to Tim Hunter, who had been one of the Amherst police officers that arrested me on November 30, 2007. I had known his family for many years and I thought once he had seen our documentary, it would set him straight. After giving him the DVD, I had asked that he take it home and view its contents, thinking it would prove to him who the real criminals were.

We put out 1000 copies on the first run and I could not keep them in the house. It seemed everyone wanted a copy. More importantly, Christian put our documentary up on YouTube and now there are many sites hosting the film he produced. "Run from the Cure" sends a very powerful message and it has a great impact on many when viewed. I think it also had an effect on the legal system as well. Now that the truth was available to the public, would they dare put me in prison? I already had a very large following that was growing every day and the legal system was well aware of this. If they put a man in jail for curing cancer, it would probably not sit too well with the public and how could they explain their actions?

The day of my sentencing, I was talking to the lawyer who had represented me during my Charter challenge and the local Chronicle Herald reporter at the courthouse. The lawyer was quite apologetic and said, "Rick, I'm a lawyer and I can't even explain to you what the legal system is doing any more. You took them on and exposed the truth and I think what they have done to you is disgraceful." He looked at the Chronicle Herald reporter and stated, "Rick's oil is medicine. You don't find it on the street for sale." The Chronicle Herald reporter agreed. Then the lawyer started to make comments regarding how my oil had been tested. To my surprise, he stated the RCMP had sent some of my oil to their lab out west to determine its contents. The lawyer explained that the results proved this sample was the strongest and purest oil the RCMP had ever analyzed. I knew the oil I had been producing was very potent and pure, but up until that time, I had no idea that it had ever been scrutinized by the RCMP.

Shortly afterwards, Duncan Beveridge called me into a side room off the hallway in the courthouse. Now he was going to try another tactic. He was no longer arguing about whether the medicine worked or not. Suddenly it was, "The truth of the matter is, Rick, the government wants the researchers to bring this out to the public." This statement really brought out the rage in me. I exploded with, "Duncan, do you really expect me to believe what you're saying? We have been waiting over 100 years for the researchers to bring the truth forward. They have had this information available to them for decades. But they have done little or nothing to bring it to the public's attention. There's also something else I want to ask you, Duncan. If one of yours had cancer, would it be safe to say you would be looking for this oil yourself?" Down went his head.

At the time, I was thinking, "What a lawyer." He knows everything I have been saying is true, yet he is more than willing to let our government's corruption turn me into a criminal in the eyes of the public. In addition, he seemed to care nothing about all those who were in desperate need of this medication, which were currently suffering and dying. I am really not trying to make Duncan Beveridge out to be any worse than others I had the misfortune of dealing with in the legal system. Still, I found what he did to be truly disgusting and he certainly did not mind charging a big fee for doing nothing other than going along with this horror show. Now this same lawyer is a Supreme Court judge. I can only pity anyone who is seeking justice in a court he presides over, for no doubt it will not be found.

A few minutes later, I was standing before the judge, waiting to be sentenced, thinking, "Man, this is going to be good." Many of my supporters had showed up to witness my sentencing that day. Before any of us were even allowed to enter the courtroom, we were all put through a metal detector. Never before had I ever heard of metal detectors being deployed in the Amherst courthouse. It looked to me as if all these legal types were a bit more than uncomfortable and may indeed have been in fear of their lives. If the general public had known the facts surrounding my case, as they would have if it had been reported by the news media properly, no doubt these legal eagles would then have good reason to be afraid to show their faces.

There were quite a number of my supporters present and it was obvious many of them were not in a good mood. The judge started off by saying that under different circumstances I would be winning awards for the work I was doing but no awards were given out in a court of law. He then stated that in the 34 years he had worked in the legal system, he had never encountered a case like this. There was no criminal intent. The people in attendance all clapped and there was no doubt I had their complete support. When the judge had made this statement, it was almost laughable to me. I already knew from past experience that there was a great deal of criminal intent regarding this case. Throughout my trial, what the legal system had done and were now doing had criminal intent written all over it … their criminal intent.

Then the judge came right out with it. He admitted, "The scientific evidence does exist to back up everything Mr. Simpson is saying." This brought about even more applause from the audience. During the trial, I had not been allowed to introduce this evidence, now the judge was openly admitting to those present that it did exist and was indeed true, even though he would not allow it to be introduced in court. This was just getting better and better.

He then stated, "Mr. Simpson has a great number of people who have used this oil for their conditions and they, too, back his position." He did not hear any testimony from patients during my case, because he would not allow them to testify. Now here he was, telling thc audience that this too was true and that obviously the oil could do what I had claimed. Knowing what this judge knew, why had he not allowed the patients to testify? Is the Canadian legal system not concerned about the truth? Did they not realize their actions were keeping the cure for cancer from the public? To my mind, what was going on here could only be termed as being pathetic and all these people who had worked so diligently to convict me were no better. Instead of crying out for joy that the medicine of our dreams was now available, the sentencing went on as if what had been exposed meant nothing.

The charges I had been convicted of carried a very stiff penalty and I was facing a possible twelve years in prison. The sentence to be handed down is left to the judge's own discretion. I really do not remember how much prison time the prosecutors were asking for, but I feel they should be the ones to serve it, since I knew they were both as guilty as sin. In the end, the judge gave me a $2000 fine and a firearms restriction.

When one is convicted of trafficking in Canada for some unknown reason it carries with it an automatic gun restriction. Why I was given this restriction really made no sense to me, since there were no firearms found in my home during any of the raids the RCMP conducted and they were not threatened in any way. I did know some RCMP officers who certainly should have such a restriction put in place against them, but giving me this penalty seemed somewhat absurd.

With regard to the 2000-dollar fine I was forced to pay for healing people, I can only surmise it had something to do with the way I spoke out against what this judge and the prosecutors were doing during my trial. If indeed I hurt their poor little judicial feelings by exposing them for what they really were during my court appearances, it was no more than they had coming to them. Rather than pay the fine I was given to the court, I felt these funds should go to the Salvation Army, but the legal system wanted the money for themselves and refused. Now I and others want to make it clear to Judge Cacchione and the rest of the world that we feel he or the legal system he supports should return this amount. A donation to the Salvation Army from them in my name for 2000 dollars would do nicely. All I would like is the paperwork proving the donation was made. The 2000 dollars I was forced to pay them belonged to me and I think that under the circumstances I have the right to demand that this amount should go where it can do the most good. At least then I would not feel as if the money was simply stolen.

This case has to go down in history as the biggest miscarriage of justice that ever occurred in Canada or anywhere else for that matter. What the Canadian government did had a detrimental effect upon every man, woman, and child on this planet, and they should be hanging their heads in shame. The true North, proud and free. What a bad joke, for, in reality, Canada is little more than a police state that is being run by criminals.

On a funnier note, when Duncan Beveridge left the courthouse that day, he was cornered by one of my supporters. Flute Wood walked up to Duncan and really gave him a piece of his mind. Beverage stood there and took it and you could see he was more than just a little nervous about what was transpiring. Flute Wood is not someone to mess with and Beveridge knew if he opened his mouth the wrong way, Flute would have picked him up and broken him in two. After taking a good browbeating from Flute, Beveridge scurried to his car and quickly left Amherst.

On the way back to Halifax that day, he must have realized the confrontation he had just gone through with Flute had been provoked by the corruption of both himself and the legal system, of which he is a part. Flute Wood had every reason to go down his throat for what they were doing, since there is no rational excuse other than greed, as to why our legal system would react to this issue in such a manner. Flute is a dear friend of mine and a real man, which is a lot more than I can say for anyone I have met in the legal system.

During my sentencing that day, I had not seen Rick Dwyer present. I was wondering where he had gone, but when I went to the parking lot, there he was. He wrapped his arms around me and you could see the relief on his face. The oil had helped many members of Rick's family and he is a man that can become very emotional about this issue. He told me he thought it would be best for him to stay outside during my sentencing, for if they had sent me to jail, he said he didn't know what might happen. Rick is one of my most trusted friends and I understood the way he felt, but for now all was well.

CHAPTER 10

MY FIRST CONTACT WITH JACK HERER

I cannot place much blame on the local Chronicle Herald reporter for his efforts in trying to get the truth out. After my sentencing, he did go and do interviews with people who had witnessed the healing power of this substance. To the best of my knowledge, he did write an article but those in control at the Herald apparently felt it should not be published. If the Herald had done so and published it along with the statements the judge had made at my sentencing, I am sure it would have went a long way towards clarifying to the public the real truth about this matter. As far as I know, this never occurred. That is why I would never waste my money subscribing to the Chronicle Herald. When I buy a paper, I want to read the truth about the subject they have written about, not some made-up version, which hides the facts.

All the papers which had done articles about this subject thus far had done just that, so I quickly reached the point where I no longer even cared to have articles written. I remember one article printed by the Amherst Daily News that called me a modern-day Robin Hood. In the next paragraph, this learned reporter with no medical background stated marijuana should never be made legal. What did this reporter know about the subject? He had no medical experience with this substance. Why were they refusing to bring out the truth about this? Often, these articles were so misleading that in the end I am sure it cost some people their lives.

One write-up this paper had published about a local woman who was suffering from pancreatic cancer stated she had approached her doctors about using hemp oil to treat her condition. The doctors had then informed her that using the oil would cause inflammation and therefore would be detrimental to her treatment. Anyone suffering from this condition or other medical problems were given the impression they should avoid the use of hemp oil to treat themselves because it could have an adverse effect on their health.

I wrote a rebuttal, disputing what had been said in the paper, and delivered it to them in person. I then explained that articles like the one they had published were misinforming the public and doing them harm. The piece I had written was ignored and, as far as I know, it never appeared in their newspaper. Therefore, the general public remained ignorant of the real facts, with the result being that many people were now afraid to use the oil because they thought it would cause them harm. The truth is hemp oil is the greatest natural anti-inflammatory on the planet and indeed could very well have saved this woman's life. Instead of taking a medication that could have helped her situation, the doctors talked this lady and her family into using chemotherapy as a treatment and in a very short time she passed away.

What the news media and medical system were telling the public about the use of hemp oil as a treatment was truly grotesque. Unfortunately, when big money controls the mass media and will only print articles that suit their own agenda, what else could you expect? I was so disgusted with what I had seen happening in Canada to date that I was seriously considering leaving the land of my birth. All I wanted to do was find a country that was run more honestly, where I might continue my work and keep my sanity. I was very tired and disappointed by this stage, but I still had another trafficking charge to face.

This case came up only a couple of weeks after I had been sentenced by Judge Cacchione. By this time, Duncan Beveridge had been appointed, a Supreme Court judge himself and could no longer act as my lawyer. Bruce and Val had already paid the fee for Beveridge to represent me, so arrangements were made with a new lawyer their law firm had hired to appear in his place. In reality, this new lawyer's presence meant nothing. I had already decided to simply plead guilty to this charge to get it over with. All my attention at that time was focused on getting away from this system and leaving Canada to find some peace.

In the end, this case was just a walkthrough. I pleaded guilty and it was over. I already knew there was no sense in trying to fight the same charge again. The legal system would find me guilty no matter what, so why should I spend all that time and effort to watch them display their corruption once more? I was sentenced to time served, in other words the four days I had already spent in custody, and that was the penalty I received for helping the young woman who had been suffering from stress and back pain. For me it was time to look for greener pastures. I had many friends and supporters in the area, but everything that had gone on had taken its toll on me. Now all I thought about was leaving Canada to find a better way of life, but the patients kept coming. How are you supposed to react when you have people calling you crying on the phone, begging you to help them? As tired and depressed as I was, I could not turn my back. The patients who were contacting me were in desperate need, so onward I went.

After a while, I began to level out and slowly I got back into the swing of things, but I continued to look into other countries, where I might find what I was looking for. Then one day, while talking to my son about moving to South America, he started laughing. "What's so funny?" I demanded. Mike responded, "Dad, I know you and you can't walk away from something of this importance, you would never be able to live with yourself. You're going to stay here and prove to the public and the criminals who have been running this country which end is up." I stood there for a moment and just looked at him. Then we both started to laugh. I was now back to normal again.

From the time I started providing this medication until the present, I was always hearing about well-known people having cancer or some other serious condition. But from the position I was in, how could we get the information to them? It's not that we didn't try. A great number of e-mails were sent to different well-known personalities with medical problems. The only reply I recall came in 2010 from Senator Ted Kennedy, who was suffering from brain cancer. As I remember, there was not much in the reply and he was taking some other treatment, but at least he acknowledged our information. It's too bad he did not act on it, for it might have saved his life. In the Czech Republic at that time, we were successfully treating a terminal patient with the same type of brain cancer that eventually killed Mr. Kennedy.

Through the years, I watched people like Farrah Fawcett, Patrick Swayze, Steve Jobs, and many other well-known personalities die horrible deaths that might have been prevented. Like you or anyone else, I had no choice other than to watch them suffer the ravages of their disease along with the cruel and inhuman treatments they were given. It's very easy to send e-mails and messages to well-known people, but in most cases don't expect a reply.

In 2010, we were contacted by a man who told us we should get in touch with Michael Douglas, since at the time it had been reported that he was suffering from cancer. He informed me that he was a friend of some business associates who were closely connected to Mr. Douglas. Then he started going on about how this could be mutually beneficial to both our cause and this well-known movie star. We e-mailed him back and told him that if he was truly connected to people close to Michael Douglas, he could get the information through to him easier than we could. We told him to see that Michael gets on the oil as quickly as possible and he might yet have a chance to survive. It's almost as if many believe we should be chasing celebrities around begging them to take the oil. I don't look at the life of a Hollywood star as being any more important than the lives of you or me. I will not beg anyone to take this medication. The choice is theirs.

In the early spring of 2008, we received an e-mail from Chuck Jacobs, telling me he was Jack Herer's assistant and that Jack was interested in my work. I knew that Jack Herer was well known, mainly because of the variety of hemp that was named after him. I had run across his name many times, but I really knew little about him. I had never really considered myself to be a hemp activist. I thought of myself as being more of a researcher than an activist. I knew Jack had written a book called "The Emperor Wears No Clothes" but I did not attach any great significance to it at the time. We were more into scientific studies.

One afternoon a couple of weeks later, I received a call. The man's speech was slurred badly and he hesitated a great deal, but finally he got it across to me that he was Jack Herer. The first thing he asked me was what the oil could do for leukemia. I told him leukemia is usually one of the easiest types of internal cancers to deal with. When you ingest the oil, the THC goes right into the bloodstream and often brings this type of cancer under control very quickly. At the time, I knew nothing about Jack's friend "Captain" Ed Adair, who had died from this condition almost 20 years earlier.

Jack asked if I would be willing to go on his Internet TV show. I told him I would love to, but I cannot travel into the States because of the criminal record I now had. Jack started laughing. He then explained, "Rick, years ago I used to go to Canada every summer, but now I'm not allowed to enter your country, either." We both had a good laugh over that one. The two big bad criminals that can't go to each other's country because of pot charges. Jack then asked if I could simply call in to the show. I told him nothing would make me happier and that night I was on Jack's show for the first time. Working with Jack was just great. He let me go on and on about the oil and its healing abilities. He never seemed to tire of it. I truly enjoyed doing his show and I just loved some of the things Jack would come out with. Once I understood the condition Jack was in, knowing that he had suffered a stroke and was also a diabetic, I said, "Jack, get on the oil. If anything can help your condition, it's the oil." Jack decided to take my advice and try to do as I had requested. Before we finished for the night, he asked for my address and told me he was going to send me a copy of his book.

A couple of weeks later, I went to the mail and there was the parcel. I opened it up and found two autographed copies of "The Emperor Wears No Clothes" and two DVDs of Jack's documentary "Emperor of Hemp." I thought this gesture was very nice on Jack's part, but what could be in his book that I hadn't already learned elsewhere? All the research we had done, I can only surmise, had made me somewhat smug. I felt the only reliable information would come from researchers in the field. After arriving home, I watched Jack's documentary three times in a row. What an amazing source of knowledge! Then I started to read his book and I do not recall ever having a more humbling experience. Between its covers was practically everything of importance I had ever learned about the hemp plant. I became an instant follower of Jack and I consider his book to be a priceless gift to mankind. Long live Jack Herer, the one and only Emperor of Hemp!

In 2003, I had contacted Marc Emery about all this, but had never heard anything back from him. Then in the spring of 2008, he got in touch with me and asked if I would do an article for his magazine *Cannabis Culture*. I was very busy with patients, but I agreed to do what I could and I sent him the article within a few days. A short time later, Marc contacted me and stated he would not publish what I had written because I was editorializing. I responded with, "Look, Marc, I'm a very busy man and I'm certainly no journalist. Send a reporter down and I will take him to the patients." I heard nothing further from Marc about doing this article.

The next time I was talking to Jack, I told him about what had taken place with Marc. At first, he did not seem to know who Marc was. I explained, "You know, Jack, the Prince of Pot." Jack replied, "Oh, you mean the little seed salesman from the north? Can you send me a copy of the article you wrote for him?" Once Jack had gone over its contents, he said, "I can't understand why Marc Emery would refuse to publish it. This is a good article." I explained that as I understood things, it seemed our Mr. Emery has quite a big ego. He might be looking at me as a threat to his position here in Canada and perhaps that's why he refused to publish the piece. They do call him the Prince of Pot and you know how these princes can be if they get upstaged." Jack then asked if he could put the article up on his website. I said, "By all means, please do."

A short time before Jack Herer came into my life, I began to be contacted from radio stations in the United States, asking if I would do open-line talk shows, to which I readily agreed. No one could make a valid argument against this medicine's use. I already knew no doctor or any other medical professional would dare to come on the air to try to dispute the truth in what I was saying. I had become very good at exposing what doctors were really doing with their dangerous allopathic approach to medicine and I was perfectly at ease doing these shows.

One broadcast I took part in was with Clayton Douglas and I did have a little trouble understanding his southern drawl. Still, he is a great guy and a dyed-in-the-wool believer in the hemp plant and freedom, so Clayton and I had no trouble seeing eye to eye. I also appeared on a show hosted by Mike Hagan on Orbit Radio in Columbia, Missouri. It lasted three hours and gave me the opportunity to answer many questions. It was a complete success and I found Mike to be a real pleasure to work with.

Another night, I did a show called *Feet to the Fire* with James Arthur Jancik in Chicago. Shortly after the show began, James said, "Rick, you are talking about supplying medicine for practically nothing. How could you do such a thing?" I explained by saying, "Imagine a field of corn. Now, imagine the field next to it planted with hemp. What's a pound of corn worth?" James replied, "Well, practically nothing." I asked him, "If hemp were grown freely, do you think it would be worth any more than corn? It's the corruption of our system that is keeping the price of good medicinal hemp so high and nothing more." James responded with, "I'm sure you are going to get some arguments from people who will be calling in about what you are saying." I was on the air with James for two hours and not one person called in with a valid argument against the statements I had made. It's a strange feeling for someone like me who dropped out of school in Grade 9 to go on open-line talk shows and be able to take on anyone in the world about this subject.

I was on Jack's show many times and our friendship grew every time we came into contact. Even though the broadcasts we did together would usually last for an hour and a half or more, Jack would just sit back and let me roar. I really enjoyed every show I ever did with this amazing man. About seven weeks after I had first come on the air with Jack, Eddy Lepp and I did Jack's show together. He told me he had been there the first time Jack had taken a dose of oil. He stated, "You could see the improvement in Jack's condition every day." Within a week, Eddy himself also began to take doses.

During the show Eddy told me, "A few days before this broadcast, Jack and I attended a hemp rally in Oakland. Jack was all over the grounds where the event was staged, talking to everyone, he had time to speak with. Rick, when Jack started taking the oil 45 days ago, he couldn't walk 15 feet. Now he's bouncing around like a teenager." The oil had healed the diabetic ulcers on Jack's legs and every time I talked with him, I noticed improvements in his speech. Jack's wife Jeannie even called me one night and thanked me for bringing her husband back to her.

Often, people in Jack's condition cannot function well sexually, so I assumed that this is what she was alluding to and mentioned it in the first edition of this book. But later I was to find that what she was referring to was the fact that Jack had taken a bad fall in the bathroom and damaged his ribs, after which the doctors said that it would take months to heal, but with this medication's use he was fit as a fiddle in no time. This is why Jeannie had called to thank me and it had nothing to do with sexual dysfunction. The reason I had speculated that this was the case, concerned the simple fact that I had received so many reports from patients informing me about the tremendous impact using the oil had exhibited on their sexual prowess. So, as you can see, it was just a simple misunderstanding on my part but all considered, Jack was truly having great results with this medicine produced from the plant that he had fought so long for us all to have free access to.

Shortly afterwards, while talking one night with Jack, he surprised me with, "You know, Rick, you will be going to the Cannabis Cup in Amsterdam, Holland, and they will make you a star." I did not consider what he had said to be realistic, so I asked, "Jack, what are you talking about? What does the Cannabis Cup have to do with me? I'm just about the medicine, not the smoking aspects." Jack just laughed and replied, "We'll see." Apparently, Jack Herer understood what was going to take place in the future when at the time I could not. From my point of view, I felt it was highly unlikely that I would ever attend the Cannabis Cup.

One night Jack told me about the way he felt the first time he had watched "Run from the Cure". He went on to explain, "Rick, I was blown away. With my knowledge of the hemp plant, I knew everything you were saying had to be true. After watching your documentary, I thought of course the oil could provide the medicinal aspects you described. I just cannot believe that I didn't see it before. When I watched "Run from the Cure," it was like being run over by a truck." I found it very funny the way Jack had worded it, because when I read his book and watched his documentary, I felt about the same.

Jack and I never did meet face to face. Still, through our conversations, we became very close to one another. I guess Jack and I could be considered birds of a feather. We both believed the only way cannabis could be made legal once more would be through the medicinal aspects of this plant. Once people knew hemp can cure cancer and is a cure or control for practically all medical conditions, there would be no holding the hemp plant back. Who in their right mind would then try to stand against someone growing hemp or using it medicinally?

When the public finally learned the truth, the smoking aspect of hemp would no longer be of any consequence. Just as it had been throughout history, until Big Money had learned they could fill their pockets even more if they denied the use of this plant to the public. Jack's book vividly described the many uses of this plant and how, if used properly, it could solve most of our current problems. Then I had come along and exposed its true medicinal values by supplying the essential oil from it to patients in need. With a combination like that, Jack and I both felt it would be impossible for the system to carry on with its deception regarding this plant's many uses for much longer.

Back in 2003, I had decided to give up watching most of the shows that were available on television. At this point, to me almost everything that was being aired on TV programming consisted of soap operas and lies. The only programming I continued to watch at all was the Discovery and History channels. In a short time, even they too lost most of their appeal. I no longer even watched the news and weather. The news was mostly fabricated anyway and they never seemed to be right about the weather, so what was the point of watching? I guess you could say, I had begun to deprogram myself and as time went on, I started to see the real world.

Documentaries that exposed the truth, like "Loose Change," began to catch my attention. Now here was something I could really sink my teeth into. The facts such documentaries presented were just too glaring to be ignored and it certainly fit in with what I had seen of the system thus far. As time went on, I viewed hundreds of various documentaries and became fully aware of what the so-called system was really about. I strongly advise others to educate themselves and find the truth, for without it we are lost. What's really going on in our world can only be found on the Internet, since the mainstream media is controlled and will not bring such things to the public's attention.

Take the time to look on the Internet at the work of Max Igan, David Icke, Alex Jones, Aaron Russo, Ken O'Keefe, Ben Stewart, and many others. I think you will find it to be a very sobering experience. Some documentaries that I feel we all should watch are Jack Herer's *Emperor of Hemp*, Max Igan's *The Awakening* and his new documentary *Trance-Formation*, Aaron Russo's *America: Freedom to Fascism*, Ben and Dan Stewarts' documentary *Ungrip*, and the revealing work Alex Jones is doing at infowars.com, but there are hundreds more who have put a lot of work into documentaries that should be viewed. I would like to thank all these individuals for making this important information available. Their work goes hand-in-hand with what I have been doing. Together we will awaken those who inhabit this planet to the sad reality of the depths to which we have fallen.

In the spring of 2008, there had been some rumbling on the Internet that NORML (National Organization for the Reform of Marijuana Laws) was trying to discredit my work. We then received an e-mail from Allen St. Pierre, the national director of NORML in the US. He stated I was misrepresenting the work of Manual Guzman, a Spanish researcher in this field, and what I was saying about the medical aspects of hemp was unsubstantiated. I e-mailed him back that I had never stated Guzman's research indicated hemp oil cured cancer, but his research did show THC played a role. I then suggested that NORML perform some basic research themselves.

I told Mr. St. Pierre to simply take a small amount of good bud material and produce the essential oil. Once this was done, find someone with a diabetic ulcer, skin cancer or severe burn and use the oil to treat the condition. Just apply the oil to the affected area and cover it with a bandage, then reapply the oil every three days and watch what happens. I then asked that NORML openly report their findings to the public. To me, this seemed like a sensible request to grant, since this organization's stated role was supposedly to legalize hemp once more. I have never met Mr. St. Pierre in person, but he must be a real piece of work, because this is what he came back with.

"We are NORML, we know all about Guzman's work and what you are providing is snake oil. You are simply making a flaccid attempt to move your own agenda forward." When I read his reply, I just shook my head. Here was the national director of an organization that was supposedly trying to legalize hemp, calling high-grade hemp oil, the most medicinal substance on this earth, "snake oil"? Evidently, NORML could not be bothered doing the simple research I had requested, or they would have found out the truth about the oil this plant produces for themselves. I e-mailed Mr. St. Pierre back, telling him he and NORML, the organization that he represents, were a fraud. I also informed him that if he was truly looking for something flaccid, he should take a long look at himself in the mirror, for there is nothing flaccid about the oil or anything I am doing.

A few months later, I attended a meeting at Dalhousie University in Halifax, chaired by Marc-Boris St-Maurice of NORML Canada. He started off the meeting by stating hemp was not a cure-all and it did not cure cancer. There were many people in the audience that day who had used the oil. Even some that had cured their terminal cancer with it were present, so his remarks were not well received. I countered his statement with, "You are saying hemp oil does not cure cancer. On what are you basing this assumption?" He replied, they had treated a woman in Montreal and it had not worked. I asked him how much oil she had taken. He replied they had only given her a small amount. I asked if she had shown any improvement. He said he didn't know, since he had never seen her again.

I gave him a brief education by explaining, "There is a protocol that must be followed. You said yourself that you have never seen her again, so how do you know if it worked or not?" That one stopped him cold in his tracks. Up to that point, he had certainly said nothing to impress the audience. He then went on to state that Jack Herer was "a fraud." I could not believe my ears. The leader and founder of the hemp movement we have today being trashed by the director of NORML Canada? In the past, NORML had given Jack Herer awards for his work, but, apparently, this man knew nothing about such things.

Shortly after this meeting, I was doing a show called "Time 4 Hemp" with Casper Leitch. When he mentioned NORML, I told him what I thought of this organization; Casper said, "If I can get Keith Stroup, the founder of NORML, on the air, you won't bushwhack him, will you?" My response was, "Casper, I'm not here to bushwhack anyone, I'm just here to bring out the simple truth." It surprised me but Casper called Keith Stroup and he was willing to come on the show. When Keith came on the air, I started to explain my experiences with Allen St. Pierre and the director of NORML Canada, Marc-Boris St-Maurice. He tried to brush this all aside and told me NORML thought what I was doing up there in Canada was just great.

I replied by stating, "Then why aren't you doing something about it?" He replied, "We are. In three or four years, this is going to be legalized." I countered his statement by saying, "Keith, but what about all the people who are going to suffer and die in the meantime?" He did mumble something back, but I didn't catch it. To me, it was of no matter anyway. I already knew all I needed to know about NORML. An activist named Joe Barton who I know quite well told me he was there when NORML was formed. He stated that from his point of view, right from the beginning their agenda was not what it should have been, and judging from what I was seeing now, his statements rang true.

In the beginning, when NORML was formed, their intentions may possibly have been slightly better, but, as I understood it, NORML was taken over completely by the lawyers in the early 1990s. Sometimes an organization can start out with at least some good intentions, but in the end simply become a corrupted nightmare. I think that possibly, this is what happened in NORML's case. There are many good people involved with

NORML, but they should start looking at the intentions of those who are running the show, for the leadership in this organization is sadly lacking.

A short time later, I was again on Casper's show and continued to listen in, when my time was up on the air. The next thing I heard was an advertisement that was trying to raise funding for NORML. I called Casper back and told him, I had nothing against him or his show, but I could make no further appearances, since I would not be party to anything that was trying to raise funding for an organization I knew to be a fraud. From my perspective, this would be no different than allowing my name to be used to raise money for the Canadian Cancer Society. Casper didn't seem to be too happy about what I was saying, but he said he did understand my sentiments, so we parted friends.

The complete legalization of hemp is the most important issue of our time and a lot depends on cooperation. The hemp movement has gained quite a bit of ground over the last few decades. Still, much more could have been accomplished if all these people and organizations would simply start pulling together for the common good and what is right. If this were to happen, we would all have the freedom in a very short time to use this plant once again in whatever way we like with no restrictions.

Too often, with regard to issues like this, egos, hidden agendas, and bad intentions come into play. Not all who are involved in the hemp movement are in it for the right reasons. Many so-called activists seem to be willing to allow restrictions to continue and even have expressed their willingness to pay tax to those who have restricted its use in the first place. I do not call such people activists. From my point of view, what they are doing is simply an insult to all of us who want to live in freedom. In time, I hope we can get together and work out our differences, but in the meantime, the complete legalization and free use of cannabis must be the main goal of all who are looked at as being the real activists in our movement.

CHAPTER 11

HIDDEN AGENDAS AND TALKING HEADS

In the summer of 2008, I spoke at a hemp rally in Dartmouth, Nova Scotia. Venues like this provided an opportunity for me to expound on the healing power of this plant before a good-sized audience. Therefore, I made it a habit to attend as many functions like this as possible to get the message out. That day Jim Leblanc had come along with me to speak to the audience about his recovery. I always liked it when Jim took the time to attend such events because what he had to say was of such importance and he was living proof of what the oil could do.

While I was speaking, someone in the audience yelled, "Rick, what do you think of drug-testing people to see if they have THC in their system?" I told the audience I was completely in favor and felt such testing was necessary. I informed them that when producing the oil on a large scale becomes a reality, I intended to see those involved with its production were tested frequently. Most of the people present were looking at me as if I had two heads because to them for someone like myself to make such statements sounded insane. I kept a straight face and explained, "Everyone who works there will be tested on a regular basis. If these tests prove they have no THC in their system, we will then have to inform them that their services will no longer be required."

The statement I had just made caught everyone off guard. Most found what I had said rather funny, considering the subject it concerned. I then added, "We will not employ self-destructive people. If you do not have THC in your system, it will prove to us that you are just such an individual and your presence will not be tolerated." Everyone took what I was saying as a joke, but I was quite serious about some of the statements I had made, although in reality I am totally against testing of this nature. By that time, I had come to look at hemp oil as an essential part of everyone's life if they wanted to remain healthy. Having THC in your system was hardly a joke to me, it was simply good common sense.

After I was done speaking, a local man who owned three grow shops informed me that his business had tripled since I had first begun informing the public about the wonders of this medicine. He then stated that he wanted to introduce me to a man who wrote for *Treating Yourself* Magazine, an upper-end Canadian hemp publication. I was then introduced to Gord Hume, aka Zardoz. Gord told me they were very interested in my work and wanted to do a story about my activities. He said he would contact me in a couple of weeks and we would then get to work on the article, so I agreed and we parted company.

About three months later, a terminal cancer patient came to my home to make some inquiries about what the oil could do to help his condition. I explained it all to him but he left without asking me to get a treatment together. A couple of days later, I received a call from the same patient, inquiring if I knew of a man named Gord Hume. Gord had never contacted me back about doing the article but I told the patient I was aware of who he was. He informed me that his stepson lived close to Mr. Hume and that Gord had supplied the oil for his treatment. He then asked if I would mind examining the oil, which had been made available.

I asked him to bring it to me and I would look it over. About an hour later, he arrived with his stepson and passed me a bottle that contained the oil he wanted me to examine. Upon removing the lid, I was surprised when a small amount of its contents spilled on the floor. I asked, "What's this supposed to be? It's not the medicine I produce. The oil I make is like a thick grease that will not spill at room temperature even if the bottle it's in was turned upside down."

They asked if there was anything I could do to make the oil fit for the patient to use. I told them I had no idea what was in the bottle they had given me, but I would see what I could do. I poured the contents of the bottle into a large stainless steel measuring cup, added a small amount of 99% alcohol, and placed it on a coffee warmer. The idea was to heat the substance up and then filter it to see if I could take out the impurities. Since this substance had been produced by someone else, I had no way of knowing what had been used to manufacture this so-called oil, so it very well could contain something that might harm the patient. Even if I could turn it into something that resembled the oil that I produced, I would then be responsible if the substance had an adverse effect. I began stirring the contents of the measuring cup, but noticed there was some type of black substance present, so I stopped what I was doing. I let the oil-alcohol mix cool for a few minutes and poured its contents back into the bottle, which they had given me. It had a very strange smell and a thick dark substance remained on the bottom of the measuring cup. I then removed this dark material and stuck it to the lid of the bottle I had just poured the oil-alcohol mix into.

When I was finished, I turned and passed the bottle back to the patient's stepson. I instructed him to take whatever this substance was back to Mr. Hume and tell him to wise up and produce the oil properly. The stepson seemed quite shocked by what I had said and explained that Gord was just trying to help. I replied, "You don't help a terminal cancer patient by giving them trash like this. Don't you realize if he had taken this stuff that it could have killed him?" The next day, the patient came back and asked if I would supply the treatment. Six weeks later, I received a call from him and he informed me that he was now almost cancer-free. He was amazed by what the oil had done for him and was still in a state of disbelief. I replied, "I hope you didn't think all this was just some kind of sick joke." He answered, "At first, I didn't know what to think but I want to thank you for saving my life."

People who supply improperly produced low-grade oils and other concoctions give hemp medicine a bad name and can cause serious harm. If there really were some big mystery involved in producing good oil, people like Gord might be forgiven. Sadly, this is not the case, since high-quality medicinal oil is very easy to produce. All you have to do is watch our documentary or go to www.phoenixtears.ca and follow our instructions.

Once I had seen the oil Mr. Hume provided, it was more than clear he had not followed my instructions. Apparently, he used his own methods to produce what he called hemp oil and if the patient had taken it, who knows what would have happened. The public must become aware that oils produced by growers and dealers are not always safe to use or even medicinally effective. For serious internal conditions like cancer, the oil must be made from the highest-quality starting material and the proper methods must be followed in its production. I don't think people like Gord are intentionally trying to hurt others, but if this medication is not produced in the right way, that could be the result.

A few days later, while doing Jack's show again, I told Eddy Lepp what had transpired and that Gord Hume had never contacted me back about doing the article that *Treating Yourself* had requested. He stated, "Rick, I do articles for *Treating Yourself* Magazine. Would you mind if I did the story?" I replied, "Of course not." A couple of days later, I called Eddy and gave him the story but to the best of my knowledge, it was never published.

A few months afterwards, Marco Renda, *Treating Yourself*'s editor-in-chief, did a show with Casper Leitch. He told the listening audience he had not done an article about me because I used poisonous solvents to produce the medicine. Indeed, the statement he had made was quite true. I do use poisonous substances like naphtha and alcohol to produce this medication. Although this is the case, if the process is done properly, there is no residue left behind that could pose a danger. Even if there were a slight amount of solvent residue left in the oil, it would be neutralized by the effects the oil has upon it. I have been taking this oil myself for over ten years with no ill effects and I also provided it to thousands of people who also experienced no problems.

Mr. Renda, if you are really worried about people being exposed to poisons, why don't you do something about the pharmaceutical industry? Have you ever looked into the effects of chemo and radiation or what drug companies use to produce the pills doctors feed us? If you are truly concerned for the public's safety, perhaps you should focus on what is really posing the danger. Once this is done, it should become more than obvious to you that the oils I produce using my methods pose no threat to the public.

From where I was sitting, it looked as if both *Cannabis Culture* and *Treating Yourself* Magazine were doing their best to avoid this subject. To me, there seemed to be no rational reason why these Canadian hemp publications were not jumping all over this issue. If Marc Emery had published the article I provided to him, it could have done much to improve his situation. Instead, in North America, it was *High Times* that was the first to put "Cannabis Cures Cancer" on their cover almost two years later. I believe if Marc had been the first to bring this information out, it could have done much to alleviate the legal problems he was having at the time. The American government was trying to have Marc extradited, so they could put him in jail for selling hemp seeds to Americans. If Marc had published the article I had sent him and had brought the truth to the public in his magazine, the situation he was in might have turned around completely.

Who would then have taken this so-called crime he had committed seriously? If he had made the public aware of what medicine from this plant could do, what would he be guilty of? Selling seeds from the plant that cures cancer to Americans? That doesn't sound like much of a crime to me. Once the Canadian people knew what was happening, it is unlikely our government would feel very comfortable about allowing his extradition. If they were to do this and went along with the American government over something that is not even illegal in Canada, how would that have looked in the eyes of an informed public?

Marc did finally put some information about me and what I was doing on his website. Being well-known in the Canadian hemp movement, like Marc was, it would be somewhat suspicious if he didn't at least acknowledge my presence. In reality, no one can explain the actions of others but I think things might have gone much better for Marc if he had looked at this issue in a different way. I did not bring all this to the public's attention so that I could gain fortune and fame. I am doing this simply because it was the right thing to do and mankind is in desperate need of this medication.

Still, I could not believe the behavior of some people over this issue. If they were ill and knew the truth, what thinking person on this planet would not want this amazing medicine made available to them? It appeared to me that the vast majority of people seemed to have been brainwashed so badly that they now lacked the common sense to see the truth. For the most part, people today are so wrapped up in this corrupted system that it seems a great many have lost their ability to think rationally. In many cases, those who are suffering have to be at death's door before they open their minds to something that can really help their situation.

Because the public is kept misinformed, the vast majority of those with medical issues who inhabit this earth are little more than slaves to a medical system that is literally killing them and yet we allow it to continue. I was always taught that we should be living in freedom and that we have the right to know the truth, so being enslaved by those who are doing harm to you and your loved ones makes no sense to me whatsoever. It is time to take off our blindfolds and really examine what is going on around us. The brutal reality of it all should make it more than clear that our current medical system is doing little to help anyone.

All you have to do is take a look at what the system has done to keep this plant's medicinal use from the public. If the hemp plant really did present any real danger, all this could be looked at differently. Instead, the hemp plant presents no danger. Man's use of this plant in medicine for thousands of years proves this to be true. Many of the greatest healers in history, and I believe that includes Christ himself, used hemp to produce medicines to help their fellow-man.

In history, there are many accounts of how legendary healers put this plant to good medicinal use. For example 200 years after Christ, the Chinese were using a mixture of hemp resin and wine as an anesthetic. In their writings, it is said that with the use of this mixture they were able to do organ manipulations and amputations painlessly. From my own experience and observations, I have no doubt what they described is true. There are accounts that even Queen Victoria used hemp as a medication to ease her premenstrual problems. Yet, we, the people who inhabit this Earth today are forbidden to use it. I have two simple questions to ask our society with regard to this issue. Who in reality thinks it's within their jurisdiction to deny the medicinal application of this plant and who gave them the right to do such a thing?

Even the behavior of some in the hemp movement itself was more than enough to make me wonder where they were coming from. Are they real or could they just be talking heads with hidden agendas and I am not the only one who had thoughts of this nature?

One night, I received a call from Jack and he was very irritated. He asked, "Rick, how many hemp activists are there on this planet?" I replied, "Jack, every second guy that smokes a joint considers himself to be an activist." Then, Jack surprised me with, "Rick, there are only two, you and I. The rest are only activists when it's convenient for them. We are the only ones doing this 24 hours a day. What are the rest of them doing?" Upon thinking about it, I had to agree there was quite a bit of truth in what Jack was saying.

At that time, I had been providing the oil for about six years and I was feeling the strain of trying to deal with all of the patients who were looking for help. Not to mention the fact that I had to contend with countless phone calls from people with questions 24 hours a day. I knew where Jack was coming from, for now it seemed there was no time in my life for anything but hemp. Even my girlfriend Leah, whom I have been seeing for many years, said to me one day, "I could understand losing you to another woman but I lost you to a plant." I found her statement to be more than accurate and I knew she was right. Since I had become aware of what this plant could do, my involvement with hemp had distanced me from everything else.

This plant and the medicine that can be created from it had completely taken over my life. Even if I went somewhere and didn't mention the subject, someone else would. In the last few years, well over 90% of the conversations I had with other people involved this plant and the medicine. I really believe if I had not been ingesting this oil, I never could have accomplished this much. One of the most wonderful aspects of this medication is its ability to keep me on an even keel. The last few years had been a constant series of ups and downs. One day, I would be getting calls from people telling me the oil had controlled or cured their medical problems. The next day, there would be a cop at my door, looking to arrest me because I was helping them. But through it all, the oil kept me going.

They say there is a spirit that dwells within this plant. Because of the way I have been behaving over the last few years, I might be living proof that this is true. Often I have the feeling I am being guided. Sometimes, when I am writing, the words and sentences seem to come from nowhere. Possibly a certain amount of the spirit within this plant has made its way into my body as a result of all the oil I have ingested. Whatever the reason, I feel the oil has done nothing but good for me and all those to whom I have supplied this substance.

I have always tried to keep my temper under control, but most knew that my buttons could be pushed quite easily and I never hesitated to speak my mind. To my way of thinking, there is only right and wrong and I always had a low tolerance for nonsense. If I had not been taking the oil during my court appearances and other situations I encountered, things could have turned much more ugly than they already were. After all, the people in authority I had come in contact with thus far seemed more than willing to stand by and watch us all be slaughtered, when in fact it was their job, plus their duty as human beings, to put an end to this travesty.

Since they were unwilling to do anything to help us, should we be showing such people respect? Or would it simply make more sense to ignore them and do what must be done? Often, things have been said about this wonderful medication and me that literally made my blood boil, but the oil would kick in and keep me calm. If I had lost my temper, and I did have good reason on many occasions, it would have done more harm than good for the cause. The oil kept me standing there through thick and thin and, many times, allowed me to do things I could never have dreamed possible. To me, this is a do-or-die situation and if, by chance, I do die fighting for this cause, then so be it. This oil has given me back my life. It is a different life than the one I led in the past, but it has provided me with a much more meaningful existence. If I had not stumbled onto the truth and used this medication, I have little doubt I would no longer be alive.

By 2001, the medical system had basically fried my brain with their chemicals. Imagine, even if I were still around, the shape I would be in today if I had continued to take what they call medicine? I find it incomprehensible that anyone thinks they have the right to tell someone with a serious medical condition like mine that they are denied the use of this natural harmless medication. Who could possibly believe anyone should have such a right? The human race are much like billions of ostriches with their heads stuck in the sand that are being picked off one by one, but refuse to lift their heads to see what is attacking them from all directions. We call it the system, which sounds quite benign, but in reality it is the most destructive and deadly force on this planet. At the present time, what is being done to the human race can only be termed as outright genocide. Yet some seem to think if we keep our heads in the sand, maybe it will just go away. This seems to be the assumption a great number of people are using in trying to handle the situation we are in. If they really do believe everything is going to be all right in the future and that we should just allow our current system to work things out, good luck.

From my point of view, thinking of this nature proves such individuals must have an IQ similar to a wad of bubble gum, for obviously they have no common sense or reasoning abilities. A glaring example of what our future holds in store is exemplified by the actions of companies such as Monsanto, who think they have the right to poison the land and genetically modify our food supply. For us to allow them to be doing such things is pure insanity and of what possible benefit could it be to the human race? We need foods that are high in nutrient value to survive and remain healthy. But in reality, such companies seem to want to provide just the opposite. If we allow these companies to carry on with this madness, in a short time we will all be suffering the consequences.

Additionally, the system has implemented Codex Alimentarius, the outlawing of the natural, to restrict the public from access to vitamins and nutrients, which their bodies require. This will ensure that the general public will encounter more health problems and will then require even more medical attention. Certainly, this would guarantee more profits for drug companies and we would require even more doctors, but of what possible benefit could it be to the public? What the system is trying to do is simply a form of genocide, to which some have applied the term nutricide. No matter what we choose to call what is currently taking place, it is simply designed to cause more suffering and death, so as far as I am concerned, it should be brought to a halt.

When I first started providing this oil to patients, I figured there had to be a great number of others who were doing the same. With the medical history this plant has, plus the fact that hundreds of millions worldwide were consuming and growing hemp, how could something as simple as what I had discovered go unnoticed? Yet, as time went by, I was to find this had been the case and of course I soon realized that it was those with vast resources and power who had brought this about. Believe me, in the beginning it was a very lonely and possibly somewhat dangerous position, in which I had placed myself, for many people who have tried to expose the truth about issues such as this die under strange circumstances and are no longer around. For the most part, the public do not like to dwell on this, but no one can say such things do not take place. That's the reason I was so happy when I found that experts in the field like Raphael Mechoulam, Lumir Hanus, and others were also beginning to become more vocal about this subject. There seemed to be more support behind what I was doing every day and it was continuing to build.

Even to this day, I still hear people uttering nonsense like "there is no scientific evidence." The greatest experts and hemp researchers in the world have stood up and backed my position. All the best hemp publications are doing articles about the miraculous curative power of properly produced hemp oil. Do you actually think large publications like these would blindly print huge articles on the basis of my word alone? Not likely. Would someone who was unknown like myself in the hemp movement be crowned Freedom Fighter of the Year at *High Times* Magazine's annual Cannabis Cup, if everything I was telling the world was not based in fact? If you want scientific evidence, simply Google PubMed, then punch in cannabinoids and cancer. I think this will satisfy your scientific concerns.

As for the lack of medical documentation regarding people who have used hemp oil to treat their conditions, you can thank the medical system for that, since they have been somewhat less than cooperative in releasing such information. Instead of doing the right thing for the public they are supposed to serve, it seems they are much more concerned about their jobs and position. The longer they can help the system keep the truth hidden, the longer they can fill their pockets and maintain what authority they now have. The medical system currently operating in Canada and in the vast majority of the rest of the world is not designed to help the patient. Indeed, it seems their goal is just the opposite. If someone would like to try to prove me wrong, then please do. With the evidence now before you, I cannot imagine how anyone could believe it to be otherwise.

CHAPTER 12
FALLING OFF THE BANANA BOAT

By the spring and summer of 2008, I was no longer being contacted by only people who were looking for help. Now we were receiving more and more e-mails and calls that concerned a wide variety of topics. Still, in my little world, it didn't seem that this issue was becoming that well-known elsewhere. After "Run From The Cure" was released, our website did receive many more hits, but I was so busy now with the demands people were putting upon me that I had little time to notice.

Larry had done a wonderful job taking care of our website, but the increase in traffic had made running it on dial-up impossible. We needed high-speed access, which would allow us to keep up with all that was happening. To solve the problem, Steve Ridgway, a man that I had come in contact with from Amherst, volunteered his services to run our site. Steve had a high-speed connection in his home that was still not available to us in Little Forks, so I talked it over with Larry and we decided to take him up on his offer. Even though, it had been Larry's efforts, which had made the site possible, he graciously stepped aside and let Steve take the helm. Although Larry no longer plays this role, I want the public to know the important contribution both he and his wife Ruby have made. Without the efforts of these two wonderful people, I doubt very much that "Phoenix Tears" would have been a success.

Running the Phoenix Tears website had turned into a major headache and Steve soon started to feel the pressure of his new role. He is a strong believer in what this medicine could do for the public and he has put a great deal of effort into running the site. I might also add that he has made thousands of copies of our documentary available, so that we could distribute them free of charge, and Steve has been a great ambassador for this cause. I have lost count of the number of printers he has worn out, just trying to supply the paperwork needed for distribution. All in all, I don't believe we could have found anyone more capable or freely giving of their time than Steve Ridgway. Many seem to think I am solely responsible for what is taking place, but as you can see, that is hardly the case. What is happening right now is based on the efforts of many people who have nothing but good intentions for the human race.

One day in the late spring of 2008, I received a call from Terry Bremner, who was with the Chronic Pain Association of Canada. Terry had been to one of my seminars in Halifax a few months earlier and asked if I would be willing to speak at a large meeting they were having in the fall. Of course, since my aim was to spread this knowledge, I could do little else but agree. We talked for a few minutes and Terry stated, "Rick, I hope you're not going to go after the doctors too much." I replied, "Terry, you know me better than that, you've heard me speak," and we both laughed. I really didn't have much of an idea what the Chronic Pain Association of Canada even was, but it did have an important-sounding title.

At the time, I thought Terry's intentions were completely honorable and above board. He had heard me speak in the past and what could be better for chronic pain than hemp oil? Later I learned Terry apparently thought when we had spoken that I had agreed to tone it down. There was definitely some miscommunication going on, because I had not taken our conversation that way at all. Indeed, if I had, I would never have even agreed to speak, since toning this subject down would have been completely unacceptable.

At first, he had asked me to speak for about 45 minutes, so I prepared a seminar that would fit this time slot. Later, he called me back and I was then informed that my speaking time had now been reduced to ten minutes. He said he was very sorry about all this, but they would like me to come back and speak at a meeting they were having in January. I can't say I was at all thrilled by what he was now telling me, but I thought maybe they just wanted me to do this ten-minute piece to prepare them for what I would be saying in January. So I agreed and told him I would be there and set about writing the piece I would present.

The meeting was held in November 2008 at Dalhousie University in Halifax and there must have been about 300 people present. When I entered the hall, in which the event was to be staged, I noticed there were many displays that had been set up by drug companies. I was trying to find out why all these displays were here, when suddenly the meeting got underway. Terry spoke first, followed by a reporter and then finally the main speaker took the podium. Her name was Dr. Mary Lynch and she was to be appointed the new head of the Chronic Pain Association of Canada.

The talk she gave was about doing exercises similar to *tai chi* to help patients suffering from MS. To me, what she was doing was ludicrous; since I already knew from past experience that hemp oil could cure or control MS very effectively. Now here was this doctor, telling people with a very painful spasmodic condition to do exercises. I was disgusted. Finally, it was my turn at the microphone and of course, I teed off on the whole medical system. The small 10-minute piece I had written was short, but it was certainly to the point. A few in the audience, whom I presumed to be doctors, just sat there and glared at me, but the vast majority liked what I had said. It appears the statements I was making caused Terry to panic. What I was saying must have been far too strong for him. Terry came up on stage behind me, while I was addressing the audience, and you could see how frustrated he was. There was no question he wanted me off the stage and he tried to interrupt, but I continued until I was finished.

I was later introduced to Dr. Lynch and I swear I could see the hate right in her eyes. When she spoke, it was all this negative nonsense like, "It would take hundreds of millions of dollars to bring this medicine out." I explained to her, "Look, anyone can grow this plant and practically anyone can produce the oil. I don't see where all this money you're talking about has anything to do with it. This medicine works and we would have to be complete idiots not to start using it again. All you have to do is look at the real medical history of the hemp plant; its benefits are undeniable."

Needless to say, Dr. Lynch was not impressed with what I had said and nor was I with her uncaring attitude. How could anyone who calls himself or herself a doctor ignore what I was saying, if they had any real concern at all for the well-being of their patients? After listening to the way Dr. Lynch spoke, it soon became perfectly clear to me that the Chronic Pain Association of Canada cared little or nothing about those who are suffering from chronic pain and other conditions. I had succeeded in reaching a good number of people that evening but it was more than obvious that the medical professionals who were present did not enjoy the statements I had made.

A few days later, Terry called me all in a huff. It seemed they would no longer require me to speak in January. He stated, "Rick, your little speech has cost us thousands of dollars in funding." It was almost as if he was expecting an apology, but instead I said, "Funding from who?" "Why, the pharmaceutical industry, of course," he stated. To me, his answer had made no sense, so I replied, "Terry, think about what you're saying. Isn't it the pharmaceutical companies that are causing all of this suffering and are they not the ones standing in the way of this medicine's use? Shouldn't the first concern of the Chronic Pain Association of Canada be to help those who are suffering from chronic pain?" I continued, "Terry, the organization you're connected with is a complete fraud. Before this is over, there will be many such organizations exposed to the public for what they are." Not surprisingly, I heard nothing more from Terry Bremner or the Chronic Pain Association of Canada.

By the late spring of 2008, my activities were becoming quite well known, so CJCH radio in Halifax contacted me to ask if I would be willing to come on the air. Rick Howe had an open-line talk show, which aired on this station that was very popular, and his broadcasts had a large following in Nova Scotia at the time. Since Rick has an easygoing personality, I found working with him to be a pleasure and the interview went very well. Of course, since the show I was taking part in had a large listening audience, it gave me the perfect opportunity to challenge the medical system to a showdown.

What I proposed would involve twelve cancer patients, six who wanted treatments provided by the medical system and six that wanted treatment with hemp oil. I told the listening audience that if this was done openly before the public, it would prove once and for all what I had been stating was true. As expected, the medical system shied away from my challenge and since there was no outcry from the public, nothing happened. Nevertheless the broadcast we did that day was very powerful and one of the first to call in was a man who had cured his terminal cancer using the oil. With the large following that enjoyed listening to Rick's show, I knew we had reached a great number of people with the truth, so I felt my time was well spent.

During the summer of 2008, two very good friends of mine, Eric and Debbie Donkin, left Canada to see what Ecuador had to offer. They, like myself, had become very disillusioned with Canada and were in search of something better. When we met, I had provided the oil to Eric's father Keith, who was suffering from terminal lung cancer. The first time I came into contact with Keith Donkin, he was sitting there with a cigarette in his hand, and he stated, "I suppose you're going to tell me I will have to quit smoking."

Keith was 79 years of age, he had cancer in both lungs, and his breathing capacity was down to 70%. When he was diagnosed, his lung cancer was so far advanced that they did not even offer him treatment, they simply told him that he had three months to live and sent him home to die. Since he had been smoking for decades, I told him, "I don't care if you smoke or not during the treatment," and I believe that is the only reason he agreed to take the oil.

Rick Dwyer was with me that day and you could see he was not in agreement. Later, when we were on the way home, he stated, "You can't say things like that, Rick. You know smoking is bad for you." My answer was, "Of course it is, but Keith has been smoking all his life and I think it would do little good to force him into quitting. Look, we are both in our fifties and have been smoking since we were children. If smoking was really that deadly, why are we still around? We both know chemicals are added to the tobacco we smoke to make it more addictive and harmful, but in this situation I think it will make little difference." He just made a face at me and shook his head, but that was the end of our discussion on the subject.

Keith smoked two packs a day during his treatment and it had no detrimental effect on his recovery. Ninety days later, both lungs were clear and his breathing was back to 100%. He was now cured and completely free from the disease that doctors had said would bring about his death.

Eric himself was in his early 50s when we first came into contact, but he had a number of serious health problems. By the time we met, he had already endured four open-heart surgeries and he was suffering a great deal of pain from damage left behind by a blood clot he had experienced in his lower leg. He was certainly not a well man and to me at the time his complexion was almost gray looking. In his quest to find relief Eric had tried all the medical system's nasty addictive chemicals to ease his pain, but had found they were doing nothing to help his situation and their side effects only gave him more problems.

So he, too, went on the oil, but at a much lower rate of consumption than a cancer patient like his father would require. I was talking to Eric at his home one day about four months after he began ingesting the oil. By this time, he was really looking much better. During our conversation, he mentioned that his kidney function was now back to normal. Every time you go through something like open-heart surgery, your kidney function is reduced. Eric had been through four such surgeries, so he had little kidney function left, before starting the treatment I provided. Now his kidney function was back to normal, we were both very happy about the improvement and knew exactly why this had taken place.

He also told me the shoulder and arm he had injured years before were now working properly again. About ten years previously, Eric had torn the tendons and ligaments in his shoulder, while trying to pull a four-wheeler out of the mud. After his injury, the use of this arm had been badly impaired and doctors told him to get used to it, since there was nothing that could be done. Eric stated, "A few nights ago, my head started itching and I was sitting there scratching, when I realized something had changed." Not thinking, Eric had scratched his head with the arm that had been damaged and suddenly realized, he could move it properly once more. By this time, to me such things were not unusual, since it seemed that every day people were contacting me about miracles the oil had worked for their conditions.

Debbie and Eric have both experienced nothing but wonderful effects from this medication. Eric can now also walk much better and no longer requires the use of a leg brace. If he has any pain now, at least it is something he can tolerate and the damage the blood clot had done to his lower leg and foot has been greatly reduced. After what Eric and Debbie had seen the oil do, they became two of my biggest supporters.

As time went on, the inaction of our system with regard to this subject had frustrated them. They were sickened by the lack of concern about this issue on our government's part and now all they wanted was fresh air and freedom. I hated to see them go and I knew I would miss them both but, happily for me, they returned from South America about a month later. They had both enjoyed the lifestyle in Ecuador, but at the time did not find things as stable there as they had been led to believe. In addition, they had found the weather in that region was not all it had been cracked up to be. They explained that there was a lot of rain and often roads were washed out, making it very difficult to travel.

Not finding what they had been seeking, they had returned to Canada and nothing could have made me more happy. Eric and Debbie bought a beautiful little place seven kilometers from the nearest power pole and they are as happy as two squirrels. The simple truth is, it's a great shame the world does not have many more such people who are able to find happiness by living off the grid and becoming one with nature again.

Shortly after Eric and Debbie returned, a friend of theirs from Amherst, who was suffering from prostate cancer, gave me a call. After speaking with me, he decided to produce his own oil and use it to treat his condition. About two months later, he called and said that he would like me to drop by and pay him a visit. When I arrived, I was told that he was now cancer free and it was more than obvious that he was very happy with the results of his treatment. We then sat down to drink a coffee and he asked, "Rick do you know what the medical system was planning to do to me?" I informed him that I had a pretty good idea of what they had in mind and that I was very pleased he did not take their advice.

He stated, "The doctors were going to fill my prostate with radioactive beads and they told me that afterwards I would no longer be able to have sex with my wife." In addition, he was also informed that he could not even allow his grandchildren to sit on his lap. The expression on his face said it all and he then exclaimed, "What the hell do those idiots in the medical system think they are doing? If I had allowed them to do this, they would have ruined my life and if I had found out about this cure afterwards, I'm sure someone in a white coat would have been doing some suffering too."

Over the years, I have heard several people make similar statements and I'm sure many of them would have backed up what they were saying by seeking vengeance. Yet, unbelievably, doctors continue to mutilate many of their patients in the same manner, so I think it's just a matter of time before this occurs. Quite possibly, such things are beginning to happen already, since I know many patients I treated have voiced their disgust to doctors who were treating them. If indeed some violence is already being directed towards doctors, don't expect to hear too much about it in the news because if it was reported openly, it would cause all the other doctors to panic.

After our documentary had been released by Christian Laurette, the number of calls and e-mails we received went through the roof. Many people started getting in touch with us about get-rich-quick schemes, in which I had no interest. From the time I had started providing oil to people to treat their conditions, I have always made it clear that I would not allow the oil I produced to be taken over by a pharmaceutical company. This medicine belongs to the people and drug companies have no right to control its production or use and neither does anyone else. My plan had always been for Phoenix Tears to remain an entity that works for the greater good of mankind. People who are sick and destitute should be given free access to this medicine at no charge. Can you imagine a drug company doing such a thing? I think you have to admit that it would be highly unlikely.

Since this medication can be produced so cheaply, making it available on a donation basis or even free to those with little or no money would be completely viable. If I was in charge of an oil-producing facility, it would be run with an open book policy to the public. Anyone who wanted to know what we are doing could simply come in and take a look at our books and nothing would be hidden. This way, we could build something of great benefit to mankind without the presence of corruption. I hope to live to see the day when every country on this Earth will have an oil-producing complex to supply their people's medicinal needs.

When this begins to come about, I would be happy to work with any government that has the proper mindset in helping to see that this can be accomplished as rapidly as possible, if their intention is really to help the people and not themselves. It is not about choices any more. Something must be done if the human race expects to survive. As Jack Herer has always said, "Hemp is the only rational answer." Look at the multitude of jobs that could be created in earth-friendly hemp-based industries. Have we not poisoned this planet enough and is it not time for us to change our ways before it's too late?

If this world is ever to become what it should be, we must apply the use of common sense. With the use of such thinking, hemp would be by far the biggest industry on this planet and we would have a hemp-based economy in a very short time. It baffles me as to why so many people cannot see what is right in front of them. Do we behave this way because we are all ignorant of the truth, or are we truly that out of sync with what is happening right before our eyes? We have done more damage to this planet in the last few decades than in all human history combined. Who out there really believes we can go on this way indefinitely? No one, that's who. Yet we stand like a flock of sheep and watch big money interests destroy the very Earth on which we must all live.

If you happen to be one of those people who are waiting for technology to save us, don't hold your breath. Much of the horrible situation mankind now faces was brought about by the use of some of our wonderful new technologies. Hi-tech and no common sense, the perfect combination to destroy our planet, which we need if all living creatures, including our own species, are to survive.

In the summer of 2008, Susie, the big female dog we had owned for years, finally cashed in her chips. She was at least six years old when she came to live with us, so she was easily 18 or more when she finally died. She was just one big lovable character, who liked nothing better than to lick you to death. She didn't have an aggressive bone in her body and everyone loved her, but I have to admit she was a pothead. If you sat down with a joint, in seconds she would be right in front of you, as if she were saying, "Give me a hit." She was a real comedy and we thoroughly enjoyed having her around for company.

About a year and a half before she died, we noticed she was really slowing down. I had already provided oil to other dogs to treat cancer and different conditions, so I knew the oil would do Susie nothing but good. It was funny watching how the oil knocked her down, but she certainly didn't seem to mind. As soon as the effects wore off, she would come and lick some more right off your finger. We gave her the oil twice a day for five days. Suddenly she was a new dog. She was running around like a pup again and it was great to have her back. After the ten doses I had given her, all went well for over a year. Then one night when I was talking to my son Mike, he said Susie was slowing down again. At that time, he had been keeping her down at the other house in Salt Springs. So I gave him a tube of oil, saying, "You know what to do," but before he could get it to her, she had passed away.

I often used Susie as an example when I was talking to people about this medication. I would tell them things like, "You know, dogs are much smarter than humans. If a dog is sick, it will come and lick the oil right off your finger, because dogs have the sense to know what is good for them. What a shame the human race does not possess such senses themselves." A statement like this did get the attention of many and helped to drive my point home. A dog's senses are so keen that when I tried to give Susie lower-grade oil, she would not even look at it, but when I put the high-grade in front of her, it was gone in a flash.

Being one of those who had awakened after falling off the banana boat can be quite hard on a person. I had become fully conscious of what was taking place in the rest of the world, but I found it hard to grasp why more individuals were not doing something to change things. There was certainly no shortage of evidence available on the internet, proving that we are all on the road to destruction, but still so few seemed to care. Why people were not reacting was a complete mystery to me, and trying to figure out the cause gave me a great deal of frustration.

I have always encouraged everyone to educate themselves, but I found some who tried could not handle the information they encountered easily. For many, the horror of it all is just too great and it can cause some to fall into a depressed state of hopelessness. Obviously, that was not my intent, so I suggest to anyone who feels overwhelmed by what they are learning to proceed more slowly. Give yourself time to grasp it all and do it at a pace which you can handle, you do not have to find out about everything that is wrong with our world in a week.

By the summer of 2008, I was spending hours every day just answering the questions of patients who called me on the phone. The calls were coming from everywhere. Many people were even getting angry with me because my line was always busy, but I had no control over such things. Due to all the calls I was now receiving, often those who wished to speak with me would just come directly to my home instead of trying to call.

All of this was becoming a tremendous strain on me, for in reality, I am a one-man show, even though I did have some wonderful people around me and they have all worked very hard to further the cause. Still, it was me that everyone came to when they were looking for medicine and I was the one who dealt directly with the patients. Supporters like Rick Dwyer could see all the stress that I had to endure to carry on and one day he stated, "Rick, you have to stop doing this before it kills you." My reply was, "If you were on the other end of that call and you were suffering, would you want me to pick up the receiver?" The statement I had made certainly caused him to rethink what he had said, yet still he was absolutely correct. With no help from those in authority, sooner or later, my own health would be in jeopardy as a result of my activities, but what was I to do?

By August of that year, I could no longer even supply those in need. Over the preceding months, I had bought up all the high-quality bud in a radius of 50 miles from my home. In our area, there was nothing left to be found, so when people called, I had to tell them they would have to find the hemp required for their treatment themselves. Many times, they did just that and I would produce the medicine for them. I did not like doing it this way because in the beginning, often dealers would rip the patients off. Sometimes people would come to my door with a pound of hemp bud they had paid thousands of dollars for, which did not have the quality necessary to produce the medicine properly.

It was quite easy for me to get the right hemp because I knew what I was looking for, but unfortunately, many who tried to acquire their own did not. After they became aware of what I was doing, I have to say that most dealers were quite good about it. Once they learned the hemp was required to produce medicine to treat cancer or other medical problems, they usually tried to supply the best material possible. Some dealers even sent patients elsewhere if they felt other suppliers might have something better to work with at their disposal. When I first started buying material on a larger scale from other growers, quite often they would try to sell it to me when it was still somewhat damp. I told producers, "If you are not willing to supply the material completely dry, then I can't do business with you."

In the end, they agreed to comply. Even though I had to pay top prices, at least the material they supplied was dry. Growers liked doing business with me, since they no longer had to try to sell their goods on the street and with me they always received cash on the barrel head. If they had good material, usually I would buy up their whole crop and turn it into medicine. I was the guy who was producing the oil and I knew quite a few suppliers who were growing good medicinal bud, so in many instances I ended up being the middleman between the growers and the patients. With my experience, it was a role for which I was well-suited, and both the patients and the growers seemed to like this arrangement.

Producing this medication by doing two washes of the bud material provided about 60 grams (2.1 ounces) of high-grade oil per dry pound on average. There are strains that can produce more oil and those that can produce less. So if you get 60 g out of a dry pound of good material, be happy, you have got your money's worth.

In 2008, the small valley behind my home had flooded and this ruined practically all my crop that year. Luckily, I knew others who had been more successful and I could always turn to them for what was needed. It would not have made any difference even if the flood had not occurred, since the shock-and-awe boys were at it again. The police had helicopters flying up and down the valley and hovering in my back yard three times during the late summer of 2008. Even if the flood had never taken place, these diligent public servants would still have stolen the crop. I almost had to feel sorry for the RCMP in their flak jackets and yellow striped pants, since Mother Nature had beaten them to the punch.

The RCMP and the military seemed to take a great deal of interest in searching the area where I was living and hovering just a few feet off the ground with their helicopters in my back yard. Yet, strangely, not one patient who acquired the oil from me was ever stopped or bothered by them upon leaving my property. Even to a casual observer, it would have been apparent I was still supplying the medicine. Often, my yard was completely full of cars and there was a constant flow of patients coming my way. I suppose that if the RCMP were to stop cancer patients who were leaving my home with the oil in their possession, it would create a very ugly situation in court. To avoid the embarrassment, it appears they decided to lay low and not bother the patients who were going home with the medicine. Even before the RCMP were done fluttering around with their choppers, I turned to the other growers I knew to supply material. It took me a few weeks to catch up with the backlog of patients who were waiting for the medicine, but catch up I did and the crusade went on.

CHAPTER 13

THE HEMP PUBLICATIONS BECOME INVOLVED

In the early fall of 2008, another federal election was called in Canada and some of my supporters wanted me to run again. I knew from the last election it was basically a waste of time, but letting the public know that this issue had never been resolved could help to spread the word further. We did all the legwork that was required to get the paperwork ready and it was submitted to the proper authorities. The last election I had taken part in showed that many of those who were putting on these political events did not want me to speak, and in this election, it was even worse. I was only invited to speak at one event during the whole campaign. This time, it didn't bother me so much that this issue and I were ignored, since I didn't have the time to travel and speak anyway. I was too busy trying to keep up with all those who were coming my way looking for help.

The first time I ran, 524 people had given me their support, so Rick Dwyer asked me how many votes I expected to receive in this election. It had been almost two years since the last election and my activities had become much better known to the public, so, joking, I answered, "525." Rick found what I had said quite humorous, since we both expected I would do much better after all the notoriety I had received. When the election results were known, if memory doesn't fail me, I believe I received 551 votes. Everyone around me said this can't be right; they thought I would have done much better and felt possibly someone had played with the numbers. Even I started thinking that something like this may have taken place, because almost everyone I was coming in contact with said they had voted for me.

If what I was doing had not been so important for them to keep hidden, it might be said I was just someone crying in his beer, because I had received less votes than expected. But with the perversions I had seen the system perform in the past, it was easy for me to suspect that they could very well have played with the election results. There is only one reason that anyone would do this and that is to send a message to the public that what I was doing had little support. Elections today are not run honestly and in reality, they never have been. When I was young, I clearly remember all the pints of whisky and rum that were passed out at voting stations in brown paper bags to bribe those who were casting their ballots to vote the 'right way'.

What I am describing was common practice when I was a youth and although such things are not done so openly today, should we really expect current elections to be managed more honestly? Judging by the Bush-Gore presidential election in 2000, manipulation, it appears, is still alive and well and is certainly not unheard of. I have no proof that such a thing transpired in my case, but when the system is trying to keep something of this importance quiet, they will stoop to any level.

I never really thought there would be any possibility of me being elected to Parliament anyway. The idea would just be too outrageous. Talk about a bull in a china shop ... if I had been elected, Ottawa would never be the same, once I was done with them. So, I always thought there would be very little likelihood that I would ever become a Member of Parliament. All in all, running in this election was a waste of time, but it did let the public know I was still around and that no one had been able to disprove anything I was saying. Many people were starting to realize what I was exposing had to be true.

If not, why were no medical professionals standing up to debunk me and the use of this medicine? To more and more every day, it was becoming clear who was deceiving them and it wasn't Rick Simpson. Canadian doctors continued to avoid me like the plague, which in the end proved they had little or no concern for their patients. Only one doctor from Canada ever asked me to contact him directly. I supplied the oil to a man with terminal prostate cancer that had metastasized to the bone. He was stage IV with no hope of recovery according to his doctors when he came to get the oil. A few days later, the patient called me and said his doctor wanted to talk to me, since he was concerned about this treatment.

I called the doctor's office and asked him what the problem was. "Oh, no problem," he replied. "Mr. Simpson, I just wanted to let you know, I would be happy to keep you informed as to the patient's progress." Now that was a new one, "Maybe this guy really did want to heal people," I was thinking. I thanked him for his cooperation and of course never heard another word from him again. Since this doctor had told the patient he was concerned about this treatment, it appears to me that he was trying to put doubts about this medication in the patients mind.

By using the ploy of telling the patient that he wanted to talk to me directly, he may have thought that I would not dare to contact him. If I had not done so, it would prove to the patient that this treatment was not effective, because I would not defend its use. I think it came as a bit of a shock to this doctor when I didn't hesitate to contact him and I believe that is the reason he tried to feed me this cock and bull story about keeping me informed as to the patient's progress. Three months later, the patient contacted me and reported he was now cancer-free. Shouldn't a doctor who had seen his own patient cured of terminal cancer with the use of this oil have done something?

I have seen this same scenario played out over and over again. Not one of these Canadian doctors was willing to expose the truth about this medication, so that it could be recognized and used by others. Over the last while, a few patients have been telling me that their own doctors had sent them my way. In a couple of cases, the patients who were sent informed me that they had a very close relationship with their doctors. I can only assume these medical professionals wanted the best for them, but why were more patients not sent to me before they were too badly damaged by chemo and radiation? From my perspective, it appeared that doctors were only sending patients that they knew well and cared about. I know how terrible this sounds, but when you take their advice, how do you know what that guy in the white coat is really thinking? Would they send patients with whom they are closely connected to get treatment with something they knew could help, while giving the vast majority of us chemo and radiation? You be the judge.

Certainly, it can only be said that they were doing little or nothing to bring the use of this medicine forward. Some patients informed their doctors as to what they were using, while others waited until they were cured and then told them. In all the years I have been doing this, I only know of one patient personally who was ever bothered by the police because his doctor reported him, but I'm sure there must be many more. Norm Peterson is a local man who had used this medication to treat his cancer. When the cancer was gone, he then told his doctor how this had occurred. Apparently, the good doctor was upset that his patient had been cured by the oil and he had then called the law. A short time later, the police arrived at Norm's home to ask about his use of the oil. Norm replied that yes, he had used it, but now he did not have any left. The officer asked him, "Did it cure your cancer?" Norm replied that it had done just that. The officer then gave him a smile and walked away.

Since my sentencing last February, the police had stayed away completely except for the nosing around they did with their helicopters. Everyone knew what was going on, since I had provided the oil to police officers and their families, too. It seemed that when police officers were sick enough or a loved one's life was in danger, whatever inhibitions they had against this medicine's use went into the trashcan. This proved to me that at least a few of these law enforcement types did have some reasoning abilities after all. Every time I dealt with a police officer after the medicine had worked its magic, I always told them they had better start looking at cannabis hemp in a whole different light and they would agree. Unfortunately, their jobs prevented many from discussing it openly and most were forced to remain quiet about what they had learned, while those who worked with them continued on trying to eradicate this plant, which is so beneficial to our health and wellbeing.

One case I remember well involved the twenty-year-old daughter of a local police officer, who had been suffering from Crohn's disease for eight years. We had known each other for a long time and when he came to my home, he asked if what he had been hearing about the oil's healing abilities was true. I stated, "Do you think I would be doing this if it didn't really work? I believe by now you should know me better than that." He laughed, then went on to describe what the medical system had done to his daughter. She had been suffering since she was twelve years old with no improvement and was steadily getting worse. He felt that if something was not done quickly, in the near future, this horrible disease, which causes so much suffering, could bring about her death.

I explained to him that if anything could help his daughter, it would be the oil and I supplied him with a tube to get her under treatment. About six weeks later, he returned to my home and told me that now his daughter no longer had the disease. One six-gram tube of oil had solved her medical issues and now she could go back to living like a normal human being. With results like that, I expect this officer told many of his friends and co-workers, who were having health problems, about the miracles this oil can produce. But if he were to start making too much noise about what he knew, I'm sure it could have cost him his job. To the best of my knowledge, the officer I supplied with oil is no longer on active service, but still I see no need to reveal his name. If I were to do so, it would probably bring some unwanted criticism his way and, under the circumstances, I really don't think he should be bothered by others who, if put in the same position he was in, would have done no differently. But if the need ever arose, I am sure this officer would be happy to verify everything I have stated.

Those employed in law enforcement always used the same old tired excuse, "We are just doing our jobs." From my perspective, they are certainly doing a great job killing people for the government, but is this the role they are supposed to be playing in our society? Those who have been employed as police officers to protect and serve the public, for whom they are supposed to be working, obviously have their wires crossed. You do not serve the public by stealing a natural medicine that can heal them. At that time, I would say about 50% of the police officers in our local area would have preferred that I be left alone. Legal or not, it's nice to have someone at your disposal that can really help if a health crisis should arise in your family. Still, this did not prevent many of their counterparts from carrying on with the raids against both myself and others who were growing for medicinal purposes.

I found the late fall of 2008 very depressing. Eddy Lepp was going to be sent to prison for 10 years because much like me, he had been growing large amounts of cannabis. I wrote a letter in defense of Eddy but it fell on deaf ears. How could our system have become so decayed that it would send a man like Eddy to prison for trying to help the human race? Jack and I were totally disgusted by what was happening. We were both well aware that millions of years in prison time had already been served for the simple act of growing and using this plant. We also knew that those who had caused the incarceration of such vast numbers were indeed the ones who should be serving time for their actions themselves. Still, what could we do, since as yet we did not have the support to change things?

In January 2009, I got together with some supporters and we decided I should try to do a tour across Canada that coming summer. I knew by the time summer came there would be no material left available around our area to produce the medicine from anyway, so why not give it a try? We all felt a Canadian tour might be just the thing to break this issue wide open, so we put a request up on the Internet for donations. It was very disappointing, but by spring, we had only raised $2900. For me to do this tour properly, it would take much more funding to accomplish the task. We planned to do big well-advertised seminars in 28 cities and I would have to be on the road for about four months.

You would have to be insane to set out on such a venture with only $2900 to fund the project. The tour had to be cancelled, so we explained to the public what had happened and made our apologies. The price of a decent house would have covered the expenses to put on the tour we had in mind. Sadly, the 2900 dollars we received in donations was far from the amount that would be needed to even begin staging such events. The only thing I could do would be to continue passing out information and put more clips from seminars up on the Internet. At least that way we could still reach some people.

Jack Herer was not pleased the tour had to be cancelled. He insisted, "Rick, do the tour, it's important." I told him it was impossible and that we just didn't have the funding. For me to even begin the tour, I would have to drive 4500 miles to Vancouver, British Columbia to get things under way. This was necessary because the citizens of British Colombia were much more open-minded about this issue. If we began the tour there, it would have a much better chance of succeeding. I had planned to put the seminars on with no admission charge to bring in more people. We did not have the funding to pay for the halls and advertising necessary to make it a success, let alone keep us alive during the tour. Finally, after I explained the situation, Jack relented. Still, neither of us was happy about it, but what could be done? I had no choice in the matter. Even if we could have come up with the funding to do the tour, I'm sure the government would have thrown as many obstacles as possible in our path. With this in mind, all in all, it appeared that canceling the tour may have worked out for the best in the long run.

The winter of 2009 was very busy. They were coming at me in all directions. An ex-American football star named Eric Affholter drove all the way from California just to meet me and see the process I used. Eric was very nice and we got along well, so he stayed at my home for about a week. When he went back to the States, he was completely sold. He had seen what this oil could do with his own eyes and was a total believer. A few weeks later, another young man named Jordan Fierro, who was involved with Jack Herer, also spent a week at my home filming and doing interviews.

Then a photographer from England named Yvonne Poland came and stayed with one of my supporters for a few days. She took many pictures and she was not only a great photographer, she was also a wonderful cook. Eve is a vegetarian but she could produce dishes you would swear had a great deal of meat in them. After she had departed, Eve was instrumental in bringing what I am doing to the attention of David Icke and Max Igan. Because of this, her efforts have done much to help the cause.

Around this same time period, a supporter contacted me and said he had found a song that I needed to hear. Its title was Tree of Life and it was put out by a group called Human Revolution. After listening to its lyrics, I was truly astounded. They had put everything that Jack and I had been saying to music. Many wonderful songs about this plant are available, but I have yet to hear anything that compares to Tree of Life. As far as I know, Human, the young man who heads up this group, wrote the song himself and I have become his biggest fan. In one rendition, the whole group does the song and I must say that they did a very good job. But there is another version, where Human himself just goes off into a field of hemp and cuts loose with his guitar and this is the version I like the best. If you have the time, please go on the Internet and give it a listen and I am sure you will see why I consider this song to be so important to the cause.

Everything was going well, but many times it seemed there were not enough hours in the day. As usual, I had bought up all the good hemp for miles around. Now I was starting to find it very hard to get the high-grade material required to produce this medication that was needed so badly. One day in the late winter of 2009, I was again doing a seminar at Dalhousie University. One of the people in the audience shouted, "Rick, your instructions on how to produce the oil have been published in *Weed World*." Suddenly, I was now being told that one of the largest and most read hemp publications on the planet had published my instructions.

Later that day, I purchased a copy of *Weed World*, volume 79, and sure enough, there was the article. I had been doing this for years and no one seemed to be willing to publish anything about this subject. Now, to my surprise, *Weed World* had just gone ahead and published my instructions without my knowledge. Even though they did not ask my permission, this was quite all right by me and I would like to congratulate *Weed World* for being the first hemp publication to bring the truth to the public's attention.

Around this time, I received a call from Justin Kander, a young man from the United States whom I had talked with many times in the past. He had been in touch with Marc Emery and Marc wanted Justin to do a story detailing my activities. I told Justin I would be happy to help and gave him the story. I explained to him what I had already been through with Marc Emery and told him that I doubted the article I had given him would be published in *Cannabis Culture*. Justin did the story and sent it to Marc Emery, but to the best of my knowledge, it was never printed.

In the late winter of 2009, a man of native descent named Stan Castonguay from New Brunswick came to meet me. He stated, "I just had to come and meet the man who saved my life face to face." A few months earlier, he had contacted Scot Cullins to get the oil to treat his terminal cancer and he was now cancer-free. Scot was just one of many from all over the world who had contacted me offering to help others. Of course, in most cases, they could not provide the oil for free and the patient had to cover their expenses. Even though the oil could not be supplied at no cost, at least they were making the medicine available.

Stan asked if I would be willing to come to Saint Anne, New Brunswick, to put on a seminar. He informed me that he could get a good crowd together and Scot would also be in attendance, so I agreed. It is over a five-hour drive from my home to Saint Anne, but I wanted to do the seminar and meet Scot in person. We had a successful event that came off well and I was fortunate enough to meet some very important tribal leaders, whom I spoke with at length. Scot and I also got together and had some time to talk things over, which left me with a very good impression of this man.

Mark Allen, one of my supporters, had come with me to attend the seminar and afterwards he and I stopped in at Scot's on the way home, so we could take our discussions further. I took an instant liking to Scot the first time I met him. It was more than apparent his heart was in the right place. All he wanted to do was help others and he did not seem to be about the money that could have easily been made. People with this type of mindset and I tend to get along quite easily, since there is no conflict and our aims are so similar. I was very glad that I had been given this opportunity to put on the seminar and to meet Scot in a relaxed setting.

At the time, I had people in Europe, Africa, South America, the US, Canada, and elsewhere, who had volunteered to help supply the oil. Unfortunately, Scot was the only one of these suppliers I ever had the chance to meet in person. When people in other countries contacted me, I would always encourage them to acquire a pound of material and produce the medicine themselves. Often they did not have the right contacts to provide the bud material that was needed and would ask if I knew anyone that could just simply supply the finished oil. In cases like this, I would send the patients on to someone who had contacted me and offered to supply the medicine. I made it perfectly clear I could not be held responsible for the quality of the oil or the business practices of those they were about to deal with. Many seemed to be convinced that I was the head of some big international organization supplying oil to people worldwide, but that was hardly the case.

Overall, I have to say in the beginning things went fairly well and many people were helped. Sometimes I would receive a complaint, then I'd get on the phone and contact the supplier if I felt they were at fault. This worked quite well in the beginning and most situations were easily resolved. Suppliers at that time were depending on me to provide them with customers; if they did not comply with my wishes, I would simply not send anyone else. To me, it was all about the quality of the medicine they were supplying. If they were not willing to do what is right and provide high-quality oil at a decent price, I would not instruct patients to contact them. I had to insist that suppliers provide the best medication possible, because those who should live could die if they were given an inferior product and hemp medicine would be given a bad reputation which it did not deserve. Unfortunately, the number of complaints continued to increase until it got to the point I could no longer put any trust in what most others were producing. After that, all I could do for those in other countries was tell them it would be best if they produced their own.

The price was often an issue and people would always ask how much these suppliers charged for a treatment. I explained to them it really depended on how much the suppliers had to pay for the starting material. I knew of one lady in New York, who paid $7500 for a pound of good bud to produce her medication. To me, such a price was highway robbery, but when your life is at stake, what choice do you have? I always encouraged growers and those who were producing the oil to keep their prices as low as possible, so that patients could afford the material or medication they required. You have to keep it about healing ... the minute greed comes into play, healing goes out the window.

In the late spring of 2009, all hell broke loose. Jack Herer contacted me to do a chapter for the upcoming 12th edition of "The Emperor Wears No Clothes." I was floored by Jack's request. This book had become my bible. Now Jack was providing me with another way to reach the public in his wonderful masterpiece. Tickled pink are not the words. It seemed Mr. Herer was going to have a very big impact on the rest of my life.

At about the same time I was contacted by *Weed World*. They wanted me to write some articles about the oil for an upcoming special edition they were planning to put out. To supply what they had requested required about 35 pages of written text. The special edition *Weed World* put out in September of that year contained five articles I had supplied. They did a great job putting this edition together and, at the time, it was badly needed.

Then I was hit with the big one. Jindrich Bayer from the Czech Republic asked if I would answer some questions for the Czech hemp publication *Konoptikum*. He stated that there were other publications in nearby countries, which were also interested in having me do articles, so I agreed. When I received the questions, he wanted me to answer, I just about fell off my chair. There was page after page of them, and I knew they would keep me occupied for quite some time. As I recall, I sent Jack about 40 pages for the twelfth edition of "The Emperor Wears No Clothes," but to answer the questions Jindrich had supplied required 70 pages.

Believe me, I now had a much better understanding of the term writer's cramp. I was swamped with phone calls from people seeking help and now I had weeks of writing in front of me to satisfy my obligations to everyone. Somehow between all the calls and people coming to see me, I found the time to do all this writing and got the paperwork in question sent to the right people. I'll never forget the day Jack called me and said he'd gone over what I had sent him and had given it his approval. My statements about this subject were going to be expressed in what I viewed to be one of the most important literary works of all time and I could not have been more pleased.

In the spring of 2009, I came into contact with members of the Freeman on the Land movement. Previously, I had taken the time to watch some of Rob Menard's documentaries on the subject. At first, I must admit it all sounded a bit crazy, but the more I found out, the more intrigued I became by what he was expounding. Then one day, I received a call from a man named Darrell, who lived in Sackville, Nova Scotia, inviting me to speak at a Freeman's meeting they were having in the near future. On the appointed day, I arrived and spoke about the wonders of this medicine. Of course, there were many in attendance who were experiencing health problems, so they took a great interest in what I had to say. At the end of the meeting, a good number of those present took some oil home to see what it could do for their medical problems.

At the next meeting held a month later, they were all talking about the wonderful effects this medication was having on their conditions. I enjoyed listening to their comments about what they had experienced with the use of this substance, but I was becoming more and more interested in what this Freeman on the Land business had to offer. I acquired a good deal of information about the subject, but had little time to go over it, since I was so busy elsewhere. Becoming a Freeman on the Land is supposed to put you back under the old Common Law System, under which growing hemp is not a crime. After what I had been through with the authorities in Canada, all this sounded good to me, so I said, "Sign me up." Shortly afterwards, all the paperwork was sent in and since those in control did not voice an objection, I was now a Freeman on the Land.

In reality, I was so busy I felt I didn't even have time to grow a crop that summer. However, thanks to the paperwork I now had in place, my legal status was very different and if I chose to do so, I should be able to grow as much hemp as I liked without interference from the police. Normally, by early June, I would already have the hemp planted in the ground, but out came the seeds and by the end of June I had about 250 plants in my back yard again.

Shortly after the crop was planted, I received a call from Jimmy Flynn, a very popular Canadian entertainer and comedian. He had visited my home a few weeks previously and told me that he had lost his son to cancer 12 years ago. What I explained to him that day made him realize this medicine could have possibly saved his son and might prevent others from going through what his family had to endure. Afterwards Jimmy had become an instant supporter and was now calling to tell me I was being mentioned on a popular maritime radio show that was then in progress. Jimmy and his manager gave me the number so I called in to the show to clarify what I was doing to the public. After finding out who I was, they asked if I would be willing to do a 20-minute segment to which I readily agreed.

At one point, the show's host, Tom Young, asked me if I was growing any hemp this year. I told him, "I am growing it right my back yard, as usual." He replied, "But you're not allowed." I then explained to him, I was now a Freeman on the Land and under Common Law, growing hemp was not a crime. If memory does not fail me, I believe I also told him I now had three of the original land grants that surrounded my property in my name, which totaled 1500 acres. The Tom Young show is very popular in the Maritime Provinces and as far as I know, the show was aired several times. Right after I was done with my part of the broadcast, Jimmy Flynn came on in support of what I was doing. In addition, a person who had treated their terminal cancer with the oil came on the air and spoke about their experiences, so this show had a very positive effect.

I must admit at the time I really didn't know what would happen. During this broadcast, I had just told every cop in the Maritimes that I had hemp growing in my back yard again. I figured, if the RCMP were going to come once more, it might as well be now. At least then, I would not have to guard the crop like a watchdog all summer only to have them come and steal it again. The summer went by and nothing happened. Everyone knew the hemp was there, including the police, but no one came near. In addition, during this time period I had a couple of patients who were looking for oil tell me that friends of theirs who were employed by the RCMP had told them to come to me for treatment. At that point, by all appearances, it seemed I was finally going to be left alone.

In regards to the original land grants I now have under my control, I would need permission from local Indian leaders to make what I have in mind a reality. If those who speak for the Indian Nations will comply and have no objection to these grants being in my name, we may be able to have a decent sized hemp plantation right in Cumberland County, Nova Scotia. If what I have been told is true, this land would have the status of a country within a country and the Canadian government would have no say in what takes place there. On this 1500 acre grant, I would provide the law, not the RCMP, and the land in question would be under my jurisdiction. As I remember, I think information about these land grants was sent into the authorities when I declared myself to be a Freeman On The Land.

I had sent all this paperwork in to various government agencies, including the Prime Minister's office and our local RCMP detachment, but I had received no reply from any of them disputing that I have the right to do this. Once I can purchase the property from those who currently own it, this land would be completely under my control. I know the individuals who now own the property and since they too back the use of this medicine, I am sure they would be happy to comply.

Unfortunately, I never had the time to arrange this with the tribal leaders before I was forced to remain in exile following the last RCMP raid in the fall of 2009. In the coming months, I will try to contact native leaders to see if we can get the details worked out, if so, then we may all witness something good happening for a change. After what the Canadian government had put me through in the past, having my own little country within the boundaries of Canada seemed to be the only logical thing to do. If this can be accomplished, it would then provide me with a place where I can conduct my research without interference from anyone. In addition, this is the only way I would feel comfortable in returning home to stay and who in my position would feel otherwise?

CHAPTER 14

INVITED TO EUROPE

By the beginning of summer 2009, I ran out of material to work with. I had bought up all the high quality bud in our area and even local pot smokers were upset with me because they couldn't find anything good to smoke. Now I was compiling a list with names of those who wanted the medicine as soon as it became available. It's very hard to tell someone who is dying from terminal cancer that their treatment cannot be provided until harvest time. But, too often, this was the case and many people were becoming more angry over the government's behavior towards this issue. I was more disgusted than most over what was taking place, but even though I did not have the medicine to provide treatment at the time, there were still a few rewarding moments.

One day, I was about 140 miles from home visiting patients and stopped to fuel up my truck. When I entered the convenience store to pay for the fuel, a man was present that looked familiar. He walked over to me and said, "Are you Rick Simpson?" I replied, "Yes," but I still couldn't figure out who he was. Just then, his wife appeared and looked our way. She lit up like a 1000-W bulb and came straight in our direction, throwing her arms around me in a bear hug. When I saw her, I remembered her face and knew she had been to my home, so I asked her how she was feeling. In reply, she stated, "Rick, when I came to you a year ago, they had given me two months to live, how do I look?" I replied, "For someone who is no longer supposed to be with us, you look rather well." I have dealt with so many people it's impossible to remember all their names, but she had been suffering from terminal cancer and was now cancer-free. I have to say moments like this were pure magic and helped to give me the incentive to push on with what I was doing.

Because of the supposedly illegal nature of this medicine, quite often after the patient had received the oil from me, I would hear nothing further from them. People often seemed to be afraid to contact me for treatment or to report their experiences while taking the oil. This no doubt had a lot to do with the laws that are currently in place, which restrict this medicine's use. No one wanted trouble with the system and many suspected my phone may have been tapped by the RCMP and quite possibly it was. From my position, I really didn't give such things a second thought. If the RCMP wanted to listen in, let them go ahead. All they would hear would be the conversations I had with desperate suffering people looking for my assistance. Still, I did not want to see any trouble brought to the doorsteps of patients who were using the medicine, so I didn't insist that they remain in contact.

It seemed only about one in ten of those who used the oil would speak out freely about what this medication had done for them. A great number of people kept their communications with me as minimal as possible and, under the circumstances, if I were in their position, I would probably have done the same. Quite frequently, I received calls from patients who were looking for treatment and they would mention the name of someone they knew who had used the oil. Often, this was the way I finally found out the oil had worked for them. This medication was making its own reputation, because it was so effective for all conditions and word was spreading fast.

By this time, I really didn't need much feedback from patients anyway, because I already knew how effective the oil was in the treatment of practically everything. I received very few complaints about the oil and, if a problem did arise, it was usually caused by pharmaceuticals, the patient was needlessly trying to ingest. The oil seems to have the ability to replace the vast majority of pharmaceuticals and may end our dependency on them entirely. When one starts ingesting oil, the idea is to get off these harmful chemicals as quickly as possible. As time goes on, the oil detoxifies the patient and replaces the drugs they were taking and these harmful substances will then disappear from their bodies.

Using the oil as a medication is very beneficial, since it is effective and harmless, but the healing power of this substance almost defies description. At first, I thought the oil would just replace the pharmaceuticals to control the conditions of many who came to me. In no time, it was plain to see the oil was not only controlling the problem, but in a great number of cases was providing a cure. Many who had come to me with so-called incurable conditions were now healthy once again. High blood pressure, diabetes, arthritis, Crohn's, AIDS, cancer, multiple sclerosis, chronic pain, etc. All these serious conditions and many others became much easier to deal with when the oil came into play.

This substance seemed to have the ability to work miracles on all medical conditions. But still, there was a large segment of the population that continued to believe the propaganda the system had told them about hemp. Many were still trying to reject the truth, or showed no interest in supporting this medication's free use. Patients who had used the oil were scattered all over Canada. This made it virtually impossible to get enough of them together to draw attention to this subject. The oil was proving itself to more and more people every day, so even then I knew the system was losing their battle against this amazing plant.

During the summer of 2009, I was again contacted by Jindrich Bayer. This time he asked if I was interested in doing a speaking tour in Europe. I thought about his offer and contacted Jack. I was so busy I thought my time might be better spent right where I was. As soon as Jack heard about the tour, he urged me on by saying, "Rick, do it. You can reach so many more people that way." At first, I had been somewhat reluctant to do the tour, but talking to Jack had changed my mind. During our conversation that day, I asked Jack if he would be willing to come along and he agreed. I e-mailed Jindrich and informed him that, if he liked, Jack Herer was also willing to become involved. This offer really got his attention. He contacted me right back, saying he thought it would be wonderful if Jack was willing to do the tour, too. He then told me Lumir Hanus, a hemp researcher who was world-renowned was also interested in taking part. With Jack Herer and Lumir Hanus present, the success of the tour would virtually be guaranteed. Lumir Hanus and Jack were both very well known in the Czech Republic and the rest of Europe. This really looked like the beginning of something big.

Around this time, a young man contacted me who had produced the oil to treat his grandfather's cancer. The oil had worked wonderfully and his grandfather was now cancer-free, but he told me he could not believe the attitude of their family doctor. He had taken my advice and not told the doctor what he was using to treat his grandfather. Then one day he was called to the doctor's office and was told his grandfather was now cancer-free. The doctor then stated he knew what had been used to accomplish this and told the patient's grandson he could get himself in a great deal of trouble.

He stated, "Rick, I couldn't believe what I was hearing. My grandfather was cured and this doctor was upset with me because I had used the oil to save his life. I have seen for myself that many doctors are little more than monsters, so I am now in the process of looking for one who isn't." I wish I could say people contacting me with information about their doctor's contempt for the use of this medication were rare. Yet, sadly, this is not the case. There really are a great number of people in white coats and other professions who are trying to keep this medication from being used freely. From my perspective, I can only imagine that their behavior towards the use of this natural medicine is based upon their desire to protect their incomes and positions. If indeed I am correct, such people have committed horrendous crimes against us all and their inhumanity towards their fellow-man seems to have no limits.

Obviously, this issue was being well covered by hemp publications in Europe, but to date, it had received no coverage in North America. Around the end of August 2009, Steve Hager from *High Times* Magazine decided to come to Nova Scotia and do a story about my activities. We made arrangements so I could pick him up at the airport in Halifax, but at the appointed time, there was no Steve. Finally, I found out he had been held up in Customs, but after four hours, he was finally released. Steve was now in a great hurry to get the story completed, since he had been ordered by Customs Officials at the Halifax airport to be on the next flight back to the U.S. at 6 AM the next morning.

He had planned to stay three or four days, but now thanks to Canadian Customs we could only spend about eight hours together. I took Steve to my home and there he interviewed several people who had experienced the wonders of this medicine. Since we were so rushed, I thought, "How will this man ever be able to write a comprehensive article about this subject?" Later that same night, Steve and I had a long conversation about the oil and its use, while I was driving him back to the hotel at the airport. Within days, Steve phoned me and read the article he had put together. Considering the circumstances, under which he had to work, he still somehow managed to write a decent article that didn't have too many mistakes. He then made arrangements with a photographer in Halifax, who came to my home and took the photographs *High Times* required.

The photographer was a very nice lady and I had to laugh at her reaction when she realized what was standing in my back yard. She asked, "Is that what I think it is?" I replied, "Yes that would be hemp." "But that's illegal," she stated. I explained, "Dear, when your life is at stake and medicine from this plant can save you, who cares about illegal?" I told her what the essential oil from this plant could do and she listened to what I had to say with great interest. She took many pictures and talked to some people that came to my home, who had successfully used the oil to treat their conditions. By the time she left that day, she had acquired a great deal of information. Once she understood what was really going on, she then seemed to be very supportive towards our cause.

By September, I had a long list of patients waiting for treatments. Luckily for them, a local grower had brought in a fairly large early crop. On September 1st, I started producing medicine at a furious rate and, in no time, his whole crop had been turned into oil. The grower was paid for his efforts, the patients received their treatments, and everyone was happy. It took all of September but, by the end of the month, I had caught up with the backlog of patients who had been waiting. A few who were awaiting treatment had died during the summer, but at least by the end of September I was able to supply oil to all the rest that had been in need and waiting for so long.

The crop that was planted behind my home at the end of June was doing all right. Still, the plants had lost a month of growth, since they really should have been planted much earlier. In late September, on average, the plants were six to eight feet tall, but were very slow to form bud. That September, the police and military were again flying around in their helicopters, looking for hemp and of course all this was being paid for at the public's expense. My son and I saw them from the house three or four times, flying back and forth, searching nearby. It seemed from our observations that they were staying away from the 1,500-acre land grant I now had in my name. There is no question they knew the crop was there, since it was right out in open sight only a few feet from my house but yet, they did not come near.

In previous years, they always sent helicopters to check my back yard and quite often, they did it more than once. On top of all that, Tom Young's radio show had informed everyone including the police that the crop had been planted. If the police were looking for hemp, one of the first places they would have checked was my property. I had not been able to take the time to really look into it, but by all appearances, this Freeman on the Land business carried some weight, for why else would the police be staying away? Finally, after all I had been through, I was starting to think the old Common Law system might just be the answer to my problems. If one can get the paperwork in and declare themselves a Freeman on the Land, they are now again supposed to be under Common Law jurisdiction. Possibly, under the rules of Common Law, someone like me could find a little freedom in Canada after all. Our present system does everything possible to hide our rights and it does take some effort to find the truth, but it looked as if the Common Law form of justice might solve my dilemma.

Just before the end of September, I received word that Jack Herer had been stricken with a heart attack. Over the previous weeks, Jack had been speaking at hemp rallies across the US and traveled thousands of miles by van to attend these events. A man of Jack's age and delicate health should not have been doing such things. But that was the way Jack had always fought for the cause; he felt compelled to be there to provide his message to the people no matter what the circumstances. At first, I didn't know how bad things really were. All the reports I received said he was in the hospital and they had put him in an induced coma. A couple of days later, I learned that a brain scan showed Jack did not have any brain activity. Of course, I was screaming, "Get him on the oil!" and somehow those who were around him at the time succeeded. A few days went by and then I received another call, telling me Jack had been scanned again, but still his brain showed no signs of activity. The caller asked me if I felt the oil might affect the results of such a scan. I told them that the oil is deeply relaxing and since they were giving him very large doses, this could be a possibility.

A few days later, I heard the doctors were trying to bring Jack out of the coma, which they had induced, but were not having any success. So I instructed those who were giving Jack the oil to back his dosage down. After they had done this, Jack came out of the coma and, to everyone's surprise, seemed to be doing quite well. I had been informed that after his heart attack, Jack had gone with no oxygen flow to his brain for about a half an hour. When the brain is deprived of oxygen for this length of time, massive damage occurs and even if the person survives, there is little hope that they will be able to function properly again. But apparently, Jack was trying to speak and followed the movement of people around the room with his eyes, which gave me hope that my friend might be able to make a comeback after his ordeal. He had gone through two brain scans that showed no activity, but now he was awake and improving. To me, it looked like another hemp oil miracle was in progress. The Emperor was still with us and I could not have been more pleased with the effect the oil was having thus far.

When I had received word about Jack's heart attack, I almost cancelled the Czech tour. After everything that had happened, I didn't know what was to be done. It may sound strange to some, but I swear I could hear Jack's voice urging me on. When the Emperor speaks, you must obey, so I contacted Jindrich about all that had transpired and we decided to carry on, even if Jack could not attend.

A few days after Jack's collapse, I received a call from a woman in California who was talking about making a movie. She seemed to think I knew all about it, but I had to inform her I didn't know what she was talking about. She then introduced herself as Melissa Balin and seemed surprised that I knew nothing about her. She exclaimed, "Jack never told you anything about me?" I replied, "I'm sorry, dear, but he never." She then explained about the movie they were trying to make out of Jack's book and she wanted me to take part. She stated, "You'll be going to the Cannabis Cup in November to put on a seminar and I'll be coming along to get it all on film."

I had no knowledge about any of this, since Jack had never said a word. Maybe he was planning to surprise me. If so, he succeeded. She then asked me about the Czech tour and I told her it was still going to happen. "It would be wonderful if I could come and film that, too," she offered. I explained that the tour I was doing really had nothing to do with the Cannabis Cup, but she said it would be great to have the footage. I considered her offer and replied, "All right, if you will give me copies of the footage you shoot, so we can put some of it up on the Internet, I will talk to Jindrich and see if they can cover your expenses." She replied, "That would be just awesome."

We were still often contacted by people asking us where they could find the scientific proof. If I could put footage of me with one of the greatest researchers in this field up on the Internet, it would go a long way towards answering such questions. It would also allow people to have a great deal more confidence in the effectiveness of this medicine. To me, it sounded like a win-win situation; we could both get the footage we desired and everyone would be happy. So I contacted Jindrich and arrangements were made for Melissa and Jack's assistant Chuck Jacobs to come along on the tour.

A short time later, I received a call from Steve Hager. Steve, too, was also devastated about what had happened to Jack. He stated, "This may sound a bit eerie, but a few days ago, I talked to Jack. Rick, it's almost as if he knew something was going to happen to him. He told me if anything came up, the torch was to be passed on to you. We would like you to stand in for Jack and come to the Cannabis Cup in November, where we are going to crown you Freedom Fighter of the Year."

Melissa had just told me I was to attend the Cup, but until I talked to Steve, I really did not believe what she had said. I was very honored by the award they were offering to bestow on me, but in my heart I knew no one including myself could replace Jack Herer at the helm. I told Steve I would do the best I could to help out, but I was not a suitable replacement for Jack. No one was. Both Steve and I knew not just anyone could simply step into Jack Herer's shoes but, in this situation, I had little choice.

Over the last while, Jack and I had become very close but, for the most part, other big names in the hemp movement had no idea who I was or what I was doing. At that point, even I didn't really feel that I had much to do with the hemp movement. I was just the guy who produced the medicine. I thought if I went to the Cannabis Cup and tried to tell those present I was filling in for Jack Herer, many would probably be offended by my presence.

For years, Jack had been recognized as the undisputed leader of the movement. At the time, I didn't understand the deep respect Jack Herer commanded. When he made his wishes known, people listened. I guess you could say they didn't call Jack the Emperor for no good reason. In many circles, his exploits had given him a legendary status that was well deserved. For someone like me, who was virtually unknown at the time, to come out of nowhere and announce to the hierarchy of the hemp movement that I was taking Jack's place seemed somewhat absurd. Not only would I now have to explain this plant's medicinal use, I also had to try to make it clear to the hemp movement that I was someone worthy of speaking on Jack's behalf.

At the time, as far as I knew, Jack's condition was improving. With any luck, I felt the Emperor would soon be out of his sick bed and back on his throne where he belonged. I knew Jack would want me to go to bat for him in his absence, so all I could do was try to follow his wishes until he returned. So much was happening so quickly that I felt overwhelmed. I had a hard time getting my head around the fact that what was taking place was even real. For years, I had been running around everywhere speaking to individuals and audiences at my own expense, but all my efforts seemed to have little impact. Now individuals from the Czech Republic were willing to fly me to Europe and cover all the expenses if I would come and do a series of lectures. But Canada, my own country, had already spent vast amounts of money in an effort to keep what I was doing quiet.

The fact I had never been to Europe in my life was also very unsettling. Around our local area, I had done all right, but in no way did I consider myself to be a public speaker. With so much riding on me, I was really wondering if I would be equal to the task at hand. It was hard enough for me to get my message across here in Canada. In Europe, the language barrier would necessitate the use of translators. I had never worked with an interpreter before and I expected that it would be much harder for me to explain myself. This and the fact that I couldn't speak the languages in these countries made me quite edgy about the upcoming tour.

One serious problem I was facing in going to Europe was the fact that I could not take my medication along. Where was I to get the medicine I required after my arrival? I could try to take some with me, but if it was discovered at one of the airports, I would be in a world of trouble. Luckily, this problem had already been taken into consideration by Jindrich, who informed me the medicine would be supplied when I arrived. They were as good as their word and shortly after I flew into Prague, I was given some high-quality oil to fulfill my medicinal needs.

Jack was right, as usual, when he had told me Europe was very important. He seemed to love Europe and its people. He had stated, "Rick, you really don't understand, things are very different over there." If Jack had not collapsed just before the tour, I'm sure his presence would have done much to ease my mind. Even though it would not be possible for Jack to be present, still, it all sounded great. Lumir Hanus was going to be there and apparently, they had lined up many venues at which we were to speak.

All my supporters in the local area were excited about the tour, but they didn't really seem to be happy about my departure. No matter if they liked it or not, I knew if I was to spread the word, it must be done. In early October 2009, I was worked up about the upcoming tour, but I was also thinking about the backlog of patients I would be facing upon my return. People were literally coming in droves now, quite often as many as four to five at a time. I knew from past experience and the increase in the number of patients trying to acquire the oil that I would exhaust the local supply of hemp in no time. Still, with the tour coming up and then the Cannabis Cup in November, I figured by the time I returned to Canada from Amsterdam, some doors that had been previously slammed in my face should soon begin to open.

To me, it seemed the end was in sight and soon, I expected this medication would be available legally. The police did not come near me, I was a Freeman on the Land and I had the original land grants for the property around my home under my control. In addition, a very large bond had been put in place in my name that was supposed to afford me some protection. The whole world was now rapidly finding out that what I had been saying about this plant's healing power was true. So what could go wrong?

At that time, I had only been doing seminars for about four years. During this period, most of the audiences I spoke to were small, but I knew the Czech tour and the Cannabis Cup would be a whole different ball game. I was a bit nervous about what was coming; even when I did seminars in Canada, it could not be said I was at ease in the beginning. Once, when we were driving to Digby to put on a seminar, I asked Rick Dwyer who was accompanying me, "Do you think the people in Digby will even be aware of what I'm doing?" After driving hundreds of miles from my home to do a lecture about this subject, I expected those attending would have little or no knowledge about any of this. A great number of people had already been to my home from all over Canada. But Digby is a long drive from where I live and I didn't think there was much chance that past patients would be in attendance. When the hall had filled up that day, I was relieved to see five or six faces in the audience that I recognized.

Shortly after the meeting started, an older man, whose face I remembered, put up his hand. He then stated, "I bet you don't remember me." I replied, "I think you were at my home a few months ago and I believe you had prostate cancer." He seemed surprised and stated, "That's right." I then inquired, "How did you make out with your cancer?" At moments like this, you really don't know what's going to happen. Possibly, he had done as I instructed and used the medicine properly. Yet, he could also be someone who had ignored the instructions and was there to cast doubt on what I was trying to tell those in attendance. It was a somewhat tense moment, but he then stated he had taken the oil as directed and his cancer was gone in six weeks. After a statement like that from someone in the audience, believe me, we had a very lively seminar.

Now I was going to Europe to do lectures about this subject, but there was no one in Europe who had used the oil I produced. I never sent this oil to foreign countries, because of all the restrictions that were in place, and if I had, I probably would have ended up in jail. Since there was no living proof at my disposal in Europe, I didn't know how the audiences would accept my statements. I figured they would either listen to what I had to say, or I could find a lot of tomatoes coming in my direction. The only thing for me to do now was to take whatever was coming head-on and try to get my point across to those in Europe who had open minds.

The tickets and passport were taken care of and everything needed for my departure now seemed to be in place. The crop standing in my backyard was still not ready to harvest and there was very little bud present on the plants. In past years, I had witnessed buds grow from tiny little nugs to beautiful big buds in two to three weeks. I thought that possibly if we had a little good weather while I was in Europe, the buds might have time to fatten up. Then, when I returned in three weeks, they could be harvested. So, arrangements were made for the plants to be watched while I was gone. Everything was under control and if the tour went smoothly, I could not imagine too many difficulties in the future. I had watched the Canadian government and everything they control stand in the way of this issue for years. They had branded me a criminal and continued to let innocent trusting people suffer and die. I had no use for government Canadian-style and their systems of medicine and justice. Now very soon the whole world would know my sentiments.

CHAPTER 15
THE CZECH TOUR

On October 7, 2009, my son dropped me off at Stanfield International Airport, just a few miles outside the city of Halifax. After much anticipation, I was finally on my way to the Czech Republic. I had flown a few times in the past on aircraft of different sizes and possessed a fair knowledge of aeronautics. Still, I had always looked at these big jets with a certain amount of distrust because I always wondered how well they were maintained. There is a lot of competition in this industry and, under these circumstances, I am sure there are companies that might be willing to cut some corners. I also, have little use for all the scans and inconvenience we are put through at airports, even though they try to tell us it's for our own safety. Those who are employed in such places seem to look at us all as if we are nothing more than smugglers or wanted felons. Every time we turn around, they are putting us through metal detectors and at some airports you are even being scanned with radiation.

I guess you could say I am not a fan of George Bush and his bogus war on terror. Perhaps, if the United Nations and some of their member countries were not pursuing policies of oppression against other nations, our travel could be much less dangerous and there would be no need to subject us all to scans that can cause harm. Going through an airport today makes one wonder, "Whatever happened to "Fly the Friendly Skies?" and why has the world we live in become such a dangerous place? The only positive thing I can report about my flight to Europe is the fact that it caused me to come up with a new way in which I could take my medicine. Obviously, I could not bring any with me, so before entering the airport where it would be awkward to do such a thing. I took out my upper teeth and applied a good amount of oil to them, using it in the same way as one would apply a liner to their dentures. I had applied three quarters of a gram or more and its long lasting effects made what was to come much easier to deal with.

When we were flying over the Atlantic that night, there was a lot of turbulence and the flight had been very rough. You could see that many passengers were distressed and afraid, but the effects from the oil kept me relaxed and calm. I also have no fear of flying, so this too may have helped but still I have to give the medication I had taken most of the credit. It was still about an hour before dawn, so to help break the boredom, I looked out the small window to see if anything was visible. Miles below, streetlights formed a golden spider's web that stretched out before me as far as I could see. To me, it was truly an amazing sight, for I had never seen anything like this in the past. At that point, I think we were over the British Isles. A short time later, we landed in Frankfurt, Germany, and there I boarded the flight that would take me to Prague.

Upon landing and exiting the airport, in Prague. I was met by Jindrich Bayer and Milan Romsy, the owners of Bayer & Romsy (www.konopnamast.cz). Jindrich had been a translator, so he could speak English fluently and we all got along very well. Bayer & Romsy are a hemp cosmetics company, which led me to ask Jindrich how they had become interested in the healing aspects of this plant. He explained that they produced their cosmetics with the use of an extract taken from the buds of industrial hemp and had witnessed surprising healing properties in the cosmetics they were distributing.

Before they had ever heard of me, they already knew even industrial hemp had some healing abilities. When they found out what I was doing on the Internet, it all made perfect sense to them. I was working with some of the most medicinally active hemp strains in the world to produce the medicine. Simple common sense told them what I was saying about the medicinal properties of potent strains of hemp was probably true. It was more than apparent that Jindrich and Milan were just as excited as I was about the healing capabilities and benefits this plant could bring to mankind.

On the way into Prague, one of the first cars we came up behind was a Ferrari. Since expensive foreign cars like this are very rare in Canada, I had only seen pictures of such vehicles and now here we were driving along behind the real thing. I was really starting to wonder what other surprises the Czech Republic would hold in store for me. Then we drove into the city of Prague and it took my breath away. To anyone given the task of trying to describe Prague, it is almost impossible to do this city justice. To me, it was like driving into a fairy tale. Towers, turrets, steeples, castles, bridges, and palaces, Prague had it all and much more.

This city literally reeked of history. Its beauty and historic sites are something I will never forget. I thought, possibly, I had just arrived in Camelot. The architecture in Prague is its most amazing asset; this city is timeless. Sometimes, I felt like it could have been the year 1500 instead of 2009. Everywhere I went, people seemed to be happy and I found the vast majority of those I encountered to be very friendly. This country was presenting an entirely different picture than what I had envisioned in my mind.

The first night I spent in the Czech Republic, we stayed in what had been a manse next to a beautiful old church in the village of Zehun. The owner of the manse, a young artist named Jan Pospisil, and his girlfriend, Vlasta Samohrdova, welcomed us and provided a place to sleep. The next morning after breakfast, I took a walk around this ancient village to see the sights. While I was strolling around, suddenly this feeling of familiarity came over me and it felt as if I had been there before. Had I seen a picture of this village in the past or something of that nature? The sensation was just too strong to be ignored. It was a pleasant feeling, but still it made me a little uneasy since I did not know the cause.

When I got back to the manse, Jan showed me some of his work and I was very taken with his talents. Not only did he do artwork using many different materials and subjects, he also built giant creatures for movie sets. Vlasta is a very creative artist in her own right regarding photography and design and she gave him two beautiful children. When we left, Jan told me I was welcome to come back and stay any time. It was a real pleasure meeting Jan and Vlasta and if all goes well, I think their talents and skills will carry them very far in life.

A short time later, we were back in Prague and again, I was awestruck at the sheer beauty of this city. I was then introduced to one of the world's top hemp researchers, Lumir Hanus. Over the years, I had become quite adept at getting a handle on the nature of the person I was dealing with simply by looking into their eyes. They say the eyes are the window to the soul and from my experience, in most cases, this old saying holds true. In the eyes of Lumir Hanus, all I could see were good intentions and we became instant friends.

While eating at a restaurant that afternoon, I was to meet Melissa Balin and Chuck Jacobs face to face for the first time. Chuck was very easy to get along with, but Melissa was a whole different story. Apparently, she had come here to get everything possible on film, but I can't say I was comfortable with the way she was behaving. Later that day, I was scheduled to give a short talk, but suddenly it was decided that I should do a full seminar. As I had understood things, I wasn't scheduled to speak until Monday, two days in the future, which would give me a couple of days to get ready. While still in Canada, I had put together a seminar, which was very political in nature. I planned to tone it down a bit over the weekend, but now there was no time to make changes.

Lumir spoke first and did a great seminar. This man is a consummate professional. Then it was my turn to speak and I really must say, I felt sorry for the poor woman who was trying to translate my words. The lecture I gave was very strong politically and I did mix up a couple of pages, but somehow we made it through. Lumir sat passively during the whole seminar and I couldn't tell if he was in agreement with what I was saying. I could only hope the hard line I took with politics did not offend him. Before I had spoken that day, I thought it might be best to just speak and not follow what I had prepared. Still, there were many important points to be made, so I followed the script I had written. All I could do was say my piece, then wait and see how the audience reacted. After I was done speaking, no one seemed to be upset by what I had said and I think they understood why I felt this way about the Canadian government's behavior towards this issue.

Lumir proved to be a real pleasure to work with and we got along very easily. His presence gave what was being said at the seminars much more weight. Chuck was doing a good job speaking on Jack's behalf and Melissa was filming it all. When I talked to

Jindrich about the tour, he seemed a little distant. I asked him if there had been trouble with the funding. He explained that there had been and almost all the sponsors and media had backed out when Jack had fallen ill. It seemed we did not have anywhere near the budget we had been expecting to complete the tour. It literally meant that Jindrich himself was paying for most of the tour out of his own pocket. I told him not to worry, my needs were very minimal, just a full belly and a warm place to sleep was all that I required. It cannot be said I was not worried about whether or not there would be enough funding to complete the tour but, given the circumstances, all we could do was try.

Right from the beginning, Melissa and I bumped heads. She was acting as if she was running the show and seemed to feel she had the right to order everyone around. The minute you start trying to tell someone like me that they have to do anything without good reason, you can expect an argument, and she got one. I told her to wise up or she would be back on the next flight to the United States, at which point she turned on the tears and said, "If Jack Herer was here, you wouldn't be talking to me like this." I then replied, "You're right, if Jack were here, I wouldn't be talking to you like this, he would."

I was very serious about sending this woman home and if she had pushed any more of my buttons, that is exactly what would have happened. She must have realized the situation she was in, for she cooled down a bit and began to behave more properly towards everyone. I think, in the beginning, we were all under a lot of stress and not having the funding everyone thought would be available did nothing to help the situation. I have to give Jindrich and Milan a lot of credit, they held it together, and somehow we went on with the tour.

A few days later, Lumir and I spoke at two events in the city of Olomouc. In the morning, we gave a lecture in the hall of Palacky University in Olomouc and later that day, we gave another in a theater known as Divadlo hudby (Musical Theater). Of course, by this time I had toned the political side of my seminar way down and focused more on what this medicine could do to help the human race. After I finished speaking at the university, a young medical student came up to me and stated, "You're saying doctors are committing murder?" I answered her by asking what she would call me if I were to give someone poison and they died from its effects. I then stated, "Does it really make a difference if the person supplying the poison is wearing a white coat?" This statement really got her worked up and it was plain to see she was very upset with what I had just said. She then stated, "The medical faculty of this university want you to come back on October 26th and they are going to set you straight." I replied, "Listen, dear, get every doctor in the Czech Republic here on the 26th and we'll see who gets set straight."

Jindrich had overheard our conversation and seemed to be very excited about the upcoming confrontation. He stated if the medical school takes you on, the news media will get involved." I just laughed and replied, "No one is going to take me on, I am the only one telling the truth. What could they possibly take me on with?" Not surprisingly, the university called three days later and cancelled, saying the students were not interested. I don't know how others will feel about this, but I have a very hard time believing young medical students would not want to know about the greatest natural medicine on earth and what it could do to help their future patients. If these medical students did indeed have no interest, then I can only say I feel sorry for those they will be treating, when they become doctors. In my opinion, what went on here was just the same old hide-the-truth routine I had dealt with so often in Canada.

Lumir and I spoke at many different functions together. What he and I were saying about this subject went hand-in-hand and I was so pleased to have this great hemp researcher at my side. Chuck provided a somewhat less serious side to these functions and often had the audience laughing. It was a nice mix and we were well received at the events where we spoke.

Now that the official part of the tour had ended, it was time to go freewheeling. Jindrich had lined up several clubs and venues where Chuck and I were to speak. From then on, there would be no further scripts to follow. Many people in the past had told me I got through to an audience more effectively without a script. Most times, it seemed all I had to do was cut loose over the sound system and I could get my point across to those who were present. We would simply go to these events and play "Run from the Cure" with the Czech subtitles Jindrich had provided. Then I explained to those present what this natural medicine could do and why its use had been forbidden. We would then do what was usually a lively question-and-answer period and after Chuck was done speaking, we would bring it to a close.

After the seminars were over, the music would be cranked up and then we could relax and take in the atmosphere. To say these Czech clubs rocked is an understatement. Even my old bones couldn't sit still when the music started. I think it surprised many to see someone my age could move so freely. It was more than apparent to anybody watching me that there was no arthritis in my joints. I always loved to dance anyway and I felt it was important for people to see what this oil had done for me and my overall health. I guess you could say I considered myself to be an example to the public of what this medicine's use could do for them. After the seminars were over, I would talk to dozens of people about the amazing qualities of this medication and I thoroughly enjoyed the whole experience.

Many years ago, I had lost my taste for alcohol and it was unusual for me to even drink a beer. After sampling the world-famous Pilsner Urquell produced in the Czech Republic, I must say my distaste for this substance changed somewhat and when I was out, I often tipped a couple of Pilsners during the evening. I spoke at many drinking establishments during this time period, but my favorite watering hole was a little club in Olomouc called the Metro. Although the Metro is quite small, when compared with many other clubs, I really enjoyed the time I spent there.

One day, we did a seminar at a nice hall in Kojetín and we stayed at the home of a local couple for the night. They were very nice people and their home was just lovely, with well-preserved antiques everywhere. The next morning, I was in their back yard, looking at the well-maintained herb garden they had on their property. It seemed they were growing just about everything one can imagine. Then, a small greenhouse at the back of their garden caught my attention. It was filled with different species of cactus and to me this came as somewhat of a surprise. The last thing I expected to find in the Czech Republic was cacti, but here was a small greenhouse overflowing with them.

Later, I took a walk around the neighborhood and Mrs. Kalovska, the lady we were staying with, told me that before the Second World War this area had been home to many Jewish families. I knew what had been done to the Jews and others during the war and here I was strolling through the same streets where many of these atrocities had taken place. Seventy years earlier, German soldiers had been rounding up Jewish families here to fulfill Hitler's mad dream of the final solution. It gave me an eerie feeling, just knowing this had occurred on the very streets I was now walking. Unfortunately, man's inhumanity towards his fellow-man did not end with the final solution.

As much as I hate to say it, from my perspective, apparently hospitals had now replaced Hitler's death camps. To me, the final solution was still in progress today, yet in a much more sinister and hidden fashion, which is backed up by most governments worldwide. I almost have to laugh at the way other countries have criticized Germany for what took place during the war, when they themselves have killed hundreds of millions in their hospitals with the use of chemicals and poisons that drug companies supply, while denying their citizens the use of natural medicines, which could have healed them. I suppose the word medicine does sound much better than the term genocide, but when the end result is the same, what is the difference?

During my stay, I also spoke at the Green Pump in Chraštice, which is located in South Bohemia. On display they had many products produced from hemp such as: hempcrete, insulation, paints, varnishes, pasta, chocolate bars, and even hemp beer. It seemed there was very little that could not be produced from hemp and I learned a great deal that night. The following day, one of only three hemp harvesting machines in Europe was brought to a nearby industrial hemp field to let us observe how it worked. It was certainly an awesome monster, but I realized such a harvester would be of little value for what I had in mind. This machine seemed to work well for their purposes, but it would leave a lot of the bud and resin that I required to produce the medicine behind in the field. That morning, I also saw one of the big presses they use to produce cold-pressed hemp seed oil. The oil came out one spout, while large noodles of pressed hemp seed shells came out another. You could take one of these noodles and dip it in the hemp seed oil, which gave it a delicious nutty flavor when eaten. It seemed this plant was just full of surprises and it was truly a delight to see how some of these hemp products were produced.

We spent a great number of hours traveling by car throughout the Czech Republic and this gave me the opportunity to observe this beautiful country for myself. Everywhere, it seemed, there were well-kept farms and breathtaking mountain views, which caused that feeling of familiarity within me to continue to grow. During the tour, I learned that hemp's use in the Czech Republic seems to date back at least 26,000 years. Apparently, some ancient pottery had been discovered and when its date of manufacture had been determined, they also took note that hemp had probably been used to produce the designs upon it, when the pottery was originally produced. Maybe this was part of the reason that the vast majority of Czechs I met did not seem to be affected by all the negative propaganda about hemp. Coming from Canada, to me the Czech Republic and its people were a breath of fresh air.

One night after a function I had attended, I even smoked a joint with a Czech police officer who was in uniform and, at first, this felt very strange. But he was a nice man, who was easy to get along with and soon, I became relaxed in his presence. I asked this officer, what the Czech police thought about citizens smoking pot and if he felt the laws currently in place were just. He smiled and explained that many police officers here smoke hemp themselves and a good number of them feel that they should not be bothering the public for doing the same. After dealing with the police in Canada, I found this man to be a refreshing change and wondered why more police officers back home did not behave in a similar way. It appeared the police here had a much more relaxed attitude towards this issue and instead were interested in dealing with serious crimes, rather than chasing pot smokers around. One can only hope that maybe the police in Canada will soon be doing the same, but only time will tell.

I had come here thinking I would be visiting a quasi-police state like Canada. Instead, I found myself in a land where it seemed you could sense freedom all around you. I expect this attitude has much to do with the repression suffered by the Czech people, first from the Nazis and then the Communists. They had suffered greatly under these regimes, but finally, in 1989, the communist grip was broken. This transition was called the Velvet Revolution and it was led by Vaclav Havel, who became President of this nation a short time later. It says a lot about a country and its leadership when they can have a revolution and no one has to die. Sounds kind of civilized, does it not? Then, in 1993, the Velvet Divorce occurred. The Czech Republic and Slovakia went their different ways and became separate nations. Although the history of the Czech people dates back through the mists of time, they now had a brand-new republic. After all the citizens of this country had been through in the past, it now seems they have a burning desire to build something better and I firmly believe they will succeed.

When we visit a foreign land, the majority of us do not really expect to fit in well. In most cases, we are just there to see something different that we can talk about when we return home. This was hardly the case with me. Everywhere I went, I was met with warmth and friendliness. I could sit in a room full of people who were speaking a language of which I had no understanding and still I felt perfectly at ease with my surroundings. Everything about this country gave me the feeling I had just returned home after a long absence. I guess you could say I was developing a strong affection for the Czech Republic and its people, which I feel is well deserved.

The tour had been a whirlwind of activity. I met so many individuals with good hearts I could not help but be impressed. A world famous Czech photographer named Jindrich Streit informed me that he had started to do a photo journal of patients who were using the oil and I believe that this could do much to raise awareness. I was also introduced to activists like Leopold Svaty and his girlfriend Silvie Sedlackova, Milan Jirasek, Martin Kadlec and others who go by names like Zerock and Mr. Smokalot. Some of these names activists use may send the wrong message to some, but Zerock and Mr. Smokalot saw to it that Panacea Medicinal Seeds supplied me with hundreds of good seeds, so I could give them out to those that contacted me who were planning to grow their own. All of these seeds were supplied free of charge, so I would like to thank Panacea Seeds for their generosity and tell them that what they supplied has been put to good use.

These are just a few of the activists I came into contact with and it was very refreshing to speak with individuals of this caliber. DJ Nuff, another Czech activist I had met, brought his friend Ondrej Vetchy to one of my seminars. I was told that Ondrej is one of the biggest movie stars in the Czech Republic, so the information I provided was certainly reaching some important people. I also came in contact with Hugo Toxxx, one of the top rap stars in the Czech Republic. Hugo is a great guy and we spent quite a bit of time talking about what this medicine could do to end the suffering of citizens with medical problems living in this beautiful country. Those who are in Hugo's position can reach the masses to spread the word and I know that is exactly what he has done. A few months after we first met, Hugo even put out a song about the oil to help spread the message to the young and I could not have been more pleased with his efforts.

I can't understand how Jindrich and Milan were able to hold the tour together. They had taken a Canadian who couldn't speak a word of Czech and made this tour a great success. Because of the lack of funding, we all had to rough it a bit, but the work we were doing made any inconveniences seem of little importance. In total, I gave ten seminars in the first eighteen days I was there. In addition I spoke to many other groups and individuals as well. On average, that is about one seminar every two days. This in itself does not sound too impressive. Still, when you consider the traveling from place to place that was done, it was a very busy schedule. By the time I completed all the seminars, I was very happy with the results. We had touched a great number of people with our message and I knew the information would spread rapidly.

One day, Jindrich told me about a local nurse who had used the oil during her pregnancy. She ingested small amounts of the essential oil from the hemp plant to combat a bladder problem she was suffering from and it took care of her condition very quickly. She had also mixed this oil with hemp seed oil and used it topically to successfully prevent stretch marks. There are many accounts in history of women using cannabis during childbirth, so when her time came, she made sure there was enough oil in her system. Since this was the first time she had given birth, it was expected that she would have to go through quite a bit of suffering. When she was taken to the hospital, she received no injections, but still there was little pain involved and the baby was born in perfect health about 30 minutes later.

For many women childbirth can be a very painful experience. So why should women suffer needlessly when they can use this natural substance, which presents no danger to themselves or the baby they are about to deliver? In a short time, I expect to see hemp oil widely used by expectant mothers and I'm sure it will be of great benefit to both mother and child.

During one of the events I spoke at, someone had called me a civil rights activist and that statement had given me reason to pause. At that point, I hardly even considered myself to be a hemp activist. Now I had to confront the fact that in reality I had become a full-blown civil rights activist. Perhaps an even more proper term to use would be a natural rights activist and such rights are god given. What governments grant are in fact civil privileges, which requires adherence to their rules. Often we use terms like civil rights and don't really pay attention to what we have been duped into saying. For the sake of simplicity, I will continue to use the term civil rights, but now you are aware of the difference. What I was doing did not concern just hemp or the hemp movement. It was about the rights of us all to have free use of herbal medicines to heal ourselves. When I considered my activities from this angle that made me a civil rights activist and now I began to look at all the work Jack had done in a different light.

Jack Herer had not only been the Emperor of Hemp. He was probably one of the greatest civil or natural rights activists that ever lived. The message he was sending in his writing and speeches was not just for the greater good of the hemp movement, it was for the greater good of all mankind. On top of that, Jack had been beating this drum for 40 years and one cannot help but admire the tenacity of such a person. People like Martin Luther King were certainly great civil rights activists, but how could anyone say Jack Herer did not fall into the same category? Jack had seen what was wrong with our world and spent decades telling us how it could be made better for ourselves and coming generations.

Throughout history, people who had done great things and inspired us all to follow their example were often made saints. Judging from his efforts to make this world a better place, perhaps Jack Herer should be afforded the same consideration. I know of no one who was more dedicated to the greater good of our species, this planet, and raising awareness about the benefits of growing this wonderful plant. Given the magnitude of the contribution he provided, I think Jack should be given the honor of being called the Patron Saint of Hemp.

With the tour officially over, I had three or four days to see Prague up close and personal before my return flight to Canada. A lovely lady named Hanka Skálová showed me a great deal of the city one afternoon and we had a wonderful time seeing the sights. Hanka was not only a delight to be with, she was also a veritable fountain of information about the Czech Republic and this breathtaking city. That afternoon, we walked through the most ancient parts of the city and Hanka explained the different landmarks in detail. After strolling across Charles Bridge, we then continued onwards up the hill towards Prague's world-famous castle. Part way up the hill, we stopped at a tavern, which appeared to be very old, to get something to eat. Hanka informed me that this tavern was the longest continuously-operating drinking establishment in Prague. I asked her how many years it had been in operation. She answered, "Since 1300." I looked at her and replied in disbelief, "This tavern has been in constant operation for 700 years?" She just smiled and replied, "Prague is a very old city." I found almost everything about Prague to be memorable and enchanting. Everyone should try to visit this amazing city to see it for themselves.

Just a couple of days before my departure, Jindrich gave me a book titled "Ideas and Opinions" by Albert Einstein. I could not imagine why he would give me such a book, since my interests revolve much more around the hemp plant than they do about the thoughts of a genius. Jindrich had grown to know me quite well and was aware of the way I thought about many things. He knew what was in this book and he also knew that when I read it, I would be very surprised. Of course, in the end he was right, but at the time I could not imagine Einstein and myself having very much in common. When I opened the book, here were the thoughts of a man who looked at the world in much the same way I did. Certainly, I would never try to put myself in the same category as Albert Einstein, but his impressions about many things were very similar to mine. Reading this book was a real eye-opening experience for me and I enjoyed it thoroughly. I had grown very close to both Jindrich and Milan, plus the Czech Republic was feeling more and more like home everyday. When the time came, I really did not want to leave, but I had many things back in Canada that had to be dealt with. Jindrich and Milan said they would attend the Cannabis Cup, so at least when I went to Amsterdam in

November, I would be among friends. I knew there would be many people waiting for the medication I produced back in Canada. The problem facing me now was would I be able to deal with them all before I was to leave for Amsterdam on November 20th, only three weeks in the future?

CHAPTER 16
TRYING TO PLAY CATCH-UP

The trip back to Canada was very tiring. We were held up at the airport in Germany for quite a long time over a problem they were experiencing with their radar. Twenty-two hours after leaving the Czech Republic, I finally arrived back at the Halifax Airport in a completely exhausted state. After a few hours of some badly needed rest, I began to start dealing with the dozens of people who had been awaiting my return. The crop that had been standing in my back yard had been harvested and dried just before I arrived home. The weather had been bad during my absence and the buds did not fatten up the way I had hoped they would so I was somewhat disappointed.

During the growing season, I had removed the males as soon as the plants expressed what sex they were. Males are of no benefit for my purposes. If they are left in the garden and allowed to pollinate the females, the result would be lots of seeds but less bud to produce the medicine. When a female plant is pollinated by a male, most of the energy available to it will go into seed production. That is the reason the males are removed, unless you intend to grow hemp for seed purposes. If the males are removed and the females are not pollinated, they can then put all their energy into bud production.

After I removed the males, only about 150 females were left to be harvested. As usual, I did not have much to work with, but it was much better than having nothing at all. I took the material I had available and went to work producing the medication for those in need as quickly as possible. Back in the spring of 2009, I had supplied oil to a man from Yarmouth, named Lery Deon, to treat his son's MS. His 23-year-old son could no longer work on the fishing boats because the condition he was suffering from impaired his ability to walk. After just six weeks of treatment with the oil, he was able to return to work, since he could now move and walk properly again. Seeing the oil work on his son's so-called incurable condition was a real eye-opener for Lery and we became friends.

Lery was also involved in the Freeman on the Land movement, so we had quite a bit in common. In the spring, when we had first met, he told me there was a bond available that I should have in my possession. Before I knew it, a $500 billion dollar discharging and indemnity bond was registered in my name. It had been explained to me that having such a bond would make it difficult for the system to give me any further trouble. I just looked at the bond as if it were an insurance policy. If it kept the RCMP off my property, it was worth having.

When I returned from Europe, there was a message that Lery wanted me to deal with some paperwork that needed my signature before the bond could become active. We took care of the paperwork and then he informed me that I could monetize this bond. Lery explained that once the bond was monetized, 10% of its value would then be at my disposal. I stated, "You're telling me I will have $50 billion dollars to carry on my research and bring this medication back into mainstream use?" Lery replied, "That's right. And more, if needed." I asked, "Lery, who would make such a large amount of money available?" He just smiled and reassured me by saying, "Rick, some very important people want to see you succeed. That's the reason this bond was put in place for you."

I didn't know what to make of all this. What he was saying didn't make any sense to me, so I just replied, "We'll see." Was I really supposed to believe that powerful individuals from the same system that was trying to bring my activities to a halt were now supposedly willing to provide the money required to bring this medicine to the world? This all sounded like a farce to me and I strongly doubted that those in control of this funding would ever make any of it available. Lery stated it would take a while to get the bond monetized, but when that was done, the funds would be available. At the time, I had many other things to think about, so for the time being, I decided not to dwell on the issue.

Before parting, I inquired about how his son was doing and he told me he was getting along great. Lery had been quite vocal to his friends about the curative power of the oil after it had healed his son. Many who lived in his local area were now using the oil as a medication themselves and had achieved great results. I found word-of-mouth to be a very effective way to spread the truth about the healing abilities of this medication. Since the oil produced such amazing results for so many conditions, it made a very strong impression on those who had been lucky enough to receive treatment.

I only had three weeks before I was to return to Europe, so I rolled up my sleeves and produced as many treatments as possible. Since the crop I had grown did not produce the amount of bud I required, I had to rely on local growers to come up with some of the material I needed. As usual, the patients would come and I would instruct them about the proper way to produce this medication. If, for some reason, they were unable to do so, I would produce it for them. On most days, there was a constant stream of patients in and out of my driveway. Now, when patients came, I did not have to spend as much time convincing them that the oil worked, since many were already aware of what this substance could do before they arrived at my door. This made dealing with patients much easier and less time-consuming.

The oil continued to work one miracle after another and I was getting some amazing feedback from people who had used the treatment. Batya Stark, a lady that contacted me from the U.S., was having wonderful results with the use of this medication. Her father, who was now in his early 80s, had been diagnosed with Alzheimer's and Batya had used the oil to treat his condition. In a short time, her father was healthy and vibrant and his thinking processes were once again perfect.

Afterwards, she tried the oil on what doctors said to be an incurable skin condition her son had been suffering from and cured him in two weeks. She then started to give the oil to her uncle, who was in very bad condition and not expected to live. In no time, she was achieving wonderful results and called me often to keep me abreast of what was happening. Batya is a very patient and caring person and we connected on many levels about the use of this medication during our conversations. The healing power of the oil was phenomenal, but it also seemed to have the ability to reconnect people who had suffered traumatic experiences.

Her father is a survivor of Hitler's death camps and she always found it hard to communicate with him, because of the trauma he had suffered during World War 2. The use of this medication helps such people come to grips with what had happened to them in the past. This is what she found in her father's case and she was very pleased that the oil allowed him to deal with his past more easily. I cannot help but think this medication would be very beneficial to anyone who has experienced the horrors of war or other traumatic occurrences. Many soldiers and others have taken part in events, which can be very hard to live with. This oil could help assist them in dealing with the atrocities they have witnessed in an effective and harmless way. Both Batya and I have seen the wonderful results they can achieve and I expect that in the near future many who have experienced such things will be able to find relief. I think talking to this lady and others like her did much to help give me hope that this medication would soon be recognized.

The time was passing quickly, I had just about caught up with everything, and in a few days I would be leaving for Europe again. The police had not come near me and everything was going fine. Then I received word that Jim LeBlanc had died and the news of his passing left me totally crushed. Jim and I had become very close after I had provided the oil to treat his terminal cancer about three years previously. When Jim had first come to me, he was a dying man who had suffered a lot of damage from the medical system. The doctors had given him chemo in the beginning, which almost killed him. They then gave him radiation and his chest and back looked like red leather from the damage this treatment had caused.

When I first came into contact with Jim, he was already classified as incurable by the medical system and they had sent him home to die. Luckily for him, his partner had heard about what I was doing and they decided to come see me and give the oil a try. I told Jim, "Before this is over, you won't have much use for your oncologist." It surprised me, but he actually tried to defend the doctor with "Oh no, Rick, you haven't met this man. You can see the concern he has for me right in his face." I replied, "How do you know his concern is real, Jim? Some doctors are quite talented in the field of acting. Maybe he should change his profession and he might win an Oscar, since it seems he's not very good at healing."

A few months later, when Jim found out what this doctor was really about, he told me he felt like killing him. This so-called doctor had supplied an affidavit about Jim's condition for my upcoming court case and what he stated was simply a pack of lies. When Jim read it, he was completely disgusted and stated. "Rick, they will lie right through their teeth to keep this medicine from the public, won't they?" I replied, "Now you've finally got the picture."

Jim had the lowest tolerance for the oil I have ever encountered. It took him seven months to ingest the 60 grams, more than twice the length of time the average person requires. After taking the 60-gram treatment, when he took off his shirt, you would never know he had taken the radiation treatments. Now, he was cancer-free and really looking great. Considering the condition he had been in a few months earlier, there was no question a miracle had occurred. Even though Jim had been declared cancer-free, I told him he should stay on the oil or at least take maintenance doses and he agreed. Much later, I was to find out he did not do as I had instructed. At the time, I really had no way of knowing what he was doing, since Jim had come into contact with others who could produce the oil and he told me they would supply his needs. Jim and I lived about 120 miles apart, so I didn't get to see him very often. But when our paths did cross, he looked better and better each time, so I thought he had done as I asked.

A few months after the oil had cured his cancer, he called me in a very worried state. Jim had been suffering from a blockage of the heart and the medical system wanted to do open-heart surgery. Since he was dying from cancer at the time, the surgery had been cancelled. Now that his cancer had been cured, the medical system again wanted to go ahead with the operation. I already knew about Jim's condition and had hoped that in time the oil would clear the blockage, since it had worked so well for other patients with high cholesterol and problems of that nature. Possibly, it might have done just that if he had been taking the oil properly.

I thought Jim had at least been taking his maintenance doses on a regular basis, so to me it looked as if the oil had finally run into something it couldn't repair. Jim asked me what my opinion was concerning the operation they wanted to perform. I replied, "Go in and have the surgery. You're full of cannabinoids and I don't think they could kill you even if they tried." After our talk, he seemed to settle down and then allowed the surgery to take place. He didn't inform me that he had not been taking the oil as I had instructed, so I thought there was plenty in his system.

Two days after his surgery, I went to Halifax to visit Jim in the intensive care unit. When I walked in, he lit up with a smile from ear to ear which made it very easy to tell he was happy that I had made the effort to come see him. He then showed me the stitches down the center of his chest where the surgery had been performed. After seeing what they had done to him, I was glad I never had to go through such an operation myself. We had been talking for about ten minutes, when three doctors entered the room. The doctor in the middle, who seemed to be in charge, pointed her finger at Jim and told the other doctors, "This is Jim LeBlanc. He has just had open-heart surgery and is recovering rapidly." She then added, "Mr. LeBlanc had his terminal cancer cured using hemp oil."

Jim looked at me and I'm sure he knew what was coming. I turned in my chair and stated, "That's right, hemp oil cured Jim's cancer and I'm the guy that produces it. Now why are you refusing to use this wonderful medicine to help others?" Suddenly, it was as if there was a rattlesnake coiled up at their feet; you could literally see them stiffen. One of the doctors shuffled off to one side and tried to excuse himself by saying, "I really don't have anything to do with this, I'm an anesthesiologist." I replied, "Oh, you're an anesthesiologist but you don't know hemp is man's oldest and safest anesthetic? You also don't seem to realize that in many cases the trash you administer and call anesthetic causes brain damage!"

The three of them almost ran over each other trying to get out of the room. Jim sat there with a pillow against his chest, a great big grin on his face and tears rolling down his cheeks. Because of the stitches, he couldn't laugh normally but after a few minutes he settled down enough that he could speak again. Upon recovering his composure, he stated, "Rick, I have never seen anything like that. Those doctors were terrified of you." I told him with a smile, "All you have to do is ask the right questions and these so-called medical professionals have no place to hide."

Jim pulled through the surgery just fine and was then released from the hospital. Of course, I thought he was still taking the oil he was getting from other sources. Then, to my surprise, Jim called a few months later and informed me his cancer had returned. I could not believe it and stated, "Jim that can't be right. How much oil have you been taking?" It was then that I found out he had not been taking any. Although good material was very scarce at the time, I managed to scrape up enough oil to fill four six-gram tubes and sent them to him, so he could begin treatment again.

I asked him how many CT scans he had permitted them to perform since he had been declared cancer-free. He admitted that he had allowed doctors to give him four or five scans. I explained, "Jim, there's a very good chance it was the effects of the scans that caused your cancer to return." He understood what I meant. No matter how you slice the cake, radiation does damage to our DNA and causes cells to mutate. When a CT scan is performed, even on the scan's lowest radiation setting, the patient is still receiving about 200 times more radiation than they would receive from a chest X-ray. Even the radiation from one X-ray can do our bodies harm and people who work around X-ray machines don't use those big lead aprons for no good reason.

About three months later, I received another call from Jim, saying he was again cancer-free. I asked him how much oil he had taken and he told me he had not as yet finished the fourth tube. I warned him, "Jim, the oil doesn't work unless it's in you. I have nothing to work with, so acquire the rest of the treatment from the contacts you have that are nearby." Apparently, Jim finished the fourth tube, but he didn't get the rest of the treatment from his other contacts, as I had asked. Of course, I didn't have any way of knowing this and I thought that surely this time he would do as I had told him.

Whenever I spoke in Halifax or the surrounding area, Jim would always try to be there. Everyone enjoyed his presence at these events and his open manner was irresistible. He had joined Alcoholics Anonymous or AA, as it is usually called, a few years previously to deal with his drinking problems. Although AA is supposed to be against the use of drugs, Jim made no secret of the fact that he felt marijuana had been instrumental in helping him leave the bottle behind. When someone like Jim stands before an audience and makes statements like that, there is no question what he is saying is the truth and I truly admired the way he handled himself. His partner Sherry had written a wonderful testament to the oil's healing abilities, called "Jim's Cancer Journey". We had posted it up on our site along with their phone number, since they were more than willing to talk with others about this treatment. Jim and Sherry did a great job and talked to hundreds of people, which gave hope to those who were suffering. Often, callers would say they had talked with them before calling me and what they told people about the treatment made my job much easier.

As far as I knew, Jim was cancer-free and everything was just fine regarding his health. Then, in September 2009, Jim called me and said he had cancer again. It took a little doing, but I was able to get some oil to him before I left for the tour in the Czech Republic. I knew from past experience it would take him a while to ingest the 24 grams I had made available, so he should easily have enough to last him until I returned. Then, as soon as I came home from the Czech tour, I produced a full ten-tube treatment and sent it to him. I was so busy at the time I had no idea what Jim's situation really was. Then Sherry had called and I was told that he had passed away.

Apparently, Jim had only used one 6-gram tube from all the oil I had recently supplied. When Sherry and Jim both realized how bad things really were, Sherry told me she had asked Jim why he had not taken the oil as I had instructed. She said he just dropped his head and couldn't answer. I always tell people with serious cancers it would be best to take the oil as rapidly as possible. If they do not, then their chance of survival is often decreased and the oil may only be able to ease their way out. Jim had not taken his maintenance doses, nor had he taken the complete second treatment. This, combined with the fact that even after his heart operation he had continued to allow the medical system to perform more CT scans, leaves me with the impression that these scans could have played a major role in causing Jim's demise.

Since I had first put him under treatment, he had taken about ten CT scans. I feel that in the end the radiation poisoning from these scans and his own lack of resolve in taking the treatment properly allowed the cancer to spread throughout his body and brought about his death. Jim had crossed the line and now he had to pay with his life. Unlike most people in his situation, at least the oil's use had allowed him to die peacefully and with dignity. Even though he passed away, the oil had still been of benefit. Personally, I feel he could have lived on for years if he had taken the treatment properly and stayed away from the medical system and their scans, but who's to say? At least, the oil had provided him with about three extra years of life that had not been wasted. Jim was a great spokesman for this medicine and his presence will be missed by everyone whose life he touched. All I can say is, "Sleep well, my friend. You have earned the rest, but I will miss you always."

The inability of many people to turn their backs on a medical system that is doing them so much harm is something I find very disturbing. A prime example of this occurred when a man who was in very bad shape came to me seeking treatment. He had two large tumors in his upper stomach and a very large tumor on his throat. Six weeks into the treatment, he called me and stated the two stomach tumors were gone and the tumor on his throat was only about one-tenth the size it had been. He then explained that he intended to have a CT scan performed in a couple of weeks to see how he was progressing. I asked him, "Why would you do such a thing?" He replied, "How will I know if the oil is working?" In explanation, I stated, "You said yourself the two tumors that were in your upper stomach area are completely gone and the large one you had on your throat, has also just about disappeared. Why would you go to the medical system and take a large dose of radiation to find out what your eyes are already telling you is true?"

This is the mindset of many people I have dealt with. It seems they have to hear it from the guy in the white coat for it to be true. It's their own body and who would know better than the patient themselves about how they are doing? Must they really go back and seek confirmation about their well-being from the very same medical system that couldn't help their condition in the first place? And then take a scan that gives them a massive dose of radiation to tell them what they already know? This is what happens in many cases and quite often the cancer will return, but the patient cannot understand why. Much of the time, it's the medical system itself with their insane treatments and scans that are causing people with serious conditions all this grief. We should all educate ourselves about the treatments our doctors wish to provide and think twice before we allow the medical system to do anything that could cause harm.

Don't make the same mistakes that have cost so many others their very lives. If your doctor tries to ignore the concerns you have about the treatments they are offering, tell the doctor to take the treatment they are suggesting themselves and do not place yourself under their care if you would like a better chance to survive. What I'm saying may sound rash to some, but if you have ever seen anyone die from the effects of chemo and radiation, you will understand what I mean and realize the advice I'm providing could save your life.

My trip to the Cannabis Cup in Amsterdam was sponsored by Greenhouse Seeds. They also offered me the option of bringing someone else along and I thought it would be nice to have some company. At first, I wanted to bring Rick Dwyer since we were friends and he had been in "Run from the Cure." Unfortunately, Rick does not like to fly and suggested I take someone else, so I asked Eric and Debbie Donkin if they were available. At the time, they had many things to deal with, so they too were unable to come along. I then thought about Scot Cullins. He had been supplying people with the oil and had achieved great success, so I gave him a call and asked if he would like to come with me, all expenses paid. Scot didn't hesitate for one second. "Sure, I'd love to come," he shot back. He got his passport and everything in order and was ready to fly out with me on November 20, 2009 to attend the Cannabis Cup.

By the time I was ready to depart for Europe, I had caught up with everything, but I still had to deliver medication to patients on the way to the airport. The last three weeks had been extremely busy, but finally I felt I was ready to leave. There was nothing of any real value left to work with, but I knew I could get the needed material from other growers when I returned. The bud I had grown and some which I had purchased from other suppliers had been turned into oil that I distributed to the patients. The plant material, which was left after it had been washed, was then spread across the hillside behind my house with the rest of the material I had discarded over the years.

My home had been robbed into in 2003, while I was away on a trip, and again in 2008, while I was attending court. Although many things were missing, I never bothered to report these incidents to the RCMP, since I looked at them as being even bigger thieves than those who had broken in. I was becoming extremely tired of having my home wrecked and my property stolen by both criminals and cops. So, to keep them away, my son had found a deal on some security cameras and he installed them to provide surveillance. If there were another break-in, at least then we would be able to find out who was responsible.

Everything was ready to be locked down and I decided that, as an extra precaution, my truck should be left parked about halfway between my house and the road. It is over 100 meters to the main road and with the truck parked in this manner no one could get in with a vehicle. At least, if the thieves were going to try to clean out my home again, this time they would have to carry everything they were stealing all the way to their getaway car. I could think of nothing else we could do to secure my property and I was very happy with the security system my son had installed, so I felt there was little more that could be done.

The night before I was to fly out, two brothers from Sackville, New Brunswick, named John and Alan Spencley, had me do a radio show with them at Mount Allison University. John and Allen are connected with the Freeman on the Land movement and are both very intelligent men, so I was happy to have the opportunity to work with them. I had written another article for *Konoptikum*, the Czech hemp publication, which I read to those listening during the broadcast. I explained what was really going on and between the three of us we were able to provide a great deal of information to those who had tuned in.

On the day we were scheduled to leave for Europe, Scot arrived on time and we caught a ride to Halifax with my neighbor Ruby Bjarnason. When I had gone to the Czech Republic to do the tour, I had not taken a phone along and this had upset quite a few people. The thing is I don't believe anyone should be using cell phones, since I think their use presents a danger to us all. Today, both young and old alike walk around with these things stuck to the sides of their heads as if they were born with them, and I believe this could be putting their health and well-being at risk. I cannot imagine why so many seem to think the extended use of such devices is safe, since the microwave radiation they produce can interfere with the electrical impulses that make our bodies function properly. If the public only understood the danger that all this new microwave technology presents to our health, I am sure there would be something done about this immediately, but these telecommunications companies try to downplay the danger.

Even the radios the police use themselves to communicate are giving them cancer. You often see officers wearing these devices strapped to their upper torso very close to their necks. The microwave radiation they emit causes cancer to develop in the neck area and that is a well-known fact, but if police officers refuse to use these devices, they will lose their jobs. Police in at least thirty different countries are using this technology and the system is quietly studying how quickly the tumors develop. To those currently in charge it is all just a big experiment and I expect that it would also extend into the military of many countries as well.

The system is simply playing with the lives of those they employ in these fields and care nothing about their health and wellbeing. As I understand it, UN regulations prohibit anyone from carrying out experiments on humans without their full knowledge and consent. Those who work for our corrupted system in law enforcement and in the military are in essence protecting the very people who are doing them harm. If you would like to verify what I am saying for yourself get on the internet and listen to what Barrie Trower has to say about the subject. You can find the information by simply punching in Dangers of Microwave Technology on Youtube and I think you should give what Mr. Trower is saying a great deal of thought. Even though, as you can see, I have no use for cell phones and the rest of these new technologies, which are causing so much harm, I had to relent and purchase one just to keep everybody happy. Now the only problem was since I had never used cell phones to communicate, I didn't even know how to operate one properly.

When Scot had arrived at my home, I asked him if he was familiar with the use of these devices and he informed me that he was. I stated, "This is pretty good now, isn't it? I can produce the essential oil from a plant and cure just about everything you can think of, but I can't operate a cell phone." We had a good laugh about my inability to operate one of these devices, but in reality all those little buttons and functions on today's phones seemed to be beyond my understanding. In the near future, Scot proved to me that he too had some problems operating such things, because once we got to Europe, he couldn't get this phone to work right, either.

To me, cell phones are just another example of the modern technology we have available today, which I feel is not safe to use. Besides that, such devices can bewilder someone with my background very quickly and also cause a lot of frustration. The way I looked at it, I had lived 60 years without a cell phone, so why did I need one now? But to keep everyone happy, I didn't have much choice except to go with the flow and take one along on my journey.

CHAPTER 17

AMSTERDAM AND THE CANNABIS CUP

Scot and I really enjoyed traveling together and there were many humorous things that happened. The first escalator we encountered was a whole new experience for Scot and his reaction to it was quite funny. In the area where he and I come from, escalators are not very common. You would have to go to an airport or a city to see such equipment in operation, so his reaction to the escalator was understandable and really not all that unusual.

We both realized we were just two country boys off on an adventure to a strange land. I had already been to Europe the previous month, so I was "the big European travel expert," but, to be honest, I really didn't have much of a clue about Amsterdam. To us, the Cannabis Cup was an event you read about in magazines and we couldn't imagine really being there. After we touched down in Amsterdam, the sponsor of our trip, Arjan Roskam, the owner of Greenhouse Seeds, met us at the airport. As soon as we were seated in his vehicle, I asked him where I could get my medication, to which he replied, "Oil is illegal here." "What's illegal got to do with it?" I exclaimed. "This is Amsterdam; if the oil is available anywhere, it should be here." Arjan laughed at my statement but I realized from his reaction to my question that high-grade oil would be next to impossible to find.

Arjan took Scot and I to a nice little apartment next to one of his coffee shops and this was where we were to stay for the next few days. He was a great host and made sure we had all the hemp and hash at our disposal that was within legal limits. Later, he took me to the Greenhouse Seed Company's warehouse, then, after he had shown me around, I was introduced to the staff who work for him. He runs a very well-organized operation and it's easy to see why they have been so successful with this venture. Arjan and those who are close to him are very interesting people who all work together, producing a series called Strain Hunters. They travel everywhere, seeking out ancient strains of hemp and sometimes, I've been told, they even find varieties which were thought to be extinct. The camera work in the documentaries they produce is excellent and as I understand it, they have been aired on National Geographic specials.

The day after our arrival, Arjan and Franco put Scot and I on the back of two little scooters, which they used to show us around Amsterdam. Arjan explained that scooters were the fastest way to get around in the city and he wasn't kidding. We were zipping through traffic, crowds of people and hordes of bicycles at what seemed like breakneck speed. I have to admit it was a hair-raising way to see Amsterdam for the first time. Arjan and Franco are both excellent riders and somehow the scooters stayed together, so none of us suffered any injuries. I have driven motorcycles for most of my life and I look at them as being quite safe, but I do not tend to feel the same about scooters. They are cute little vehicles and provide a cheap way to get around, but still I have to question why the companies that build them don't install larger wheels, so they would be somewhat safer to operate?

This city was a real learning experience for Scot and I and we spent a good deal of our time lost. Fortunately for us, our apartment was very near the well-known Red Light District. If we became lost, all we had to do was ask someone where we could find this well-known section of the city. Making such inquires worked quite well but it was embarrassing to ask total strangers such a question and we did receive some very strange looks. The Red Light District was much the same as I had expected. There were scantily clad women standing in the windows and I must say they did provide some nice scenery. In addition, there were a good number of theaters that featured live sex acts on stage, which is something you don't see where I come from. I think Amsterdam and the Red Light District came as quite a shock to Scot, but he quickly learned to take it all in stride. Such things are not done so openly in Canada and a walk through this section of Amsterdam can be a real eye-opening experience for many.

Please don't take what I'm saying about this beautiful city the wrong way. There's a lot more to Amsterdam than just sex for sale and coffee shops where you can openly smoke pot. Amsterdam is really a place where there is something for everyone. Although I found it a bit on the expensive side and could not smoke tobacco in public places, including coffee shops, still it is truly a city well worth visiting.

When the Cup got under way, we went over to the Power Zone. The place was packed and I had never seen anything like it. Any and all things to do with hemp was available on display. We were made judges but neither Scot nor I understood what that really meant except that it did give us access to all the free hemp we could smoke. A short time later, we were taken to a place called The Temple, where a large number of different strains were being sampled and graded. We tried a few different varieties, but in a very short time, I couldn't tell much of anything about the quality of what I was smoking. It is one thing to smoke a joint from a certain variety and evaluate its characteristics over an hour or so. But how can that be done when you are sampling many varieties in a short span of time? To me it remains a mystery. I really didn't get too involved with the Temple and all the testing because I didn't have the time. I was at the Cup to put on a seminar, not to prove to the world how much pot I could smoke.

The day before I was to put on the seminar, Jindrich and Milan arrived on the scene from the Czech Republic and I couldn't have been more happy to see them. Finally, I was again with people I knew well and trusted. Their presence put me much more at ease and made the task in front of me much less stressful.

Before I came to Amsterdam to attend the Cannabis Cup, a supporter of Marc Emery contacted me and asked if I would be willing to speak out about Marc's legal difficulties when I was giving my seminar. I told him I really didn't know what made Marc tick but no one should go to jail for selling hemp seeds. Once I explained this to the caller, I then agreed to speak on his behalf during the seminar. I knew if I could clarify to the public what the legal system was trying to do to Marc, it would put him in a better position. After all, like Jack Herer himself, I too find it incomprehensible why anyone should be put in prison over the growing and use of this plant. Shortly after the Cup was over, Mr. Emery would give me cause to wonder if he really deserved my support at all, but this will be explained in detail a little further on in the book.

On Monday at 7 PM, I went before the crowd at the Cannabis Cup and put on the seminar. I was quite relieved when I realized the audience seemed to be in complete agreement with what I was saying. I had no human evidence with me to back up my statements but most in attendance were quite knowledgeable about the subject, so no slurs or tomatoes were thrown in my direction. After I was done speaking, we all went over to the Milky Way, which is a huge club where the entertainment was taking place. Reggae DJ Yellowman was performing that night and I wanted to meet him in person. He had been a supporter of mine for quite some time and I had heard good things about his efforts. The Milky Way was packed that night and it was just about impossible to get through the crowd. The music was very loud and in no time, my ears were screaming for mercy, so I spent most of the night outside and never did get to meet Yellowman, but I'm sure our paths will cross again in the future.

Because of my injury, I already had more than enough noise in my head to deal with and I didn't want to damage my hearing as well. But I would not be surprised if many of those who were in attendance at the Milky Way that evening awoke the next morning with ear damage. Tinnitus or ringing in the ears is usually not as serious as the problem I suffer with, but it can still make your life miserable. I have no direct experience in treating the condition, but those who have suffered this type of damage have reported that some may be able to find relief with the proper use of the oil. To anyone who has to endure this endless noise, they might try mixing a small amount of oil with hemp seed oil or some such carrier. Then take a Q-tip and try to get the substance as close as possible to your eardrums. If this is done, I'm told, often the noise can be reduced to a tolerable level and, in some cases, may even disappear. Still, I think that ingesting the oil would be of more overall benefit, because it has helped me so much in dealing with the injury I have, but it wouldn't hurt to give it a try.

The oil can also help individuals who have damaged sinus passages as a result of their misuse of drugs such as cocaine. Again, simply use a Q-tip before going to bed to put a small quantity of oil up your nose where it can begin to work its magic. Very often, this condition can be brought under control rapidly. Once your sinus passages are healthy again, this too can have an effect on your ability to hear properly and you will no longer have to deal with the infections and discomfort, which plagued you in the past.

The most dangerous aspect of Amsterdam, which I encountered, was all the bicycles. They were everywhere. I suppose that if you tried hard enough, you could fall into a canal but I found bicycles to be by far the greatest threat. When I went out for a walk, I was constantly trying to avoid these two-wheeled devices, which seemed to be coming at me in all directions. When walking in Amsterdam, to many I must have looked like a bobble-head doll. My head was constantly moving so I would be aware of any bicycles coming from behind. This mode of transport can sneak up behind you and give you a very bad day if you make the wrong move. I have great respect for this type of personal transportation but never have I seen so many in use at one time.

As expected, Melissa Balin was at the Cup and she introduced me to her parents, who seemed to be very nice people. I asked her about the footage from the Czech tour that she had promised to deliver. She stated that she had not had the time to deal with it and would send what I desired on to me later. I accepted what she said but made it clear I needed to get some of this footage on the Internet as soon as possible. She was nice about it and said she would get to work on the footage as soon as she returned to the United States. I planned to return to the Czech Republic with Jindrich and Milan to do a few more seminars after the Cup. If some of this footage were available, it would make the task before me much easier. Lumir Hanus is practically a national hero in the Czech Republic. Footage of him agreeing with my statements would be invaluable to help convince the Czech people and their government that what I was telling them about this medicine was true.

On November 25, I received word from my son back in Canada that the RCMP had raided my home once again. I couldn't believe my ears. What would they possibly gain by raiding my property while I was in Europe? Mike gave me the number that the police had left with him, so I called and got Tim Hunter on the phone. He had been one of the police officers who had performed the raid even though he was well aware that what they were doing was completely wrong. I had given Tim Hunter a copy of "Run from the Cure" personally just after it was released. Since he had known me for years, I'm sure Mr. Hunter was aware of the fact that I am not a criminal.

In disgust, I exclaimed, "Tim, what do you people think you're doing? You know what's going on here and you also know who you really should be going after." I then asked if they intended to charge me with something but he refused to answer. All he would say was the RCMP wished to speak with me, but from past experience with them I knew exactly what that meant. I replied, "Tim, why are the RCMP going along with the government in committing this crime against the Canadian people?" He then tried to explain by saying the RCMP had acted on information they had received about my activities. I considered what he was trying to tell me to be completely ridiculous. Since I was so open about what I had been doing, as far as I was concerned, the order to raid my property must have come straight from the top.

If this were not the case, why had they not raided my property after I did Tom Young's radio show in June, or when they were flying around in September in their helicopters? It had certainly been no secret there was hemp growing in my back yard all summer and the RCMP were well aware of this fact. But they had not come near my home during the whole growing season and some RCMP officers were even sending people to me for treatment. In September, they had avoided my property with their helicopters and now, after the crop had been processed and the medication distributed, they come and do a big raid on my home almost a week after I had left for Amsterdam?

I couldn't get a straight answer out of this so-called police officer and from my perspective, what they had done seemed to make no sense, unless the RCMP had another motive. Finally, I lost it and called Mr. Hunter assorted things I felt best described him. Protect and serve. What a joke! It was more than obvious who the RCMP were protecting and serving and I don't think it could be said it was the Canadian people. On top of that, a local Springhill cop I had also known for years, named Kenny Matthews, was himself involved with this raid. My house is located in the county quite a few miles outside of Springhill and town cops have no jurisdiction there. So what did Mr. Matthews think he was doing in my home? Perhaps he was part of some joint task force out to keep the cure for cancer from the public. If so, then they did a great job. What a shame the Canadian police cannot seem to catch more real criminals than they employ.

I know what I'm saying may sound a bit crazy to some but, in reality, this is how the Canadian government is keeping the truth from the public. Do as you are told and comply with their wishes or they will send the RCMP to bring a halt to what you are doing, even though it is saving lives. That is the choice you are given and that is the reason I say if you want freedom, you will never find it in Canada. With cops like this protecting the best interests of the public, what could we possibly have to complain about? Take your pharmaceuticals and do as you are told, or people with guns, badges, and very strange attitudes about healing will pay you a visit.

What was happening here? Why did the RCMP do this raid? I didn't know all the details yet, but it was becoming very obvious to me that I was probably being framed. In the past, this so-called police force have more than earned their reputation for doing such things. A few years ago, the RCMP out West had tried to frame a man named Weibel Ludwig. The RCMP tried to say Mr. Ludwig had blown up a building the RCMP themselves had destroyed. Even after the truth was known, little or nothing was done about the corruption within the RCMP. I had no illusions about the integrity of this police force, since I already knew they did not possess such a thing. If I returned to Canada, those within the RCMP that displayed no conscience would see that I was charged and jailed without my medication.

I had already been put in jail for a short time in 2007 and I knew what could happen if my medicine was not available. Since it would be my third charge for the same offence under these corrupted laws the Canadian government had put in place, I figured this time I would probably be held without bail. Returning to Canada and going to jail without my medicine was not an option. I then started wondering if all this was not just a ploy by the Canadian government to keep me out of the country.

For a long time, what I had been doing was a very big thorn in the government's backside and if they did not deal with it properly, it would only continue to get worse. Right from the beginning, I knew how much impact this medicine would have on the public and how enraged many would become when they learned the truth. So, to avoid trouble, I felt it would be best to cushion the blow as much as possible. I had hoped the government would work with me to bring this medication to the public in a rational way, but they decided to do otherwise and had done the exact opposite, which exposed their corruption to many in the know.

When they refused to act and instead chose to persecute me in their courts, I don't think the Canadian government realized how much notoriety this oil and I were then receiving. Then, as time had gone on, the oil continued to gain more attention, so I expect that they were looking for a way to bring this to a halt. I came to the conclusion they had to be aware of the fact I was in Europe again before they staged this latest raid. Maybe they thought doing a raid and having me brought up on bogus charges would keep me in Europe. If so, they were quite correct, but I doubt they were aware of the fact I was to be crowned Freedom Fighter of the Year at the Cannabis Cup. An honor such as this comes with a lot of publicity and gets the attention of a great number of people both in and out of the hemp movement.

This, plus the fact that I was now being recognized as a civil rights activist, could really put the Canadian government in a bad position. It looked to me as if the RCMP and the government they serve had really fumbled the ball this time. The raid on my property had shown many who inhabit this planet what they were really doing and now I was in the perfect position to expose them. The RCMP always loved to grandstand about what a great police force they were. Now I had the opportunity to shine the harsh light of reality upon them and their masters before the public in an honest and open manner.

It would take some time and hard work to accomplish this task, but I think this book will do much to expose to the world what the Canadian system and other systems of control worldwide are doing.

A good percentage of people already know what this medicine can do and how it can be produced. Now what more could the system possibly do to stop the truth from coming out? The clock on the time bomb that would destroy their lies and deceptions was now ticking. Years ago, if they had seen to it, a little piece of lead could have silenced me and none of this would be happening. It can only be said the system truly missed the boat on this one. If anything were to happen to me now, I think it would only make matters worse for them. Their inability to see something of this magnitude coming straight at them tells me their corruption is not nearly as well organized as one might imagine. Now that the truth is coming out everywhere, those responsible for these crimes against humanity will find there is no place to hide. How will people look at governments, such as the one in Canada, who have been hiding the truth from the world?

Do you think the public at large might become just a bit angry once they are aware of what these fools have been doing? My guess is they will, but, just for once, could we please settle what needs to be done without the use of violence? It's impossible to build something better if we start off by making the same mistakes, so please give what I am saying serious consideration. Even though I am asking that we proceed rationally, I can't say I took what was being done to me and those who were seeking treatment lightly. I knew there would be people in Canada that would die if I did not return, but what good could it possibly do them if I were locked up or dead? The only sensible thing to do was stay in Europe and try to bring them to their knees from over here.

On the last day of the Cup, word about the raid was spreading fast and many people expressed their disgust over what had taken place. Arjan had offered me some seeds from his company but we were both so busy we didn't have time to connect after the Cup. T. H. Seeds gave me one of their new strains and then I stopped at the DNA Seeds display. I was just standing there, looking at the different varieties, when one of the guys behind the counter said, "Aren't you Rick Simpson?" After I admitted to being one and the same, they invited me in behind the counter. What a great group of individuals!

The owner of DNA Seeds and his wife were present and asked me what my plans were. They already knew about the raid, so I told them I was not planning to return to Canada. I explained to them it would make more sense for me to stay in Europe and continue the struggle from over here, adding that I also hoped to get some plants growing. Those must have been the magic words, because before I left their display, they gave me thousands of dollars' worth of seeds from their best strains and I could hardly carry them all. I would really like to thank DNA for their generosity and I want them to know their seeds have been planted and are already saving lives.

While I was at the Cup, many people became aware of my background and I talked with quite a few of the vendors. Breeders that were present had already named strains after me before the Cup even began. So I guess I was better known in some circles than I had imagined. It was great to have the support of so many who are involved in the hemp movement. At least now I didn't feel so alone.

In the past, I had always been able to walk on water as long as it was 30 below zero and frozen solid. But after the introduction Steve Hager gave me at the Freedom Fighter of the Year Award that night, you would think I really could. When I was crowned with the famous tricorn hat, I could feel the support from the hundreds that were present. To join the ranks of those who have worn this hat like Jack Herer and Eddy Lepp is a great honor but sadly, it comes at a very high cost for many. Jack told me he had been jailed 32 times over hemp and Eddie had just received a 10-year prison sentence. It seems a great number of good people have wound up in jail when they began speaking the truth about this issue. At least now I knew the system could no longer just sidestep the use of this medicine with their double talk. They, were being surrounded by the truth and their days of controlling and restricting this medicine's use from us were numbered indeed.

Back home, those connected with the Freeman on the Land movement were looking into what had happened on my property. If there really was something to all this Freeman business, the Canadian government would have some very difficult questions to answer in the future. Much of this is quite complicated and it would take some time to find out exactly where I stood. Even though I was to be marooned in a strange land, I couldn't help but feel I was still in a decent position. Sooner or later, our illustrious leaders will be forced to deal with this issue and, to their dismay, I'm sure they will find that something of this magnitude can no longer be hidden. Perhaps this time, I would be able to show the whole world who the real criminals were, but to accomplish this, I still had a great deal to do.

When I left Amsterdam, it was with a heavy heart… what would happen next? Scot was totally disgusted about the raid and returned to Canada the day after the Cup ended. I hated to part company with him, but it was time for us to go our separate ways. I went on with Jindrich and Milan to attend Cultiva in Vienna where I had been scheduled to do another seminar. Cultiva is another large hemp event that is held yearly and I found out there were many such events in different countries here in Europe. I really enjoyed Cultiva; there were many speakers and great displays and the whole event had a wonderful atmosphere about it. A good number of those who were present at the Cannabis Cup in Amsterdam had traveled on to Vienna, so there were quite a few that I was already acquainted with in attendance.

After the seminar, I spoke with Remo, the Urban Grower, and his wife outside the Pyramid hotel in Vienna. This interview was very helpful in getting the truth out about the RCMP raid that was conducted on my property while I was absent. I didn't even have to convince them about how effective the use of this medicine can be. A family friend of theirs had been dying of cancer a year before and had started taking the oil. Remo told me their friend was still alive and doing well, so they had already seen the magic for themselves.

Since I had come to Europe, it had been a constant blur of activity and I was becoming quite run down. On the first trip to the Czech Republic, the oil had been supplied to me, but Amsterdam and Vienna had been a whole different matter. A wonderful lady had supplied us with a whole carton of space cakes and hash brownies before we left Amsterdam. Sadly, cannabis edibles do not generally have the potency I require as a medicine and it was showing. When I left Vienna to return to the Czech Republic, I was exhausted. The ringing in my head was killing me; I needed my medication in the worst way. Luckily for me, when I got back to Olomouc, Jindrich and Milan had a fresh supply waiting to fulfill my needs.

On December 9, 2009, I received a call from the RCMP in Canada telling me that I should come in to one of their detachments. Since I had purchased my cell phone in Canada, it had been listed under a Canadian number. This seemed to baffle the investigative efforts of the RCMP and it appears for some reason they thought I was back in Canada. The officer who called said I should report to them, since I was going to be charged in connection with the raid they had performed. I promptly told this fool where the RCMP could get off and hung up on him. Considering what officers with the RCMP had been doing, if they wanted to purge the streets in Canada of crime, the first thing they would have to do is lock themselves up. In the end, if this book does nothing more than rid the Canadian public of the strong-arm tactics and manipulation displayed by the RCMP, it will be time well spent.

A few days later, I did an interview on a Halifax radio station and that's when I was informed of what they were planning to charge me with. The announcer was really full of himself and was blowing off at me like I was some kind of criminal. He was definitely on the side of the RCMP, so I set him straight about what was really going on here. When he heard what I had to say, it must have sunk in somewhat, because he became much more respectful and quiet. I couldn't comprehend some of the things with which I was going to be charged. There was all this talk about 70 pounds of hemp being present in my home, which I knew was totally false. In addition, I was told the RCMP had found booby-traps and these brave officers had been afraid for their very lives during the raid. The announcer then went on to mention that restricted weapons had also been found in my home. Of course, I knew none of this was true, but what were the RCMP trying to pull off here? It was now more than obvious they were out to frame me, but did they really expect to get away with their plan using a pack of lies such as this?

I was truly mystified by their behavior and what they were trying to charge me with. How could an organization that is supposed to be working for the Canadian people become so misguided? I guess it could be said I already knew the answer to that question. Friends of mine in the past had tried to join the RCMP but their applications had been rejected. It seems this organization does not want freethinkers or people with too much intelligence in their midst. Given the fact I personally knew two of the officers that had raided my property, would these pillars of law and order try to set me up? I had no illusions about these two officers and many of the other people the RCMP employs to do their dirty work. All you have to do is pay them enough money and let them feel important. Under these circumstances, right and wrong means nothing to them. Their behavior is just like that of so many others who are in positions of trust that have done nothing but let the public down and bring grief to our world. All I could think at the time was, "Heaven help the Canadian people."

CHAPTER 18

THE EMPEROR'S PASSING

When Steve Hagar came to Nova Scotia to do the story for *High Times* Magazine, we talked about doing a book together concerning my experiences and the way the system was trying to hold the use of this medicine back, which he would co-author. I had given Steve's proposal serious consideration, but I was so busy trying to deal with everything that was coming at me, I felt it would be impossible to complete the task. Back then, the patients were running me right off my feet and in addition there was the upcoming Czech tour then shortly afterwards I had to attend the Cannabis Cup. So even though the book was very important and would help to spread the word, for me to even try to write it at that time would have been out of the question.

Now that I had all this behind me and was left stranded in Europe with no patients to treat, I felt this would be a good opportunity to write the book. I contacted Steve and explained what I had in mind, then informed him that I would get the rough draft to him as quickly as possible. I had two upcoming seminars, which had to be completed first, so I told Steve as soon as they were over I would get to work on the manuscript. I did well-attended seminars in Brno on December 7 and I did another in Prague on the 10th. I then went to work writing the rough draft. I found trying to write a book under these circumstances to be quite difficult. All my paperwork and information was back in Canada, so the whole book had to be written from my memories of what had transpired. To write properly, a person should be in a place they are very comfortable and familiar with, such as their own home. Being in countries where you cannot even speak the language, living out of a suitcase and trying to sleep in strange beds does little to help get your creative juices flowing.

While trying to write the rough draft, I was also being contacted by people back home concerning the raid and what the RCMP had done. My son Mike had gone to my home the day the RCMP staged their raid to check the house and was shocked to find the police were up to their old tricks again. They wanted Mike to move the truck so they could get their vehicles in my yard, but Mike told them he didn't have the keys. In truth, he knew where the keys were, but the way he looked at it, why should he move the truck to make things easier for them? Mike asked the RCMP if he could see their search warrant, but they refused to provide it and of course, this made him suspicious.

A few days later, when they finally allowed him to view what they said was the warrant, he would understand why. Mike explained to me that a judge in Halifax had issued this warrant but the times that were stated did not coincide. The color of the home described in the warrant also did not match the color of my house. He told me he suspected they had taken the warrant issued for another residence and tried to use it to justify the raid on my property. He stated as far as he was concerned, the warrant they had used wasn't worth the paper it was written on. If what my son had told me was indeed true, I could return to Canada and possibly face no charges. In a real court, a warrant such as this would not be accepted and the case would be dismissed.

Of course, by this time, I had absolutely no trust in the Canadian legal system or the government, which appears to control their actions. If I came back to Canada, I'm sure that no matter what they had to do, the police and legal system would see that I was locked up. For the time being, returning to Canada was out of the question since I had no intention of allowing them to use their brand of justice to put my life on the line. Canada could keep their legal system and their prison cells. I had much more important and sensible things to do with what was left of my life. Once I could manage to get the book published, the truth would be exposed for all to see. I also needed more time for the public to become fully aware of what was taking place and every day thousands more were doing just that. The court of public opinion is all that really matters and since this medicine is so effective and simple to produce, the public's thoughts on this issue were turning more in my favor with every passing day. Still, it would take some more time yet to build up the number of people I needed to support this issue. Therefore, any plans I might have of returning to Canada would be put off to sometime in the distant future.

I needed to know more about all these crazy charges the RCMP were trying to pin on me, so I asked Mike to explain everything he had witnessed concerning the raid. I inquired if he knew anything regarding restricted weapons the RCMP had claimed were found in my home. He replied, "Dad, I was shooting some targets with my crossbows down at your place and I left them there." I stated, "What do your crossbows have to do with me?" I was in Europe and, as I understood it, crossbows were not restricted weapons anyway. At the time, there was a store in Amherst that openly sold such devices to anyone with no acquisition permit required. According to Mike, the restricted weapons the RCMP were claiming to have found in my home consisted of his crossbows and my perfectly legal pellet gun. During their previous raids, this same pellet gun had been found, but since it has a muzzle velocity of less than five hundred feet per second, it had not been confiscated. In Canada, even a child can purchase such rifles in local stores, so the RCMP had no right to even remove it from my home.

Given the fact that I had been thousands of miles away during the week leading up to the raid, how could the RCMP even lay such a charge? I then asked my son, "What's all this about booby-traps?" He replied, "When you left for Amsterdam, there was a little bit of garbage in bags left on your sun deck." I replied, "Yes, what about them? You were supposed to dispose of them while I was gone." He explained that when he had returned that day the local landfill was closed, so to keep the bears and other wildlife out of the trash, he drove some nails in boards and placed them around the bags until he had time to dispose of them.

I inquired, "What does all this have to do with booby-traps?" Mike then told me the RCMP were saying the nails which were driven in the boards around the garbage bags were booby-traps. I replied, "These brave officers were in fear of their lives because they saw a few boards with nails in them? Somewhere on the property of almost everyone I know, you could find the same. Boards with nails driven through them are hardly uncommon, so are all these people who have such things on their properly guilty of setting booby-traps?" This was the fourth raid the RCMP had conducted on my property and never in the past had any restricted weapons or booby-traps ever been found. I stated, "Mike, I hope the RCMP never conduct a raid on a construction site or a new home that is being built. I expect they would find such an experience to be truly death-defying. They would probably stumble across such things as boards with nails in them everywhere."

What Mike was telling me really made no sense to a person with any rational thinking ability. Still, since the RCMP reported to the news media that restricted weapons and booby-traps had been found, it sent the message I was a very dangerous person. If the RCMP with the help of our corrupted news media could push this nonsense down the public's throat, it would do much to make them believe that I must have been involved in criminal activities. These are the depths, to which this so-called police force will stoop to convict people such as myself, who are in truth guilty of nothing.

You would think that sooner or later those employed by the RCMP would have to come to the conclusion that what they are doing is completely wrong and indeed they are the ones committing the crimes. Sadly, it seems the RCMP will never admit to wrongdoing on their part, until their criminal activities have been exposed and even then they are very slow to admit their guilt. When the general public finds out what really took place, the RCMP will have a lot to answer for and I expect the people of Canada will take little pride in the behavior their national police force has exhibited.

I stated, "Mike, this is becoming more silly by the second. What's all this about the 70 pounds of hemp they were supposed to have found?" He explained the RCMP dug up 70 pounds of compost from my back yard and had carted it away in bags. I protested by saying, "Compost? Now they are trying to charge me with possession of compost? Why didn't they just dig up the whole back yard? Then they could have tons of compost as evidence." What the RCMP had done was truly pathetic. Still, if they could feed this nonsense to the public in just the right way, perhaps they might be able to make them believe I really was Dr. Evil. From my experience with the Canadian legal system, I knew they would be more than happy to go along. After what they had done in the past, it would help to hide their criminal activities against the public as well if they could lock me away in one of their jail cells.

The more I learned, the more foolish it all became, but what the RCMP had done focused attention once more on this issue. According to my son, many people back home were now truly upset by what had taken place and they had every reason to be. Everyone was aware that my activities were helping many in the surrounding area and elsewhere, so to those who knew the truth, what I was doing could hardly be considered a crime.

Mike then informed me that the RCMP had also taken the security cameras he had installed before my departure. I knew they often took video tapes from security recording devices as evidence, but I had never heard of them confiscating the cameras. Why would these officers do such a thing unless they were attempting to hide what they were doing from the public? They had taken the cameras but had neglected to confiscate the digital device that had recorded all their activities while they were at my home. In no time, the footage of the raid they had staged was all over the Internet.

Apparently, this video clip came as a shock to the RCMP. They didn't like the fact this footage had been released, but in reality, they have no one to blame but themselves. After all, it was the inability of their own officers to hide their activities that had made it possible. Can you imagine breaking into someone's home and taking the security cameras to cover your tracks, but then leaving the device that was recording it all behind? This is truly the level of intelligence many in the RCMP possess. Why are we paying these officers huge salaries to go solve crimes when in fact much of the time they are acting in a criminal fashion themselves?

In addition, why do we allow the police to use the weapons they carry against the public at large in such indiscriminate ways? They say turn about is fair play, so how do you think police officers would enjoy having the public behave in the same manner they do? I'm sure if groups of us invaded their homes waving guns around and threatened their families and friends, then they might look at what they have been doing in a different way. But since they have never experienced the trauma of such things, they do not hesitate to do the same to us and our trusted governments applaud their actions. In the drug addicted and insane world we are forced to occupy, which the police themselves have helped to create, truly there are many dangers. But this has only come to pass because those who are in control wanted it that way and the police, it seems, were more than happy to comply. Certainly, there are times when police officers must use extreme measures, but in many cases today, it seems they are bringing their weapons into play for no good reason.

This behavior, combined with the use of tasers and other devices like noise cannons are simply used to intimidate the public and force them into submission. That is not the role those who police our society are supposed to be playing. Don't you think it is time that we restricted the indiscriminate use of such weapons by the RCMP and other police forces? Have they not already harmed enough innocent civilians with their tactics and, in some cases, even brought about the death of certain individuals for no good reason? With the police behaving this way, perhaps we should be the ones with the weapons to protect ourselves from them instead of the other way around. We need to get back to reality and such a thing will only come to pass when people have had enough of police forces like the RCMP and their way of doing things. I hope that in days to come, police forces worldwide will recognize the harm they are causing and once again begin working for those who pay their salaries.

Writing the rough draft proved to be quite a hard task, but I put a lot of time and effort into it and finished the draft in January 2010. Trans High Corporation, the owners of *High Times* Magazine, had advanced me 1400 euros towards the book. Steve Hager was to be co-author and Trans High were going to have it published. I contacted Steve and asked him to tell his employers to send me the contract. A couple of weeks later, it arrived, and when I looked over what they were offering, I instantly rejected their proposal. Trans High Corporation were demanding I sign all rights over to them and they would be in control of everything for many years to come.

When Steve and I first talked about doing the book, he had told me Trans High were willing to give me 50% after publication costs, which, as I was told, is almost unheard of in the publishing world. Now, according to the contract I was sent, they were offering 6% and a 5000-dollar signing bonus. This was a far cry from their original offer and, judging from what was stated in the contract, they were going to make a whole lot more than I was and have control of it all, including the movie rights. I got in touch with Steve again and asked for the address of Trans High Corporation, so I could send them back the 1400 euros they had advanced to me. Steve said I should contact Trans High and see if I could negotiate a better deal.

I told him I had no intention of contacting them. If they were not willing to give me a fair shake, then I would publish the book myself. I don't think Steve was too happy with my reaction to their offer but, to me, the contract they had sent was little more than an insult. I had been forced to remain in Europe with little or nothing to support myself and now those who were interested in publishing the book thought that they should make all the money. They might pull this type of thing with other writers, but it certainly was not going to happen in regard to this book. Steve told me there was no need to send back the advance I had been given, if I was willing to write some articles for *High Times*. In the coming months, I sent them many articles, so I feel they more than got their money's worth. As for the book, it would take me two and a half years of struggling and many re-writes before I got it to the point that I felt it could be published. With all the traveling and other distractions, completing the manuscript was a great deal more difficult than I had anticipated, but this is the finished result.

Even though I had spoken out in defense of Marc Emery at the Cannabis Cup, I now received word from Christian Laurette that Mr. Emery was saying some very unsavory things about me back in Canada. According to him, I was a coward for not returning to face the bogus charges the RCMP were planning to lay. He said something to the effect that I was an old man and if I returned, he was sure the Canadian legal system would handle this case properly. I could not believe what I was hearing. At the time, the Canadian government was talking about allowing his extradition to the U.S. where he would be imprisoned for shipping and selling hemp seeds to Americans. In Canada, selling hemp seeds is not considered a crime and seeds are sold openly in this country. Extraditing a Canadian to another country to face charges for something that is not deemed to be a crime in Canada is not supposed to be allowed.

Of course, Marc Emery would be aware of all this and he would know the Canadian government should have refused the request from the US government to have him extradited. So who would know better than Marc Emery himself about the corruption of the Canadian government and their legal system? Knowing this, why would he call me a coward for not returning? If our government and their legal system would not do what is right in his case, why would they behave differently with mine? Could it possibly be that the Canadian government or their legal system may have offered Marc a deal, which might have involved refusing his extradition, if he would try to discredit me in the eyes of the public? After all, it was my activities that posed the greatest threat to the government, because I was exposing everything they were doing against their own citizens.

Compared to what I was bringing forward, Marc Emery's seed sales to Americans would only be considered small potatoes to those who are presently governing Canada. At the time, Marc was recognized as being one of the main activists in Canada, and he also ran *Cannabis Culture* Magazine. Possibly, the Canadian government may have thought that having Mr. Emery come out against me and my work might help them maintain control so they could continue on with their crimes. What I am saying is just speculation on my part, but it's the only rational reason I can see as to why, Marc made the statements he did. If indeed that was their plan, it didn't work out too well for them. In the end, Marc went to jail in the US and the Canadian government has never been able to discredit me or the medicine I produced.

Being called a coward by someone such as Marc Emery may have been forgiven if he had not made other inaccurate comments about me and this issue in the clips that he put up on the Internet. From what I can gather, Marc openly stated he had wanted to do an article about my activities, but I would not comply. This statement implied that

I had something to hide, which was not the case. I had written the article he had requested for publication in his magazine and so had a young man from the US named Justin Kander. We had sent the articles to him but he refused to publish them, so what Marc was telling the public were outright lies.

Lately, he and a few of his supporters have even began to call followers of what I have been doing "The Rick Simpson Cult." I would hardly call people who are in favor of the use of this medicine cult members. I consider their misuse of this term as a direct insult to both myself and everyone else who would like to see change in this world. In addition, Mr. Emery, I have some more bad news for you. My "cult," as you put it, is growing at a furious rate, but I doubt the same could be said for yours. Truly, Marc Emery should never have gone to jail for selling seeds, but since he behaved no differently than the Canadian government about this issue, perhaps that is one of the reasons why he should be there.

After *High Times* had done the article about my activities and crowned me Freedom Fighter of the Year, I thought someone at *High Times* would produce a small amount of oil to prove what I was saying about this substance was true. Once that was accomplished, they could openly publish their findings in *High Times* and we would be able to bring the lies regarding this subject to an end. Instead, High *Times* published an interview with Lester Grinspoon, which apparently was put out to try to discredit my work. Rather than testing the oil and doing what was right, it seems they decided they could sell more copies of their magazine if they were to stir up a controversy. It appears more sales was their only goal and it seems to have made no difference to them that people worldwide wanted to learn the truth and were in desperate need of this medication. In my humble opinion, *High Times* could have been instrumental in relieving their suffering if only they had acted in the proper way.

I always had a certain amount of respect for what Lester Grinspoon had to say about the medicinal use of this plant, even though he works in a branch of medicine, which I feel should not even exist. After watching a documentary called "The Marketing of Madness," I don't know how anyone could put their trust in a psychiatrist, since it appears that all most of them are doing is filling their patients full of mind altering medications, so the drug companies can turn a big profit. Psychiatry has no real medical science behind it, practitioners in this field simply seem to base their diagnosis on guesswork, therefore I consider it for the most part to be a fraud.

I guess it makes little difference how Mr. Grinspoon makes his living, but considering the danger posed by the medications those in his profession use, it really surprised me that he would come out so strong against the use of this natural oil that has never harmed anyone. In the article he did for *High Times*, it was more than clear Mr. Grinspoon was against the use of this oil and that he had done no research to back up his opinions. If

Lester had looked into this oil properly and had done the simple testing required, it would have done much to save his reputation. Instead, he came out against the use of this amazing medicine and, in doing so, destroyed any credibility on this subject he had ever earned over the years. The comments that he made in this article did much to muddy the waters and keep the public misinformed, but I am sure his statements pleased those who are trying to keep the truth hidden.

I won't say Lester Grinspoon has not done much to raise public awareness about the medicinal use of this plant. Nevertheless, I feel both he and *High Times* failed miserably in this instance and could have done much more. To make matters even worse, I was informed that Lester had done an interview on Canadian radio, in which he stated the people who had come to me only thought they had cancer. Mr. Grinspoon had never met with these patients and he had no access to their medical records, so how would he know what they were suffering from? Over the years, I've heard some very stupid statements from people who were trying to hide the facts, but this one really took the cake.

If indeed those who came to me did not have cancer, then I would like Mr. Grinspoon to explain why the medical system had given these patients enough chemo and radiation to put them at death's door. The patients who came to me were suffering from cancer and a wide variety of other medical problems. For many, this oil truly worked miracles and they were healed. This fact is easy to verify by simply going on the Internet and looking at all the testimonials, which are available. After learning what Grinspoon had stated, I could only conclude that he is either very misguided, or he is involved with evil individuals who paid him to make these comments. Unlike people of Lester's caliber, if I don't know enough about a subject to voice an opinion, I say so and remain quiet. Considering the serious nature of this issue, it is too bad many others out there would not do the same. I take no joy in de-frocking those who are well known in this field, but if their statements are causing this needless suffering to continue, as you can see, I will not hesitate.

The time I was allowed to spend in the EU had run out by early February 2010. I lacked the funding that would have allowed me to stay, so it was now time for me to go on my way. Arrangements were made and I was sent to the Croatian island of Hvar in the company of a charming young Czech woman named Kristyna Novakova. She came along to help get me situated in my new surroundings and to show me how to use the little laptop computer that had been sent from Canada. Since I had spent little time around computers, getting used to operating this electronic marvel would take some effort on my part. After about two weeks on the island, Kristyna had to return to the Czech Republic to get ready for an exam she intended to take. By that time, we had grown quite close and I had almost come to look at her like a daughter. She had been a great help to me and I knew I would miss her presence after she departed. The time we spent together went by quickly, and then the day she was to depart came and I was left alone on the island to fend for myself.

Slowly, I was getting the hang of using the new laptop and this little device had once again put me in touch with the rest of the world. There was a steady stream of e-mails to occupy my time and now and then, I took a walk to take in the beautiful scenery of this enchanting island. Thanks to an amazing invention called Skype, I could now talk to people all over the world free of charge on my computer. In a short time, I was again in touch with Batya and she sent me some scientific information about the pineal gland, which she said I should go over.

For years, I had been trying to find out how this oil worked its magic, but with little success. The research showed that when THC enters the body, it causes a build-up of a fat molecule called ceramide. When ceramide comes into contact with cancer cells, it causes programmed cell death but does no harm to healthy cells. I really didn't have a problem with this explanation with regard to cancer, but how was this oil working all these miracles on other conditions? After poring over research for years, we had never been able to come up with a rational explanation as to why the oil worked the way it did. Now with Batya's new information about the pineal gland and the melatonin it produces, it all started to make sense.

When cannabinoids enter the body, they are absorbed by the CB1 and CB2 receptors of our endocannabinoid system. This natural system we all have in our bodies is there to help provide balance, and protects us from inflammation and other problems associated with our health. When diseases and exposure to such things as radiation and other harmful substances cause problems, often our bodies cannot produce enough natural cannabinoids to deal with the issue, so it is necessary to give our endocannabinoid system a boost by using cannabinoids, which medicinal strains of the hemp plant can provide. When THC and other cannabinoids reach the pineal gland, they de-calcify this gland and melatonin levels can go up thousands of times. Melatonin is the greatest anti-oxidant known to man and people suffering from many medical conditions often have low melatonin levels.

I think this increase in melatonin and the improved function of the pineal gland has much to do with the effectiveness of this medication in treating many conditions successfully. The oil also works with our bodies in many other ways to promote healing, but I think this may be one of the most important of all. If the pineal gland is not in a healthy state, it can affect how we perceive what is going on around us, and I think this is one of the major causes of conditions such as schizophrenia. After receiving various reports from many people who had used the oil to treat mental issues, I believe decalcifying the pineal gland and improving its function may indeed give many patients suffering from mental disturbances and other serious conditions a chance to have a normal life again.

I'm no doctor and I don't have a bunch of letters after my name, nor as yet do I have the facilities and resources required to prove my opinions. Everything I am telling people about the effectiveness of this medication in the treatment of such conditions is from reports that I have viewed or from direct contact with the patients themselves. If you or someone you care about is suffering from a condition like bipolar disorder or other mental issues, why not try the oil and get off all those chemicals that are doing your body harm? I want to thank Batya for all the research she has done and for helping me find a possible explanation to a problem that had been nagging at me for a very long time. Well done, dear, your input has been of great value and none of us will forget the important role you played.

After a few weeks on Hvar, I was asked to come to the Croatian capital of Zagreb to help treat a lady who was suffering from lung cancer. The patient took the oil treatment and responded well, although it did take a lot of convincing on my part to keep her away from the medical system, which at the time wished to give her chemo. It has been known for many years that chemotherapy is ineffective in the treatment of cancers such as this woman was suffering with, but doctors blindly continue to use this poison with no regard to the damage it is doing to their patients.

When the day arrived that I could once again re-enter the EU, Jiri Vlk drove his car to Zagreb to pick me up and we then returned to Prague. In the short time I had spent in the Czech Republic, I had made many friends and I felt very comfortable in this country. After my forced absence, it was really great to be back in familiar surroundings with people I knew and trusted, who could help guide my activities in the future.

The first day after my return, I spoke at the Czech Parliament. What I said about the healing power of this natural medication and why it must be used in medicine was given a warm reception by the audience, but it did not seem to create the interest I had hoped for in government circles. After I finished speaking, I went back to Olomouc with Jindrich and Milan to plan some new strategies that might get their attention. I still cannot understand how so many well-educated people could treat an issue of this magnitude so lightly. Just going on the Internet told me how fast information about the use of this medicine was spreading. Did those in positions of authority not realize the situation they were putting themselves in by not acting to help their citizens? I must admit at the time their behavior truly had me baffled, but I have since come to have a better understanding of their goals.

Even though I had only been in Europe for a short time, many more people started contacting me about doing seminars. Of course, most of those who got in touch with me had little or no experience in staging such events and funding was always an issue. Up until January 2012, I have received about 10,000 dollars in donations from people who were trying to help me achieve my aims. This amount, along with the small income that's sent from Canada each month, has done little more than keep me alive, leaving nothing extra I could put towards staging seminars.

You would think a cause like this would be receiving backing from philanthropists and others in control of the capital required to move this medicine into mainstream use. Even though what I am doing is now very well known, no one with the necessary backing has ever stepped forward to provide assistance. I have always found it very hard to understand why this issue never had the funding put behind it that it truly deserved. Do foundations and philanthropists like Bill Gates have no knowledge of what I have been doing, or do they have a different plan in mind? From the time most of these foundations are formed, big money interests are in control and they have the say as to where the funding that is available is put to use. Are many of these individuals who are in control of foundations, not the same people who are openly talking about depopulating the planet? Looked at in this way, why would they want to help bring a medicine to the people that could heal their diseases when their real agenda appears to have the goal of eliminating most of us? I cannot even pretend to understand the actions or thinking of such individuals. What right could they possibly have to depopulate this earth? Are they planning this because God has spoken to them and expressed his approval, or are they simply evil?

Back in the 1940s, Hitler depopulated vast numbers of ethnic groups he thought to be undesirable with the use of violence and death camps. If those who are pushing for depopulation today are successful, the crimes that were committed by The Third Reich would pale by comparison. I don't know how those who are planning our destruction feel about what they are trying to accomplish, but I for one would not want to try living with myself knowing I was involved with the greatest mass genocide that was ever attempted in human history. In reality, those who wish to see our demise should not have so much money and power at their disposal. Perhaps, if this were so, it would be a much better world to live in for us all. The wants and needs of a few overly rich banking families and others with twisted agendas do not overrule the wellbeing of 6.8 billion suffering people. In time, they may come to realize the error of their ways but, as yet, nothing has changed.

Before I left the Czech Republic to go to Croatia, my son also sent me a copy of this huge bond that is in my name. Jindrich had copies of it made so he could show it to lawyers he knew in the hope that they could tell us if this bond was indeed real. I also put copies of it in the hands of lawyers in Croatia when I was there to try to find out the same. The lawyers in both the Czech Republic and Croatia said that from what they could find out, the bond appeared to be real, but they had no idea how it could be activated. Back in

Canada, other holders of similar bonds were also unsuccessfully trying to find out how they could access funding from these documents. Up until the present, I'm still not sure if this bond actually carries any real weight, but from what I have seen, I have my doubts. If someone ever offers to supply one to you, I would think twice before investing any amount of money, for in my opinion the sale of such bonds could very well be just another scam.

The bond I have in my name is signed by Timothy Geithner, who was the president of the Federal Reserve Bank in New York, when this bond was issued. He is now Secretary of the Treasury in the U.S., and from what I can gather; many seem to think he is little more than a bagman for the Rothschild banking concerns. If all this is true, then I feel that it is unrealistic to expect funding from these sources. Since no doubt big money concerns such as the Rothschild's and others must have vast holdings in the pharmaceutical industry as well. In the future, this medication could put most if not all of these companies out of business, so I strongly doubt there would be much of a possibility that the ruling elite would provide the funding for me to accomplish this. In addition, if there really were powerful individuals who wanted me to succeed, why would they not make some of the funding from this bond easier for me to access, so I could get on with the task? Since none of this has ever occurred, I can only surmise that this bond is probably not worth the paper it is written on.

On April 15, 2010, I received word that my dear friend and mentor Jack Herer had passed away. Like so many others who knew the Emperor of Hemp personally, I was totally devastated by his passing. At the time, I tried to write a short piece about Jack to put up on the Internet, but the emotion was just too great and I could not complete the task. Jack was a man who can only be described as being one of a kind. Because of his exploits, he had legions of followers and many admirers. For decades, Jack had been the heart and soul of the hemp movement and now he was no longer with us to provide guidance. Even though I was grieving over Jack's death, I couldn't help but wonder about the events that had led up to his passing.

Since I have been somewhat out of touch over here in Europe, my knowledge about what happened to Jack is quite sketchy. Sadly, I do know Jack was taken off the oil and a court order was put in place, which prevented his wife Jeannie from entering his hospital room. Jack's wife is one of the nicest people I have ever had the pleasure of speaking with. Who would put a court order in place that prevented her from visiting her husband, and for what reason would they do such a thing? In addition, there is the question as to why Jack was taken off the oil when all the doctors and everyone else had seen how much this medication was helping him?

What was done to Jack Herer and his wife defies comprehension and I feel we all need to know what really transpired. It is my hope the hemp movement will not rest until we find out who was responsible. If Jack had been given free access to the oil, there's a very good chance he could still be with us today. Instead, the system filled him full of chemicals and denied his loving wife the right to even visit him. Are we to allow those responsible for what went on here to just walk away as if nothing had ever happened? The greatest leader the hemp movement has ever seen was taken from us under very strange circumstances. I, for one, would like to have some answers as to why this was allowed to occur and I hope others in the movement feel the same.

A few days after Jack had passed away, I was watching his graveside service on the Internet. Steve Hager stepped forward and told those present that Jack had wanted me to take his place if something ever happened to him. I had told Steve in the past that I had no interest in trying to replace Jack. I was already very busy on the medical front and I didn't think I had the time to take on Jack's role as well. Still, after Steve had made Jack's wishes known, there was no going back, and by all appearances, I was now the new leader of the movement. Jack had been a person I truly looked up to and, under the circumstances, the least I could do is try to honor his wishes. Maybe to some in the movement I was still an unknown but in the near future, they would come to find out why Jack had chosen me as his replacement. Up until I had come along, Jack had been the only fire-breathing dragon in the movement. In my opinion, most of the other activists were doing little more than just blowing smoke rings and their efforts were not having the desired impact. Now that Jack was gone, I hoped to bring the same passion he had shown to those in favor of the complete legalization of this plant. What Jack had begun, I intended to finish, and what greater cause could be dropped into the lap of someone such as myself? Now the only question remaining was how long it would take me to accomplish the goal Jack had set for me. Only time would tell.

CHAPTER 19

MEDICINE OR MENACE

Thanks to the seeds I had brought back from Amsterdam, there was now much more suitable material available to produce the medicine in the Czech Republic. Before I arrived, many people were growing decent sativa varieties, which for the most part I was unable to use. Back in Canada, indica varieties were very easy to find, but in Europe there was very little material from strong medicinal indica's available from which I could produce this medication properly. As more and more growers began to grow the proper varieties, it became much less frustrating for us to find the material that was required. Jindrich and Milan soon had many people under treatment in the Czech Republic with oil produced from good medicinal indica's and the patients were really responding well. Overall, it can only be said they were making very good progress and I was quite satisfied with the results I was observing.

It had been over eight months since I had done the speaking tour with Dr. Hanus, but Melissa Balin never made the footage she had promised available. I contacted her and asked why she had not done so. She then tried to tell me that it had not been sent because Jindrich and Milan owed her money. What she was saying was simply a fabrication. Since her arrival was planned on such short notice, all Jindrich did was offer to help her find some extra work while she was there. Jindrich had never met her before the tour and after he saw how she handled herself, he had realized she would not fit in with what those he knew had in mind. So, from my perspective, I think that it would be more accurate to say Melissa herself was responsible for not getting other work during her three-week stay in the Czech Republic, not Bayer & Romsy. None of us were paid to do the tour, only our expenses were to be covered. If I knew she had expected to bring a big pile of money home, I would never have brought her on the tour in the first place. During her stay in the Czech Republic, I gave this woman about 700 euros out of my own pocket and Jindrich and Milan provided everything she needed. Considering the money which was spent on her, it would have been much cheaper to hire a local filmmaker to shoot the seminars, plus, we would have had processed footage at our disposal immediately.

In my time, I have heard many lame excuses and run across untold numbers of con-artists. But to me what she was trying to pull was simply unbelievable. She withheld footage that could have helped the Czech people understand what this medicine is all about. Instead of sending the footage, as she should have, Melissa had chosen to sit on it in the hope that she would receive financial gain. I contacted her back and voiced my disgust, telling her that I do not ever want to hear from her again. It amazes me that some people can be so small and self-centered. Still, her behavior was really not that unusual, considering the fact that I had run across so many others with warped agendas and schemes that were no better than hers.

At least in other areas things were going much better. I was now receiving a constant barrage of e-mails that were very positive in nature. It's a nice feeling to be contacted by people I had never met, telling me that thanks to our information they had been able to treat their cancer or other serious medical conditions successfully. E-mails like this did not put food on the table or money in my pocket, but they did increase my motivation by knowing that so many were being helped everywhere. No longer was this just something that happened in rural Nova Scotia. The issue of the medicinal use of this oil now had the attention of the world.

Of course, with all this notoriety regarding the oil there also came many problems. Everywhere people were trying to produce and market oil to those in need of treatment. All this would be well and good if everyone were honest and cared about those they were supplying. Yet, all too often, this was not the case. Since many of those who were now providing the oil had been drug dealers in the past, their only interest revolved around making as much money as possible. Many patients had trouble finding the right starting material or could not produce this medication themselves, so they had to turn to local suppliers. It is very easy to sell oil to someone who knows nothing about how it was produced and is naive about the subject. Would some of those who were supplying this medication to unsuspecting patients mix in lower-grade oil so they could turn a bigger profit? You bet your life they would.

I am not trying to say everyone involved in providing oil was behaving in the same manner. Surely, vast numbers of these suppliers really were producing high-grade medicinal oils and they did care about the patients' well-being. But sadly, the same cannot be said for others. Judging by the number of complaints I received, it was more than obvious that many patients were simply being scammed. On a more ominous note, some had even passed away because they had been sold substandard oil, which reduced their chance of survival. As if this situation was not already bad enough, now it seemed everybody and their dog was using my name and the term "Phoenix Tears" to help sell their products. Some of the claims I came across were simply outrageous and showed many would stoop to any level to deceive the public. There were even those who claimed I was directly involved with their operations and that they were in contact with me often. Saying such things gave customers more confidence in the oil they were purchasing, but it sent a great many headaches my way.

Often I received e-mails from patients telling me that they had bought my oil from someone and it didn't work or have the same effects as those I had described on our website. I then had the unpleasant task of informing them that they had not purchased my oil and they had probably been deceived and robbed. In some cases, people borrowed thousands of dollars or had exhausted their savings and they could ill afford to lose this money. What was going on did make me feel somewhat responsible but, in truth, I had no involvement with these suppliers and I have never received a red cent from any of them. The paperwork had been put in place to protect the term "Phoenix Tears" from being used by others. No one could use this term legally but that did not prevent a great number from doing so. Since there were so many, it was impossible for me to put a stop to them all. Right on our website, I had told people about this situation and warned them that, at present, if they wanted the real thing, it's best to produce their own medication. No quality control or standards were yet in place, so how could the public possibly know what they were purchasing?

I often had to explain to those who contacted me looking for a supplier that it was not possible for me to send them on to anyone. For me to do this, I would have to meet these suppliers personally and know exactly what they were supplying. As a result of the criminal record I had been given for helping people with their medical problems, I could not even enter the US and there was always the issue of no funding to allow me to travel. So how could I possibly be aware of what quality the oil is, which suppliers were producing in other countries? In addition, those who were producing oil often used their own methods and did not follow our instructions, so I really had no idea what they were providing.

At present, some researchers are making claims, which I feel could mislead the public. These claims concern a non-psychoactive compound called CBD, which hemp oil contains in amounts that vary depending on the variety, from which the oil was produced. Some are implying that oils with high levels of this compound could be effective in the treatment of cancer and it appears their aim is to take away the high, which this medication can produce until the patient becomes accustomed to its use. What they are talking about is yet to be proven and if I had an internal cancer, I would not even consider taking such an oil. From my perspective, if the oil cannot produce the high, which I believe is medicinally beneficial, then the odds are it will probably not be nearly as effective in the treatment of patients with serious conditions.

I am not saying that this research is not valid, but often suppliers will make claims just so they can sell what they are providing. From my point of view, oils with high CBD content should not be tested on patients with serious internal cancers. Instead, I think it would be much safer to determine their healing abilities on conditions such as skin cancer and if they prove to be effective, they could then be used internally. Since the oil I have been producing has already proven itself, I don't think patients should gamble with their lives by taking oils that do not have the same qualities. Complicating things to death is a trait the human race is well known for, but I like to keep things simple, so the public can understand. If it works, it works, so why tamper with perfection, until what some are saying about other aspects of this plant's healing abilities has been proven to be true?

Ingesting any given oil should be more about the patient's own personal preferences in regard to its effects. No two of us have the same body chemistry, therefore an oil I may like the effects of, you may not. Medicinal oils from different varieties should be made available for the patient to try, then they would be able to select the ones that best suit their requirements. If this were done properly, in most cases, there would be no need for a doctor to even play a role. After all, who would know better than the patients themselves about what they feel comfortable in taking? Put simply, no doctor has this knowledge, so I feel that the patient should be left to decide for themselves how quickly the oil is taken and what type of oil they choose to ingest. As long as the oil they are using has the required medicinal benefits for their conditions, the patient is then in control of their own treatment.

I much prefer that patients try to follow the protocol I have developed for best results, but some with a low tolerance for this substance may find they need to ingest this medication more slowly. I always tell those who are planning to start ingesting the oil that it does not work unless it is in them, but it is really up to the patient how quickly this takes place. To anyone with a life-threatening medical problem, I think it's only good advice to ingest the oil as quickly as possible to bring their condition under control. I have encountered some that were considered terminal by the medical system, who took this medication more slowly, yet, quite often, they still achieved good results. If I was suffering from something like terminal cancer and I had an effective harmless treatment to combat the disease such as this oil, I would probably try to take the treatment in record time because I know it would increase my chance of surviving. In time, the public will come to realize how safe this medication is to use, and when that occurs, I expect vast numbers will then take much more interest in it.

When I brought this to everyone's attention, I believed that most would look at producing this natural medication as a basic right, which we all deserve. Now there are many who feel that my vision of what should transpire is the only sensible way to supply everyone's need for this medication in the cheapest and fastest way possible. Unbelievably, it seems that drug companies still think that they deserve a piece of the pie and some are making ready to produce hemp medicines on a large scale. Since those who control these companies already have governments in their back pocket, it is very unlikely that they will meet much opposition. All this will be just great for the profit margins of these companies, but we will be the ones paying through the nose for it. In addition, I expect governments will try to continue to prevent the ordinary person from growing and producing their own.

I am the guy who brought this discovery out and having drug companies producing this medication is not what I had in mind. I did not do all this to help these companies make huge profits; instead, it has always been my goal to do something, which would be of great benefit to us all. When it comes to the growing and medicinal use of the hemp plant, I believe in only one thing, total freedom, and, in the end, that is what we will have.

Unfortunately, it is not only the drug companies which are trying to horn in on the action. Now there are many others who seem to think they can make their fortune off the information I supplied as well. I have been contacted by a good number of individuals and organizations, trying to enlist my support to promote their products. Some have even made generous offers of shares in their companies, if I was willing to work with them. But I didn't care for the direction they were planning to take, and to me it appeared they were simply about the money which could be made, so I decided to stay on my original path.

It is true that I may be from the backwoods of Nova Scotia, but still I am nobody's fool. Now that I am becoming better known if one of these organizations were successful in having me join their ranks, they could then use my name to promote their products, which I am sure would do much to boost sales, but what about the quality and price of the goods they intend to manufacture? It has taken many years, but the public have finally come to put a lot of trust in my name and I would never allow that trust to be destroyed by some fly-by-night company that is trying to cash in.

I have no problem with others producing this medication and if they manufacture a quality product, it will make its own reputation with no need for my involvement. We supplied the instructions so everyone could produce what many are now calling the Rick Simpson Oil and often people simply refer to it as being the RSO, but, in reality, I have no control over the quality of medications and products that others are manufacturing. Since I am the real Rick Simpson and I have no direct involvement with others in this field, many are simply producing medications using their own methods, yet they still call it the RSO. I looked at this wonderful medication as being a gift to mankind, but sadly many others look at it as a great way to fatten their bank accounts.

The corporate world we have become accustomed to has given many the wrong idea and people have to get their heads out of all this rubbish about making huge profits off those with medical problems. It was thinking like this that got us in the situation we are in today, so I believe it is about time that we took a more realistic approach. If we are to progress, the average person must be given the right, if they so choose, to produce this medication themselves, or to have someone else supply their needs at a reasonable cost. The days of making hundreds or even thousands of times more than medications cost to produce are over. No doubt, drug companies and others will try to sell their medicinal hemp products and those who have government connections will probably not be bothered, but most of us will not be able to afford the medication we require because the drug companies and others who are supplying the oil will charge such enormous prices. .

In the end, I expect that the public will simply ignore the absurd laws against hemp's medicinal use and the governments that try to keep such laws in place. No one is going to pay huge amounts of money for something they can grow and produce themselves and, in a rational world, why should they? Since most will not be able to acquire this medicine due to the prices suppliers will charge, their only option will be to supply themselves. In a short time, almost everyone will be using the oil, so in the future the demand for this substance will be unbelievable. The only way to deal with this in a sensible manner is to give everyone the right to supply themselves. If governments try to do otherwise, they would have to turn the whole planet into a prison. Even if our governments were to try such a thing, I think that, realistically, their own citizens would see that they were overthrown long before they could accomplish the task. As you can see, governments and others who want to continue prohibiting hemp medicine's use are playing a fool's game that could, in the end, put their heads in a noose from which there will be no escape.

If the day ever comes when I have the time and freedom to do so, I would like to set up my own breeding program. I have sampled many varieties of hemp in the countries, which I have visited. Even though quite a few of these varieties are very well known, I have never found anything that matched the potency of some of the different types of hemp, which I was growing back in Canada. I'm not saying this because I'm trying to convince the public that I am the best hemp grower on the planet, or that seed companies do not already produce good medicinal strains. Instead, I am making these statements because some of the strains I perfected to produce the oil were so strong it was truly unbelievable.

Some varieties were so potent when I tested them that all I had to take was two puffs from a joint and it was bedtime. This was the effect I encountered from smoking very small quantities of the bud material, so you can imagine the sedative effect such varieties would produce when turned into a concentrated oil. In addition, I often found that many of the oils I supplied had a pleasant euphoric effect, which most patients found desirable for their treatment. Of course, this combination was exactly what I was looking for to produce this medication and I went out of my way even when purchasing the material from others to find these qualities.

Truly, seed companies do produce some varieties that have wonderful medicinal properties, but I think small-time breeders can often produce varieties that are somewhat more powerful. To anyone who may have such seeds at their disposal, it would be of great benefit if they could supply a few to me, so I would not have to waste time working with varieties that are less potent. Over time, I would like to breed and cross these varieties, then study their medicinal qualities by testing them on both myself and other patients with different conditions. One of the biggest problems medicinal users have today is that we are never sure what we will get when we order seeds. By doing as I am suggesting, patients would then know what they are getting and once these strains were stabilized, we could then supply them to those who wish to grow their own for medicinal purposes.

I am not talking about some big money making operation, which would be turning huge profits, since I would make sure the seeds would be supplied as cheaply as possible. If you or someone you know could help out, it would be greatly appreciated. At present, I am still traveling from country to country, but, in the near future, I hope to get a breeding program underway. So if you could help supply what is needed, please send the seeds with a brief description of what you have observed about this variety's effects to my son, so he can then forward them on to me. His address is as follows: Mike Simpson, 344 Little Forks Rd., GD, Springhill, Nova Scotia, Canada BOM1XO. Please do not send low-quality seeds, thinking you are pulling a joke; what I am trying to do is very serious and I really do not have time for nonsense.

Jack Herer was the first to connect my name with this medicine when he started calling it the Rick Simpson Oil, and soon almost everyone began referring to it as the RSO. By attaching my name, it did seem to make many realize there was something special about this oil. If you were trying to treat a serious condition, only the best would do, and soon the RSO was recognized to be just that. Still there was a downside to my name being involved and there was no shortage of people who were willing to take advantage. Even to this day, I still receive requests for me to supply medication but under the circumstances I am now living, such things are impossible. Given the absurd laws, which have been put in place all over the planet against the use of this medication, how could I be expected to provide anyone with oil? If I were caught trying to do so in a foreign country, I would be arrested and deported immediately. My mission was simply to tell people how they could help themselves and obviously, I am in no position as yet to render any further assistance until some government allows me to do so.

I am not the one who makes these laws and back in Canada, I paid them little heed since I was well aware that they made no sense. Although I am well versed in the production of this medication, for me to do so in foreign countries would bring nothing but trouble. Even though at present I am not in a position to supply this medication, what I am doing is still of great importance to the cause and I think most would agree it would be best for all concerned if I were to remain free. I don't mind fighting for our rights, but I am only one man, and I need as many people as possible behind this issue.

Isn't it time for the public to become a bit more involved with their own health and well-being? Why don't people go to their politicians and doctors demanding that something be done? Are they really that afraid of those whose salaries they are paying? Why does the public allow this to go on? Could it be that they perceive the actions of those in authority as being beyond their control? If so, I think it is time they realized who is supposed to be working for who. It is the sworn duty of those we employ as public servants to act in the public's best interests, but, thus far, this has not occurred, so it is up to all of us to demand our rights.

Indeed, it can only be said that trying to work with the public does have its pitfalls. No matter what you do, some people will refuse to listen to good advice. Those with such a mindset will often succumb to conditions that could have been cured or controlled if only they had taken the time to inform themselves about their situation. Many oil suppliers who are trying to help others with their medical problems have contacted me in frustration over the behavior of some of their patients, but unfortunately little can be done if the patients refuse to educate themselves and listen to reason. In the past, that is why I have refused to provide oil to anyone currently taking chemo and radiation or those who are planning to do so.

If they can't take the time to understand what the medical system is trying to do to them, what purpose would be served by driving myself crazy, trying to help people with such self-destructive thinking? There's no question the oil would give patients who are taking chemo or radiation a better chance to survive, but why should I try to help those who take such things, when I know what they are doing can greatly reduce their chance of survival? To me, supplying oil to someone that is willing to take these dangerous treatments would be about the same as trying to give it to someone who is going to commit suicide. Adults are old enough to make their own decisions; if they wanted to take a sensible medication to treat their cancer, then I was at their disposal. If they refused to listen to reason, they were still quite free to allow the medical system to have their way with them. My way of doing things may seem cruel to some, but the oil was so precious I felt it shouldn't be wasted, and if you or anyone else had been in my position, I expect you would have done it no differently.

Unlike humans who are supposed to have reasoning abilities, animals on the other hand, do have an excuse. They have no grasp of the way in which we communicate and are not expected to have a great deal of understanding. In addition, in many cases, I'm sad to say they can also be much more cooperative and pleasant to deal with. Quite often, I receive e-mails from people who treated their pets that had been suffering from different conditions, such as cancer. The results many have achieved are astounding. Frequently, animals such as dogs were being cured of what had been deemed incurable cancer in a matter of days.

To some, animals are of little importance, but to people who have become deeply attached to their pets, the loss of such an animal can have a devastating effect on their lives. Indeed, the passing of such a creature often brings sorrow to the whole family that can linger on for quite some time. Needless to say, we now have the means at our disposal that will allow us to treat our own animals with a natural, harmless and effective medication. The veterinarians may be opposed to the use of this oil for monetary reasons much like many human doctors. Still, should their wants and needs overrule our right to treat these animals that we have grown to love?

From what I have seen, animals that become sick are treated no better than their human counterparts. In many cases, they are given the same poison and chemical trash that is in use to treat humans. If I had a pet and it became sick, I know what I would be doing and I hope those that care about the well-being of their animals will develop the common sense to do the same. No one has the right to tell us that we cannot treat our own pets and livestock, especially when we know what is best for them, so this is just another reason for us to unite and bring these restrictions to an end.

In 2010 and 2011, more and more information was coming out on the Internet every day. People like Shona Banda, Dennis Hill, David Triplett, and many others were starting to put out some very compelling videos on Youtube, vividly describing what the oil had done for them. Many other videos of interest were also put up on Youtube by different individuals, who used names like Vitamin Cannabis and Cancer Gate etc. to spread the word. I really enjoyed watching many of these clips and I feel individuals like Captain Cannabis are doing a wonderful job. It was great to see all this evidence accumulating so rapidly, provided by those who were willing to come forward and explain their experiences with this medication to the public. In 2011, the Internet literally exploded with information concerning this issue, which indicated to me that finally we had won. In no time, a great deal about the true medicinal values of this plant will be known worldwide and once this occurs, there will be no stopping the medicinal use of cannabis hemp.

I don't want to give anyone the impression that I feel I have been fighting this battle completely alone. I found that statements in support of the use of this medicine that were put out by researchers like Raphael Mechoulam, Lumir Hanus, Robert Melamede, and others who are well known in this field have been priceless to me. I have talked with Bob Melamede extensively about the use of this medication and I really enjoyed some of the clips he has put up on Youtube. Bob expresses himself very well on this subject, but the company he is involved with, Cannabis Science, appears to be taking a more corporate approach, to the distribution of this medication. I have no involvement with Cannabis Science and if they choose to do so, it's their choice. Instead, I am much more interested in seeing that we all have the right to produce our own medication, so it seems we have two different goals in mind. I will not become involved in anything that is simply just about making money or has a corporate smell about it, since that is what got us into this mess in the first place. If the day comes that I find a group, which I feel I can work with, it will be announced on our website, so the public will be aware that I am connected to these individuals, but, as yet, nothing like this has transpired.

Luckily for us all, there are also many others who have played invaluable roles in seeing that good overcomes evil. One does not have to become a scientist to be of great value to this cause. Janet Sweeney has put together the Phoenix Tears Foundation, which at present is based in Colorado. At this time, the foundation is still in its infancy but I am sure that in the near future, they will receive much more support. In addition, Janet has successfully helped many people with their medical conditions and thus far she has been a great ambassador for the cause. I am not directly linked to the foundation, but we have communicated with each other often. So all I can do is hope that she will be able to guide the foundation properly as it gathers more support.

The list of people who have played a hand in helping to make what I am doing known to all is almost endless. The many Internet and radio interviews I have done, plus the articles that have been published about me, have increased public awareness to a much higher level. Shows like "Down the Rabbit Hole," hosted by Paula Gloria, have done much to spread our information in the northeastern United States and elsewhere. Internet and radio show personalities like Max Igan, David Icke, James Martinez, Vinnie Eastwood and many others have drawn a lot of attention to the use of this medication on their websites and broadcasts. Judging by the response from what they have done, I think their input has been invaluable to this cause and I cannot help but consider them all to be very brave for the role they have played.

After grasping the importance of what these individuals are expounding, the public can then make much more informed decisions as to how they should address their health issues. The work that these people are doing is saving many lives and helping vast numbers with conditions they had thought to be hopeless. The knowledge gained by listening to what these individuals and many others have to say on this subject drives home the fact that unless something is done quickly to change things, our world is in a great deal of trouble and that possibly we should all think twice before we follow the doctor's orders.

When you apply common sense, you see that what doctors and the medical system have been providing is not medicine. If you were to ask a ten-year-old if they thought radiation, chemicals, and poison were good for them, instantly they would reply, "No!" Now ask your doctor the same question and usually you will be told that the use of these dangerous substances and treatments are necessary to treat you effectively. If a child has more common sense and medical knowledge than a doctor, I think you will all have to agree that our medical system needs a bit of work. Since saving lives and easing suffering is their stated goal, one would think they should see the error of their ways. As yet, for the most part, this does not seem to be the case, but with a little help from our friend the hemp plant and some public outcry, I'm sure doctors will soon come around.

For many decades, doctors and researchers have been inoculating tumors in test animals with cannabinoids in their laboratories. Their results showed that this is a very effective method in the treatment of cancer, yet they refuse to do the same to a human. The medical system is supposed to be trying to save lives and for someone who is dying from cancer, what would they have to lose? To me, there is no rational excuse as to why this has not been done and I think it highlights just how pathetic our medical system has become. Do doctors or even we ourselves actually need approval from what I and many others consider to be criminal organizations, like the FDA, to save someone's life with a substance which has already proven itself to work in countless cases and conditions? I really don't think so.

Often people will try to tell you doctors have no choice other than to follow the status quo in their profession even if the treatments they provide are dangerous and ineffective. Such statements are completely idiotic. From my own experience, I know that it is very hard for any one man to go against the system, but there is strength in numbers. The first priority of any doctor must be the well-being of those they are treating and to follow their own Hippocratic Oath. So why do doctors not get together and put a halt to using substances and treatments that are obviously doing so much harm? I really don't feel that even doctors who will prescribe hemp to treat their patients are doing all they can, for if they were, they would band together and expose what others in their profession are really doing. All they have to do is follow their own Hippocratic Oath and refuse to do any further damage to their patients. The only reasons I can see as to why this has never occurred are pure greed, ignorance, either pretended or otherwise, and cowardice. Would it really be asking too much for us to expect medical professionals that have our lives in their hands to do what is right for their patients? If not, then in reality it can only be said that we do not even have a real medical system.

For quite some time, I have been telling people to read Jack Herer's book, "The Emperor Wears No Clothes." Finally, in early 2011 I had the chance to view the new 12th edition, which was supposed to contain information about me and this medicine. Even before I opened it, I knew there was something badly wrong. The book had many less pages than the 11th edition and although I did not have time to go over it properly, before the book's owner had to leave, I was left with the impression that Jack's book had been dramatically altered and I knew that if Jack was still with us, he would not be happy. Not only had the book been drastically shortened, I was also told by some who knew Jack that it now contained articles which Jack would never have allowed. In addition, all the information I had sent to Jack for the 12th edition was also missing.

It wasn't so much the fact that what I had written was ignored that bothered me, it was the disrespect I felt Jack had been shown by the new editors of his manuscript, which got my attention. At least there are vast numbers of the old editions still around that people can read to get the message Jack was really sending. In the future, if I have the money and the opportunity presents itself, I would like to obtain the rights to Jack's book, so I can reproduce the original manuscript. In addition, I plan to add the chapter which Jack had requested from me. This is what my friend and mentor had wanted, and, if possible, I will see that his wishes are fulfilled.

After supplying oil for some time, I came to the realization that not all of us were thinking on the same level. It seemed that on average about 10% of those I had dealt with could grasp what I was telling them very easily. Somewhere around 40% more also picked up what I was saying if I spent some extra time explaining it more thoroughly to them. Still, no matter how I approached it, the other 50% seemed to lack the capacity to understand and showed no interest.

To many, finding the truth in what I was telling them was no more difficult than adding two and two. But others, it seemed, were unable to think clearly for themselves after receiving their programming from the system. I am truly sorry for those who are trapped in such a state. If I lacked the ability to think rationally, I would feel life had little to offer. When one considers this medicine can be easily produced and is safe and simple to use, it defies comprehension that something of this importance could be ignored. Unfortunately, this does make the fact quite clear that we as a species still have a lot to learn. In reality, it's all about how we are brought up, what we see around us and the way in which we are educated. Such things determine our perception of what we deem to be the truth. If we are given false information and are not educated properly, sadly many of us will lack the ability to reject the misguided nonsense we were fed.

All too often in regard to our health, we allow others to make the decisions for us. Then we willingly take dangerous treatments along with the chemicals and poisons we have been prescribed, thinking such things may be of assistance. Sadly, in most instances, they are not and these so-called treatments and medications often have a very harmful effect on our bodies. The human body is mostly water. If we allow the water within us to become polluted with chemicals and poisons, how can we possibly expect to remain healthy? I am a power engineer by trade and I well understand the detrimental effects such things as chemicals and improper pH levels can have on piping and equipment. The same holds true about the poisonous chemicals we ingest as medications and the pH of our own bodies. With regard to our health and wellbeing, its importance cannot be overstated. Look what happens to fish when the water they live in becomes polluted and is not in the proper pH range, which these creatures require. Do you really think we are any different? An improper pH of soil or other growing media has very adverse effects on plant life. Plant, human or otherwise, we all need to have the right pH balance that allows us to heal properly and maintain a state of vibrant good health. All people have to do is identify what is causing them harm and then do their best to avoid any further damage. Unfortunately for us all, the world we presently inhabit has dangers to our well-being lurking everywhere and some of them are very well disguised.

Are the pills the doctor has given us really harmless to consume and are the treatments they prescribe even safe? Is the food we already know to contain preservatives, pesticides, antibiotics, growth hormones, etc. safe to eat? If you really take the time to look into it and find out for yourself, I am sure you will be very disturbed by the results. If we don't use extracts from the hemp plant to keep our bodies detoxified, in time, these horrible substances will cause untold damage to our overall health. Knowing what I now do about hemp, I am in full agreement with Jack Herer when he stated, "I don't know if hemp will save the world, but I do know it's the only thing that can." There is nothing else on the planet that even begins to have the potential to solve our health issues and also the multitude of problems the world in which we live is facing today other than the hemp plant itself.

After being in Europe for almost two years and watching the reaction of governments to this issue, I can only report they have done very little. The impression I'm left with is, yes, they know this plant will be the medicinal wave of the future, but they don't want any changes to the old status quo. Unfortunately, it appears their intention is to continue controlling the medicinal use of hemp through regulations and they would like to see its production left in the hands of the drug companies. Personally, I think these schemes that have been cooked up by our governments and the wealthy to ensure we remain enslaved are madness. I can only hope for the sake of us all that their plans to keep the use of this plant restricted never bear fruit.

Those in control of these big drug firms are often the same families who used their wealth decades ago to have government officials go along with their agendas. Now politicians have become nothing more than mouthpieces for the unelected rich who are really running the show. No matter how you look at it, under these circumstances, in reality, the public has no one to represent them. After what pharmaceutical companies have done in the past to harm us all and keep natural medicines from the public, we would have to be total idiots to allow such companies the right to even produce this medication.

The public seems to look at those who have powerful positions as being the ultimate authority when laws are put in place or decisions are made on our behalf. This is especially true when organizations with grand-sounding titles like the Council on Foreign Relations or the United Nations etc. come into play. Most of these big-sounding titles mean nothing when you consider who is really controlling them. It is abundantly clear that they were not brought into being to help the plight of the human race. Instead, they were formed to do the bidding of the money masters. Sadly in the past, with the aid of governments, we, the public, have become the victims of their policies and deceptions. In my opinion and that of many others, there is no hope for our species unless we can put an end to their manipulation.

To carry on with our journey through life in a sensible way, we must ignore the respect for the system that has been ingrained in us all. The policies of governments and the mega-rich have solved nothing and indeed have cost hundreds of millions, if not billions, their very lives. They have only served to promote the decay of our society and to further enrich individuals and families who were undeserving and already too powerful. Such people do not serve nor have they ever served the public's best interests. The only hope for us all is to find a better way.

In the past, big corporations controlled by the rich elite have scooped up the finest minds on the planet, so their knowledge could be used against us by the wealthy to keep the public under control and to help them accomplish their dream of world domination. This type of thing has been going on for a very long time and sadly, as yet, nothing has been done to rectify the situation. We need to form an organization that represents the public's best interests and is also free of corruption. Once this has been done, they could give individuals who possess skills useful to mankind, everything they need to work with. After all, shouldn't such people be working for the greater good of everyone instead of simply being bought off by the rich to fulfill their dreams of grandeur?

There are brilliant minds in many fields of endeavor, which could help to make our world a better place. All we have to do is motivate them in the right way and use their talents to help solve our current problems. Instead of the wealthy commandeering these individuals to use them against us, such people should be employed and rewarded by those who represent the people. If you want a better world for your children, it's time we rolled up our sleeves and got to work. We are the ones who are truly in control of the path we will take in the future and no longer can we allow our will to be denied.

CHAPTER 20
MASTERS OF OUR OWN FUTURE

After spending all this time in Europe, I can only say it has been quite an adventure. I don't think anyone from North America can even begin to understand the Old World unless they have spent a great deal of time there. It must be a wonderful experience for those who can afford to travel abroad as tourists to drink in the atmosphere and culture of these beautiful countries. I lacked the funds to enjoy Europe like a well-to-do traveler would. Nevertheless, I did find my experiences in all these different countries to be a real education. Being forced to move from country to country every twelve weeks is not a pleasant experience, plus always wondering where my next medication would come from was another downside. But everywhere I went, many friends were made and it was only due to their kindness that I have been able to maintain myself while staying in these strange new lands.

Upon seeing how people live in these foreign countries, I think North America could learn much from the Old World. When the financial collapse everyone is predicting does come, I have little doubt the people of Europe will fare much better than the average person dwelling in the so-called New World. Time-honored customs and the ability to use methods from the past to produce what is needed are still widely practiced in Europe. Luckily, they have not been ignored and put aside as they have been in many other countries.

I have only been directly involved in the treatment of a small number of people since I left Canada. Trying to find the right material to work with often proved to be a real obstacle in many countries I have visited, so there was little more I could do. It would have been impossible to deal with the vast number of patients who contacted me for help personally, but still I did the best I could. I understand the desperation families feel when the life of a loved one is in danger. Still, in the final analysis it would make little difference if I were there or not. My presence has nothing to do with the healing effect this medication produces. Everything depends on the quality of the oil and whether or not the patient ingests a sufficient quantity in the fastest manner possible preferably to cure their diseases or to at least bring their conditions under control.

About half the e-mails we receive concern questions that already have been answered on our website. It would have eased our workload greatly if those who had questions took the time to simply read through the information we had already provided. Many others also contacted us with far-out proposals that amounted to little more than pipe dreams. There may be those who have tried to move forward with such plans but to the best of my knowledge, none of them have achieved success. Often they did not even seem to realize that what they were proposing was still against the law. If any real progress is to be made in these countries, we would need the approval and cooperation of their governments. Without such backing, it would be no different than the nightmare I had already gone through in Canada, so I knew there was nothing to be gained by involving ourselves in schemes of this nature.

Supporters of the use of this medication back in Canada were constantly e-mailing us in an attempt to have me return and continue with my work. They did not seem to understand how much my thoughts about returning home had changed. My past experience there had already plainly shown that the Canadian government would stop at nothing to force people like me to comply with their wishes. Their aim is to simply carry on with their deceptions and try to control the masses by whatever means they deem necessary. Would a rational person want to live in such a country if they had the chance of finding a better life elsewhere?

As yet, I have not been able to find a country where my dreams can be fulfilled but I will carry on my search in the hope that sooner or later I will. Somewhere on this earth, there must be a place where I can find the freedom I desire to continue on with my research without interference. Since this medicine is now gaining recognition everywhere, this may soon come to pass. My experiences with governments thus far have been very disappointing and I have come to view many so-called honorable professions with a great deal of disgust and not without good reason.

I cannot help but wonder why so many individuals who are otherwise quite rational and intelligent would continue to do themselves and the public they are supposed to be serving harm by not acting. Finally, I have come to realize we must all share in the blame for what has taken place. Are we any less guilty than those who most of us perceive to be in control? No, we are not. For if that were true, we would have put a stop to all this long ago. We are being used like puppets by the rich elite to achieve their goal of dominating what is going on worldwide. They have the money, they have the media, and they have the means to accomplish their aims, unless we, the human race, stand up and put a stop to their activities.

We hear all this talk about the New World Order from politicians and others who are stealing our rights and freedoms and the natural resources of our countries. The ruling elite have been successful in putting such people in positions of authority to achieve their goal of controlling our existence. Who is actually behind this New World Order? It's people who are at the very top of our society that have unlimited wealth and power who are trying to bring about this evil scheme.

Families with last names like Rothschild, Rockefeller, Warburg, Carnegie, and many others, who prefer to remain in the background to avoid detection. These are the ones who are trying to bring about this New World Order and they are the same overly powerful names that have brought mankind nothing but misery in the past. Even those many perceive to be royalty like Queen Beatrix of the Netherlands and so-called blue bloods from other nations are deeply involved in this insanity. Are we really supposed to now go passively along with their new plans for us all, when we already know they are designed to bring about our destruction?

Judging by the shape our civilization is in today, we do need a New World Order but not the one the rich elite had in mind. This alternative plan for a New World Order would involve governments worldwide working together for the greater good of everyone and there would be no corruption or manipulation to please big corporations or the wealthy elite. The speed with which we can communicate and travel today is bringing us all much closer together. So indeed it may even be time for a World Government to manage the international affairs of all nations properly. Then any disputes could be handled rationally and there would be no need for bloodshed, unless the country that was causing the problem refused to act sensibly. Such a plan would keep aggressive nations in line and, in a short time, I think we could all learn to live in peace and harmony. Such a plan makes more sense to me than what those who are currently calling for a New World Order have in mind.

For quite some time, the express goal of the ruling elite has been to dramatically lower the population of this planet. Line up over there and they will happily implant a chip or give you a vaccine that possibly could enable them to terminate your existence if you happen to get on their wrong side. If depopulation is truly in order, shouldn't we start by eliminating people who display twisted irrational thinking, such as those who support the New World Order? If this planet was managed properly, there is more than enough to sustain all species and still do little harm to this earth or ourselves. No longer can the public allow themselves to be manipulated by false claims of a looming energy crisis or food shortage when such things can easily be dealt with by simply growing enough hemp to solve the problem.

Tens of thousands of people, unfortunately for the most part children, are dying every day from starvation simply because they are not allowed to grow hemp and eat the seeds from this plant. Why is it always the innocent who must suffer and pay with their lives for the crimes of others and why do we allow this to remain so? This bogus War On Terror and their much-touted War On Drugs must come to an end. It should be more than obvious to us all by now that in reality, the big-time drug dealers are the governments themselves. If this were not so, why are our troops guarding poppy fields in Afghanistan, where around 80% of the world's heroin supply comes from? In addition, was it not an American government agency called the CIA, which for many years imported huge cargo planes full of cocaine into the U.S. from Central and South

America? For governments to pretend they are not involved with the drug trade is idiotic, when there is so much evidence to the contrary.

If investigated, the War on Terror proves to be just more crimes that have been committed by our governments against us and the populations of other nations. If your country happens to have large oil reserves or other items of interest to big money concerns, but your government will not comply with their wishes, the U.S. and their cohorts know how to deal with such a situation. They do this in exactly the way David Icke describes in his lectures. First, they use false flag operations to create an event like the supposed terrorist attack on the World Trade Center in 2001. Then they use the news media to spread propaganda, which scares the public into thinking that something must be done to protect them from this menace.

After the public has been given time to accept the system's version of what transpired in the news media, they are then told that they must give up many of their rights and freedoms so their government can protect them from future attacks. Once this has been accomplished and they have succeeded in convincing the public that who they say was responsible must be dealt with, they are then free to invade foreign countries, which actually had nothing to do with the events in question. Suddenly, the leaders of such countries are labeled terrorists who have weapons of mass destruction at their disposal, or some other such fairy tale.

In the interests of protecting the so-called free world and putting an end to the danger they have told their citizens your leaders have posed, of course they are then obligated to invade your country with the real weapons of mass destruction under the guise of bringing freedom to your nation. To make these invasions easier to accomplish and to do more lasting damage, the invading military forces they have sent do not hesitate to employ the use of weapons that contain depleted uranium, which even the United Nations calls a crime against humanity. With the use of such weapons, they will bring freedom to your country, American-style.

Huge numbers of children are being born badly deformed as a result of expectant mothers being exposed to depleted uranium and other toxins that were released into the environment during the invasions of their countries. No wonder much of the rest of the world now has such disdain for the nations that inflicted these atrocities. Your homeland is now a radioactive chemical wasteland, like much of Iraq, for example, and it is now no longer safe to inhabit for eternity. Many of the soldiers from invading nations who were sent there to conquer have also experienced severe health problems because they too were exposed to these horrible substances. Before going into battle, they were also given shots and vaccines of a dubious nature, which many in the military have said caused them great harm.

From what I have learned, I cannot help but agree; all one has to do is look into what these shots and vaccines contain and I think the vast majority of us would not want such things in our bodies. Individuals like Bill Gates are trying to see that everyone including our children are subjected to the danger, shots and vaccines that are currently in use can pose. Since Mr. Gates has clearly stated that he is in favor of depopulation, I find his plans to have us all vaccinated to be somewhat suspicious. As far as I am concerned, I feel there is no need to be sticking needles in anyone. If I want to protect myself and my family from something such as the flu or other diseases, there is no better way to do it then to simply ingest the essential oil from the hemp plant. At least then, I will know I am taking something that is effective, which will cause no harm.

Do those who produce and employ the use of these vaccines and weapons that cause such harm and mass devastation feel no remorse for their actions and if so, why is this the case? Thus far, it seems they do not, which leads us all to ponder how these individuals could believe they have the right to cause these horrible things to occur and yet feel no guilt. If any of us were responsible for causing such harm, I think most would have a hard time living with themselves. So is it possible that those behind these events are simply deluded control freaks without a conscience? Obviously, they have always been able to get away with such things in the past, but do they think they can go on doing this forever without being brought to justice? From my standpoint, it certainly appears that way, but, in the information age, how much longer can this go on without the public becoming aware of their crimes?

Judging by the studies which are available and the work of people like Dr. Rebecca Carley, the vaccines they are trying to shove down all our throats have done a great deal of harm. So I feel anyone who would even consider allowing the medical system to administer these horrible substances to be badly misinformed. Then there is the issue of all these needless wars that seem to be continuously taking place. Obviously, attacking foreign nations and bombing them back to the Stone Age without just cause could hardly be said to be of benefit to us or those who inhabit these nations.

But under the cloak of propaganda which many in charge of aggressive nations employed, the world was told that this had to be done, because countries like the US and others needed to protect themselves. When they attack other nations, they often say they are mounting a preemptive strike instead of calling it what it really is, an outright invasion. So how could we hold Hitler responsible for starting the Second World War, because when he invaded all those other European countries, was he not doing about the same? In reality, these wars are staged because those in charge of nations like the US, Canada, and the UK etc. simply wanted to steal the natural resources these countries possessed. In addition, this would also allow them to set up military bases there to maintain control. Is this what freedom and democracy in action looks like or could it better be termed as war crimes they have committed against poorer nations that do not have the military might to defend themselves? From my perspective, if these countries are not guilty of outright aggression and war crimes, then we have to re-write the history books because Hitler behaved no differently.

The average North American does not seem to understand why so much of the rest of the world has come to detest them and their unwanted interference in foreign countries. Nor can many of them get their heads around the fact that 9/11 in New York and 7/7 in London were staged events that could never have happened unless those in positions of authority were involved. Would some of those who hold powerful positions in the US, England, and elsewhere go along with such a thing to enable them to get public sentiment behind their planned aggression against another nation? Look into 9/11 and the subsequent invasion of Iraq, then also check out 7/7 and what has recently taken place in Libya. Yes, they would, and indeed they have.

Again, we must ask ourselves who those responsible for this irrational and callous behavior are and what is their motivation? All you have to do is follow the money. It will lead you right to the so-called ruling elite and the bleak future that they have planned for mankind. For a very long time the elite have had their way with us and look at the consequences we must now live with that were caused by their greed and mismanagement of our precious resources.

Two prime examples of the trail of destruction that big business leaves in its wake are the Gulf Oil Spill and the Fukushima nuclear generating station disaster in Japan. What have governments done to inform the public about the danger and why have these disasters been downplayed by those in authority and the news media? Both of these events have had a catastrophic effect on our world and will continue to do so for countless years to come. Since it's a well-known fact that hemp can detoxify the ground it has been planted in, it would only make sense for us to see that it is planted in areas contaminated by radiation where nuclear accidents have occurred.

What a shame these big-money concerns did not approach the production of energy in a sustainable and more logical way. If they had done so, hemp would be growing everywhere and all species, including our own, would have reaped the benefits. In addition, our planet would be in much better condition and a whole lot less toxic. It is a well-known fact that one acre of hemp can produce anywhere between 500 to 1800 gallons of fuel we can burn in our cars or use to heat our homes. When hemp is grown and used to create biomass fuels, there is little to no pollution involved.

When hemp is growing, it takes in CO_2 and releases clean fresh air, then when it is burned as a fuel the CO_2 is released back into the atmosphere. This means we will no longer be adding CO_2 to our environment the way we have been when fossil fuels are burned. Producing fuels from hemp will prevent the Green House effect from becoming worse and climatic changes can be reduced. In addition, we will not be releasing all that sulfur which fossil fuels contain, so acid rain could become a thing of the past.

From what I can gather, ethanol can be produced for fifty cents to a dollar a gallon, so why are we paying many times that amount for gasoline and diesel fuel to power our cars? If we can run our cars on ethanol, why can we not also use it to provide the energy needed to run our power generating stations? The standard argument from today's energy providers is that it would use up too much of our valuable farmland, but this is utter nonsense. Hemp can be grown almost anywhere, so there would be no need even to use land that farmers currently have under cultivation to supply our energy requirements. Even if hemp were to be planted on good farmland, one must remember that the seeds from this plant are an abundant food source. So, in reality, farmers would not only be growing food and medicine, but an amazing source of energy as well.

Instead of using common sense, big oil companies bore holes into the ocean floor that should never have been drilled, while other energy interests build nuclear power plants in earthquake zones. No rational person who knows the dangers would even consider such lethal folly. People in general do not know much about nuclear energy but, in reality, they have harnessed the atom to simply boil water. With all the other safe alternatives that could perform this task, what right did they have to use energy sources that can cause such mass devastation?

Such seemingly intentional destructive behavior goes along with the reptilian way of thinking many of those who are in control tend to exhibit. They show no compassion for life in general and no feeling of remorse for the harm they are causing. Everywhere you look, there are those who are working in league with the power elite to keep us suffering and enslaved. The way they are going about it proves just how sick their minds have become and in truth, they are all behaving like little more than psychopaths. If we are not the ones who must put a stop to the agenda of these evil creatures, then who is?

If we ever start behaving in a rational way, as humans should, we could have a hemp-based economy in a very short time. When this comes to pass, we can produce food, medicine, energy, textiles and just about anything else you can imagine at a very low cost. Over 50,000 different things can be manufactured from what this plant can provide and its uses are almost limitless. What can be manufactured from petroleum, which is poisoning our earth at an alarming rate, can also be produced from hemp at much less cost in a sustainable earth friendly harmless manner.

There is no question great damage has been done to our planet and all forms of life it supports by a very unscrupulous group of individuals. Unfortunately, in the past, our species has developed a well-deserved reputation for being a little slow to react, even when it comes to saving ourselves. Still, where there is hemp, there will always be hope. If we so desire, it's within our power to give ourselves and this earth a new lease on life.

Even the horrible danger to the health of us all, which is being caused by the radiation emanating from Japan and elsewhere can be greatly reduced. Properly produced oil from the hemp plant can undo damage from exposure to radiation, so this is just one more reason that we should all be ingesting this substance. Years ago, I read a report that claimed insects like flower beetles and cockroaches are the only survivors from the effects of radiation after a nuclear accident or the detonation of a nuclear device. From what the report stated, it seems that these creatures have high levels of melatonin, which researchers thought could explain why this is possible.

Since consuming the essential oil from the hemp plant causes our pineal gland to produce vast amounts of melatonin. I think it would only be sensible for us all to be ingesting this oil to protect ourselves and our loved ones. Not only would this be of great benefit in preventing radiation damage, it would also allow us to stop using all these chemicals and poisons provided by our medical systems. Wouldn't it be a good feeling for many of us to no longer have to worry so much about paying through the nose for overpriced healthcare insurance? When, indeed, very often, it is really of little or no benefit anyway?

Now we can truly envision a better world and all that really has to be done for this to come about is for us to create a shift in public awareness. While this is occurring, I expect to see the system we all know and detest devour itself from within. By all appearances that is exactly what is currently taking place. It only stands to reason that not all those who are employed in government-controlled positions of public trust are as naïve as the people who have been in control would like. Sooner or later, individuals who do have a conscience will rebel against those who are causing mankind so much grief. The ruthless forces that have been controlling our governments and therefore our lives will soon realize they are no longer standing in the shadows. When this occurs, they may not feel so secure in continuing their practices.

Even if you are filthy rich, it would not be a good feeling to go through life knowing that at any time someone could seek retribution against you in a violent manner. Employees of the wealthy and those who work for the system have families themselves. They too have loved ones who have suffered harm at the hands of the so-called power elite. How will someone who is working for the system or those who control it behave after finding out that the very system and people they work for are nothing more than criminals of the first order? Once they were aware of the fact that those who have been employing them are responsible for holding back a natural treatment, which could have eased the suffering of their own family members, or may even have saved their lives, would it be unrealistic to think that some might try to see that the activities of those who employ them are brought to a halt?

I am not saying everyone would be seeking retribution in a violent way towards those who employ them, but no doubt there could be some who will. If this were to happen, many would applaud their actions but let us hope this does not occur. Just working quietly within the system and undermining their efforts to maintain control would do much to make the rich and powerful begin to feel a bit uneasy. Given the situation those in powerful positions have now put themselves, I think it would be only sensible for them to clean up their act before it's too late. If I were in their place, no time would be wasted; I would endeavor to make things right with the public as quickly as possible to avoid repercussions.

We must all evolve to a higher level of awareness if we are to avoid destruction at the hands of our own species. Those in powerful positions who resist what must take place in the end will find they are only making matters worse for themselves. Indeed, such behavior could even cause violence to be directed towards them and their families, should they persist in their abnormal way of thinking. The greater good of all life forms on this planet must be the goal of us all, rich or poor, if we are truly serious about rebuilding this earth into the Eden it once was.

If we are to succeed, there's no time to waste. Hemp must be planted everywhere possible to offset the coming shortages we are facing in the food, medicine, and energy sectors etc. Certainly, medicine and energy are very important but our food supply should also be of great concern. By all accounts, it seems our old friend the honey bee is fast becoming extinct and one of the major causes of this appears to be connected to our use of microwave technology. If this occurs, it will have a devastating effect on our food supply because these tiny creatures will no longer be available to pollinate our crops and this would be a catastrophe. Luckily for us, the hemp plant does not require honey bees or other insects to ensure pollination. All that is required is a light breeze to accomplish the task.

If hemp were grown freely, the seeds from this plant could remove the threat of starvation in the future and that would be of great benefit to our species. Since hemp seeds are so nutritious and plentiful, it is our only option if a great deal of suffering is to be avoided. The faster this is accomplished, the more quickly we can establish an abundant food supply that will eliminate the danger of large segments of the earth's population from going hungry. In the past, it seems change has always come with a great deal of bloodshed and hardship that, in far too many cases, could have been avoided.

At this stage of our evolution, is it not time for rational thinking to prevail? This beautiful planet we call home is being destroyed by power-hungry individuals who manipulate our economies to their best advantage. The sheer greed and lack of concern for this earth and our wellbeing, exhibited by those who are the wealthiest among us, speaks volumes as to why we must bring an end to the dark days of their domination.

I know many will find what I'm saying in this book to be inconceivable, but the facts speak for themselves. If given the opportunity, I would like to confront the richest and most powerful individuals who are now in control with a few simple questions. A gathering such as the Bilderberg meetings they seem to enjoy taking part in would be an ideal setting. I would like them to tell me in a truthful way what benefits their manipulation in both the past and present have brought our civilization. In their mad rush to make profits for both themselves and their investors, was the harm they were causing to this planet and the life upon it, even considered? If indeed it was, how could they possibly rationalize their behavior?

The mega-rich have access to the greatest minds in all fields to advise them. They have unlimited power and wealth, so what more could they possibly need to make the right choices? To the rich, money and power seems to be much like a drug they have become badly addicted to, but all addictions can be broken when hemp oil comes on the scene. They must stop causing this needless harm to our species and planet, not to mention the other creatures that also inhabit this earth, and begin to do things in a sensible way. If the rich and powerful are willing to work with us, then I believe this transition could be accomplished quite easily and I only hope that they have the common sense to do so.

Recently, I have received reports from back home that Doug Shatford, the Crown prosecutor who tampered with the jury during my trial was again caught doing the same thing in another case. The case concerned a man from Amherst who was producing and supplying the oil to patients, much the same as I had been doing in the past. From what I have been told, it appears Mr. Shatford again felt compelled to tilt the scales of justice in his favor. After it was discovered that Shatford had tampered with the jury and police officers had lied on the stand, the case was dismissed. I might not know too much about legal issues, but shouldn't Mr. Shatford have been disbarred from the practice of law and then be sent to prison for his actions? If you or I had done the same, I am sure we would be thrown in jail for a very long time, but it appears that lawyers do not receive such harsh penalties.

In addition, behavior such as he exhibited should cause all the cases Mr. Shatford has taken part in to be brought into question. I have no idea how many times this man has done the same to others, but after being caught twice, I think that someone should have brought, his criminal career to an end. On top of all this, why did the officers who lied on the stand not lose their jobs and face jail terms since perjury is supposed to be a very serious offence? How can the Canadian people or citizens of other nations ever expect to find justice in their legal systems, when it is apparently being run by nothing more than criminals who are serving the agenda of the rich and powerful, instead of protecting the rights of those they are supposed to serve? What our current legal systems choose to call justice could better be described as tyranny, so let's show them that we have had enough of their way of doing things.

A short time ago, I was talking to my girlfriend Leah and she told me the authorities in Canada are now stating that hemp is responsible for a large portion of the car accidents which occur. It appears that they forgot about the University of Toronto study, which was performed in 1999, that tells us the safety hazards of smoking hemp and driving are highly overrated. These findings were published in Health Effects of Cannabis, a publication of Toronto's Center for Addiction and Mental Health. It seems the Canadian government are getting ready to set the stage to levy harsh penalties and fines on Canadians who are in reality doing nothing wrong. It truly makes one wonder when those in control will ever come to their senses about this plant's effects and sadly the same agenda is being pushed in some other countries as well. Statements like this that are released by our trusted public officials are highly inaccurate and they are only designed to deceive the general public into thinking that hemp presents a menace.

Now let's look into this subject rationally. We have always been told that it is the psychoactive effects of hemp that present a danger. But one of the most psychoactive substances on Earth is caffeine, which most of us consume in coffee and other refreshments. We tend to look at coffee and soft drinks etc. as being more or less benign, but that is far from the truth. If you ingest coffee, especially some of the stronger varieties, you can definitely see its effects after only a couple of cups and if too much is consumed rapidly, it can actually even bring about your death.

If this is truly the case and psychoactive substances really do present such a danger, shouldn't our governments deny all those who consume such things from the right to drive their cars on our highways? If this were done, it would certainly be a great way to deal with their imaginary energy crisis, for then there would be practically no one on our roads. What they are saying is just more of the propaganda that is used to convince those who are ignorant about the subject that the use of the cannabis hemp plant must be denied and the plant itself should be completely eradicated. I'm sure what you have read in this book has explained why this is being done, so I see no need for further explanations.

In reality, those who have little or no experience with the effects of smoking hemp usually tend to drive somewhat differently, until they become accustomed to its use. Such people are usually quite easy to spot on our highways because they tend to drive much more slowly and carefully than the rest of us. Although driving slowly would certainly cause much less damage if an accident were to occur, I think people who are not used to smoking hemp should avoid driving until they are familiar with its effects and I feel the same should apply to those who are using hemp oil as a medication. Truly, it can only be said that highways of today are very dangerous and the effects of many pharmaceuticals and other substances such as alcohol that are in widespread use only add to the danger.

Years ago, the medical system supplied Tylenol 3 to my father and he became badly addicted to their use for quite some time. Before starting this medication, Dad had always been an excellent driver; then, after taking this substance, he appeared to be in another world and I can only say his driving skills were greatly diminished. This all took place before I knew what hemp medicines could do and I must admit that even I was afraid to be in a vehicle he was driving. Of course, there is no law against what he was doing and Dad used to drive around with his pills openly on display in his car. Now ask yourself how many others on our roads are doing the same, and since people like this are badly impaired, what are they doing on our highways? Even many police officers are taking substances that cause such effects and these are the same people who want to take our driver's licenses away, because those who use hemp have it in their systems.

It seems to me that what has been going on defies all forms of common sense and should come to an end. I really have no fear of meeting other drivers who have been using hemp on our roads. But I think we are all in peril when we encounter those who have ingested pharmaceutical opiates and other substances. If we do indeed want to make our roads safe, it's just about time our governments recognized where the real danger lays and I don't think it could be said to be the use of cannabis hemp.

In late August 2011, the time I was allowed to spend in the EU again ran out. Jindrich and I were invited to Costa Rica in the hope that we could legally get something underway to produce this medicine. Unfortunately, the information we had been given proved to be false and the support that was promised never materialized. Costa Rica proved to be a dead end street, but at least we were able to spend a couple of days with a supporter who lived there named Dale Scott. Dale had retired to Costa Rica a few years ago and is now living in the Central Valley with his lovely Costa Rican wife Ileana. We could only spend a short time with them, but we really enjoyed it and hope to return soon for another visit. It is people like Dale, who make our mission well worthwhile and I have to say meeting both Dale and his wife was the highlight of our stay in Costa Rica.

A few months earlier, Tomas Harner, who had been in Honduras for 24 years, contacted me about coming there. Given the fact we had little money and no place to go, he seemed to offer a solution to our dilemma, so after two weeks in Costa Rica we boarded a bus and traveled to Honduras. I can only say I'm glad we did, because Honduras provided the peace and serenity that has allowed me to finish this book.

Tomas, also known as the Patucawarrior on the Internet, is a big believer in the old ways of natural farming and when you throw hemp into the mix, it fits like a glove. Hemp has been an important crop to farmers everywhere for thousands of years and is historically one of the best food sources to feed livestock. Given the fact that Tomas is involved in raising pigs for market it goes without saying, he would be very interested in seeing this plant made legal again. To farmers everywhere, feed for their livestock is an important issue and once farmers again have the right to grow hemp freely, this burden can be greatly reduced. Not to mention the fact that they could easily produce their own medicine to keep their animals healthy.

Honduras does have a reputation as being a dangerous place to be. But Olancho, the section of this country we visited, has proven to be more or less peaceful. I have found the people here to be very friendly and most live the same rural lifestyle I led back in Canada. These people are still very connected to the land and their neighbors which shows in the way they behave towards one another. Honduras and other countries in this region have a wonderful climate for growing hemp. Once these countries can rid themselves of the foreign control that has stifled their progress, many things will then change for the better.

At present, it's 2012 and with all the information that is currently out there on this subject, I find it hard to believe that more has not been done to address this situation. Do governments and their masters, the power elite, actually believe they can go on with business as usual? How long do they think humanity is going to sit still and allow this slaughter to continue? If our fathers and forefathers who fought and died for freedom were aware of the atrocities being committed, such as we are, they would never have allowed this to take place, so why are we?

There will be some who will read this book and think it was written by someone who does not have their facts straight. I more than anyone else wish this were so, but who can deny what I have been saying isn't true? It can only be said that our world is on the brink of some very hard times if something is not done. In the near future, our species and many others may soon face extinction if mankind does not take control of their own destiny. The process of change must start with people being given back the right to freely grow and use the cannabis hemp plant in whatever way they choose. This simple plant could provide for the essentials we need to exist and put a stop to the damage our lifestyles are causing. Additionally, growing this plant would detoxify the soil it is planted in, which would be of great benefit to the planet and all the creatures that dwell upon it.

I look at the oil produced from strong medicinal strains as an oil of redemption. Not only can the use of this oil redeem our health and protect us, it will also allow mankind to think in a more sensible way. Then perhaps we would not be so self-destructive and we could all look at what goes on around us more rationally. Gaining the freedom to use this precious resource properly once more will bring about the beginning of a new age in both the way we think and live.

In addition, many things that have been hidden from us, which could make our lives much better, will be exposed. Those who have been in control have gone out of their way to keep the public in the dark about subjects, which could be of great benefit to both the human race and our planet. In the future, it's more than possible that we could all have access to such things as free energy. One of the greatest scientific minds in history, Nicola Tesla, was certainly having thoughts of this nature more than a hundred years ago. If big-money interests like J.P. Morgan and the Rothschild's had not put a halt to his activities by withdrawing their backing, we would have had much cheaper or even free energy and much more at our disposal decades ago. But don't despair, things like cold fusion and other less talked about subjects concerning the production of energy are showing great promise. Once we break free of this petroleum-based economy, we can begin to use these earth-friendly technologies properly and in conjunction with ethanol produced from hemp and other sources, we will be able to solve the looming energy crisis.

I firmly believe that in a few short years we will no longer even recognize the world in which we currently exist. The very thought that we once allowed ourselves to be manipulated in this manner will become repugnant to us. In the future, common sense and knowledge will prevail; there will no longer be a place for evil agendas and manipulation. Then we can finally have the better world, for which we have all been searching.

A man I mentioned earlier in this book, Jack Layton, leader of the NDP political party in Canada, recently died of prostate cancer at the age of 61. I had contacted Mr. Layton in 2003 about what this medication could do for those who were suffering from cancer and other conditions. Eight years later, Mr. Layton died from one of the very diseases I told him how to cure. Over the years, I have supplied this oil to a great number of patients who were suffering from prostate cancer. To the best of my knowledge, all who followed my instructions and took the oil properly survived. It seems individuals such as Mr. Layton are suffering from some form of mental block, which does not allow them to think in a sensible way about this subject. As Mr. Layton just proved, lacking the ability to confront the truth can cost you your life. I wonder, in the end, how many of those who have stood in the way of this medicine's progress will do the same? They have held back the use of this medicine, and many would say they deserve no better for the suffering they have caused. I have spent years waiting for Mr. Layton and many others in government circles to do something to help the citizens of Canada who have serious health issues, but to date they have done nothing.

No doubt, those who represent us are responsible but how can we condemn them, when they too suffer the same horrible treatments from the medical system that we do? Being misguided is not a crime, but when the decisions these individuals make affect the health and wellbeing of everyone in the country, they should investigate claims such as mine to see if they are in fact true and at least try to do their jobs properly. This is the role those who represent us should be playing to protect the health of us all and the wellbeing of themselves, their families, and friends. Perhaps, in the near future, the Canadian people will have a government that represents them honestly and when that occurs, I am sure things will be much improved.

Even if what I have done does expose the obvious flaw many have with their reasoning abilities, a good number of individuals will still try to reject the truth. For those who may have any lingering doubts that governments and researchers knew the truth about the medicinal value of this plant decades ago, please investigate the information available at www.lynnicewedewer.com. Lynnice Wedewer is a PhD who calls herself a Professional Cancer Survivor, since she has dealt with cancer many times from the 1970s onwards. When you go over the information she has provided regarding what has kept her alive, it is more than clear governments and researchers have been well aware of the medicinal virtues of this plant for a very long time.

Significant numbers of people think of themselves as being quite intelligent. Therefore, to them it would seem impossible that any system could control their thinking and reasoning. Even though the truth is all around them, many will have a very hard time understanding and getting over the fact that we have all been deceived. If we were really as smart as we think we are, would this world be in the shape it is in today? My guess is it would not and I think anyone with common sense would agree. I hope in the future most people will make it their business to find out the truth for themselves. I think, after they do so, it will be obvious that yes, our lives have been controlled and we have never lived in freedom and nor do most even understand the concept.

In countries like the US and Canada, we have all been living with the illusion that we have freedom and democracy, but what we have endured is far from the real thing. The only freedom and justice you will ever find is under the old common law system, which is not practiced in courtrooms of today. As for democracy, the founding fathers of the United States had little use for the concept and considered it to be the worst form of government. America was founded as a constitutional republic not a democracy and under the constitution, citizens have many more rights than those living in a so-called democracy. The late great Aaron Russo explains the difference on a short video that is available on Youtube and I think everyone should listen to what he has to say on the subject. Just go to Youtube and punch in Aaron Russo explains America is not a democracy, which was taken from an interview with Alex Jones called Reflections and Warnings. After listening to what Mr. Russo is exposing, the public should have a much better understanding of how we have all been duped into using the term democracy. If America had simply followed their own constitution, it now would truly be the greatest country in the world. But through manipulation on the part of individuals who support the New World Order, this document has been ignored. As a consequence, today the United States of America can only be considered to be a fascist police state where citizens have nothing more than the right to do as they are told.

The old saying is, "If you want freedom, you have to fight for it every day." In reality, the biggest dangers we face are not from terrorists, but from our own governments themselves. Judging by the state our world is in, it seems we have all been somewhat remiss in our duties to protect our own freedom. If by chance we can finally get it right this time, mankind may still have a bright future. It's time for us all to re-examine everything we have ever been told and decide for ourselves if it is indeed true. We cannot begin to build a better world without a solid foundation. Only truth and knowledge will provide a firm footing from which we can all begin to understand what it means to be human again. We can then move forward and with a little hard work, this earth can become the Utopia it was meant to be. To date, we have been a dismal failure as a species but that's no reason why we should allow it to remain this way. We are the human race and we shall overcome but, in the future, we must all guard against the mistakes of the past.

My vision of times to come involves all people working together for the greater good. It makes no difference what country you are from or what religion you choose to follow. We have to lose all this hate; then we can begin to work together in a meaningful way. Do we really want our children to grow up and have to fight needless wars? I don't know about you, but this doesn't fit into the scheme of things I have in mind. At present, we truly have a golden opportunity to make things right and it is indeed the duty of us all to do so.

There may be those who will say I am out to get even with people and organizations that were named in this book. This is really not the case, but nonetheless I was very disturbed by the action's of those involved and the misguided institutions they represent. Everything I have stated in this book is based in fact and it is all on public record. I simply felt the public had to know the truth and that they deserve the right to know the names and professions of those who are causing such suffering.

I feel the individuals who were named in this book are no better or no worse than millions of their other counterparts worldwide. My goal was simply to make the public and all those who work in these professions aware of the harm they are causing and to show them that indeed there is a better way. The profit-making policies and thinking of those with vast power can, and indeed does, affect the lives and wellbeing of us all. Now that the lies and deceptions, which were forced upon us have been exposed, there is no longer any reason we should not stand up for our rights and take back what is rightfully ours.

Many seem to think I have spent the last two and a half years dodging the police, while I remained in hiding. This is not the situation at all. There has never been an international arrest warrant issued for my apprehension and, to the best of my knowledge, I am quite free to travel to most countries except the U.S. I have never kept my whereabouts a secret. How could I, given the fact that I am always doing interviews and putting on seminars? I think you would have to agree that if I am hiding out, I'm doing it in a rather strange way.

Again, you have to ask yourself the question, "Are these the actions of a criminal?" If I truly had done something wrong, would I not try to keep my location a secret? When you enter a foreign country, your passport is checked and it is recorded, and many passports contain electronic chips, so your whereabouts can be traced. Under these circumstances, any government would have little trouble finding my location. At any time, the Canadian government could have tried to have me extradited back to Canada. This did not occur and I have never been pursued by the police in any country to which I have traveled. This tells me the authorities back in Canada don't know what to do in regard's to my case. Even if I were brought back to my homeland, would they dare put me on trial?

The world may soon find out just how far the political corruption will go in Canada, because once this book generates enough money, I might return to Canada for a short time. I have not seen my mother since 2009 and she is now eighty years old and not in the best of health, so I feel that I should at least go back for a visit. What the authorities have done to me since I dared to speak out has caused my mother a great deal of distress and she thinks if I return that I could be thrown into prison. After all that has taken place I do not believe it would be in the government's best interests to try to give me any further problems.

If the Prime Minister of Canada chooses to send his evil minions to persecute me again, I expect that for the government of Canada it would become little more than a very embarrassing public spectacle. In fact, if this were to take place they would find that I am not the same man they felt so free to toy with in the past. Now that this book has been published, the truth is laid bare for all to see. If they did indeed try to give me further problems, I would have nothing to say to them; if they are in need of a statement from me, they can buy this book. I would probably not even try to defend myself against the charges the RCMP intend to lay because I think what they are trying to do is just too ridiculous to even warrant my participation.

As yet, I have not decided when I will return home but it will not take place until my mother and others are at ease with me doing so. A few days ago, I was talking to my son and he stated, if anything, the behavior of the authorities in Canada towards this issue had become even worse since I have departed. If this is so, then perhaps I should wait a little while longer until the public have had time to absorb what is in this book. The speed with which this information is traveling should awaken the Canadian government to the fact that what they have been doing is now public knowledge everywhere. If I was in their position, I would waste no time in apologizing to the Canadian public for their actions in the past and I believe a complete change of attitude concerning the hemp plant is in order.

Even if this does take place, it's unlikely I would remain in Canada for very long, all I have in mind is to visit for a short time, then be on my way again. What has transpired there in the past has left a very bitter taste in my mouth and, in reality, Canada does not have the growing climate I am looking for anyway. At present, countries like Israel have huge hemp projects underway and I have talked to commercial growers there who are licensed to produce over a million plants each for medicinal use. With all that is happening elsewhere, I think my time would be better spent in one of these countries, since it seems that I am at the center of all this and in the near future it might allow me to carry on with my research.

According to the Canadian government, I am a criminal, and now, thanks to them, I have a record as being such. If I am to be labeled a criminal for easing suffering and saving lives, I wear the badge proudly. I will never ask to have my record erased, those who committed the real crimes were the ones who gave it to me, and now they can live with what they have done. Having such a record would not interfere too much with my plans anyway, since, in a short time, foreign governments and everyone else will know why I was given this status.

As yet, I am still looking for a country to call home but once the truth is known, I expect there will be quite a few nations that would welcome my presence. If you are a Canadian citizen, you are now aware of what the federal and provincial governments have been conspiring to do against both you and your loved ones. I have been fighting this corruption for a very long time and I will continue to do so no matter where I am living, but I also think it's time for the Canadian people to stand up for themselves. With everything that is currently taking place, the system's reign of terror should soon come to an end, and when this occurs, the citizens of Canada can make a brand new beginning.

Shortly after I began supplying oil, I came across some information describing what a person can expect when they try to bring something important to the attention of the authorities and the general public. The three stages one must go through are rejection, ridicule, then finally acceptance, and I have experienced all three. In the beginning, no one wanted to believe what I was saying, so for quite some time it was rejected. Then, since I persisted, I was ridiculed by many and persecuted by the legal system. Now, what I have exposed has finally become accepted and those who have stood against me are quickly fading away. This is the stage I am now at and vast numbers worldwide are beginning to recognize that indeed everything I have stated about this medicine is true.

Still it seems the Canadian government intends to continue to turn their backs on this issue and I expect they will try to do so until they have nowhere left to turn. All I can say about the actions of the Canadian government thus far is that what they are trying to do defies all forms of common sense and, in the end, I expect that there may be a heavy penalty, which they will have to pay.

Charges against Simpson Withdrawn
AMHERST – A series of drug charges against an Athol man who says he's exiled in Europe have been withdrawn.

Rickey Logan Simpson, 62, was charged with the production of cannabis marijuana, possession of cannabis marijuana for the purpose of trafficking and possession of cannabis marijuana and possession of cannabis resin following a raid of his Athol Road home in November 2009.

Simpson was in Amsterdam, Holland accepting the Freedom Fighter of the Year Award at the annual Cannabis Cup when the raid occurred and it's believe he has been in Europe since then.

Crown attorney Doug Shatford said the court approved a forfeiture application against Simpson under the Controlled Drugs and Substances Act last week. Once that occurred, he brought forward a motion to withdraw the charges against Simpson, who declared himself an exile in Europe after the 2009 raid.

"The application was made to forfeit the items that were seized in the raid and upon completion of that the decision was made to withdraw the charges," Shatford said Friday.

Under the order, Simpson forfeits cannabis marijuana and resin seized in the raid along with growing equipment, marijuana plants and seeds, syringes, three crossbows and arrows, two pellet guns - including one with scope and suspected silencer, grow op materials, video equipment, books, documents and building materials.

Shatford said one the issues facing the court was Simpson's whereabouts.

"We're really not sure where he is. We believe he is somewhere in Europe. He had been in Holland, but we're not sure if he's still there or somewhere else in Europe," Shatford said.

Withdrawing the charges would appear to clear the way for Simpson to return to Canada. Shatford is not aware of any other outstanding charges against him.

In December 2009, Simpson said via e-mail he could not return to Canada because he would be put in jail "without bail or medicine."

He said he's not afraid of jail, but could not go without his medicine. To him, returning to Canada "would be like committing suicide."

Simpson said he grew the marijuana plants, extracted the oil, and provided it free of charge. He said he has never hidden his activities from police. After he was convicted in 2007, he told the judge he would not stop.

Source: http://www.cumberlandnewsnow.com/News/Local/2012-05-14/article-2978460/Charges-against-Simpson-withdrawn/1

At first, I didn't know what to make of this and people everywhere started contacting me, saying things like I have been exonerated and that I am now free to return home. For a day or two, I did think about returning for a short stay to visit my mother, then the memory of my past experiences with their corruption brought my plans to a halt. What most who got in touch with me seemed to miss is the fact that in reality nothing has changed. The Canadian government have not altered their agenda about the use of this medicine as yet in any way, so even if I were to return, of what possible benefit could it be to the Canadian people or myself? Indeed, if I were to come back, all it would do is present them with the opportunity to use the RCMP again to try to frame me once more.

The Crown Prosecutor Doug Shatford who, in my opinion and in the opinion of many others, is guilty of nothing less than complicity in genocide himself was the one who withdrew the bogus charges that were pending against me. But all this came with the stipulation that they were to keep whatever was confiscated from my home and property and for them to do this, I think it would require my consent. I expect if I were in Canada, they would try to have me sign the paperwork that would allow them to do just that and if I did not, I would then probably be recharged. The simple truth is they had no right to raid my property again in the first place and I will never agree to allow them to keep what they have stolen. In the article, Shatford also stated that they had no idea where I was or how I could be contacted. Let me give you a hint, Mr. Shatford, as to how I can be reached. If you simply go to our website at www.phoenixtears.ca, the same as countless others have done over the last two and a half years, that may solve the big mystery for you and the corrupted legal system, of which you are a part.

All you have to do is read over the list of things which they are trying to keep and you will soon realize how ridiculous what they are doing really is. They confiscated the books I had accumulated on the medicinal use of this plant, which no one has the right to do. In addition, they also took the communications, which I received from patients that would have helped to prove what this medication is truly capable of. Then there were the weapons of mass destruction, which were discovered in my home, like my son's crossbows and my pellet guns, one of which I think was broken anyway. They even stated that a silencer was found, which they suspected I had used on my pellet rifle.

Could someone please tell me why anyone would put a silencer on a pellet gun, which makes little noise anyway and has a muzzle velocity of less than five hundred feet per second? The only way to silence the noise the spring action in a pellet gun produces would be to wrap it up in an old mattress before firing, but I expect this would make it rather difficult to point and aim. It seems that the Canadian justice system does not know the difference between weapons, which are restricted and those that are not. If ordinary pellet rifles really did present a danger, why can anyone purchase the same without a permit in local stores? What they are trying to do is truly insane and I can only assume that they threw that silencer nonsense at the public in an attempt to make me look bad. According to the article, they also intend to keep the security cameras and hemp seeds, which were stored in my home. In Canada, you can legally buy hemp seeds, so what right did they have to take mine and since when does the RCMP strip homes of their security cameras and keep them?

There is also the question of the large bond, which I had in my possession that my son has also informed me was among the missing after their last raid. Could it be that this bond really does carry some weight and they do not want me to have access to it so I can use it against them? The only thing I would agree to them keeping is the 70 pounds of compost, which they dug up from my back yard. But I think the same officers who took it should return and fill in the holes, which they left behind. In the future, when I have the funding, I intend to see that the Canadian government and all they control are brought to justice.

In reality, I think that every family who has lost a loved one to diseases, which this medication could have helped or saved, should mount a class action lawsuit against those responsible. It is impossible to put a value on the lives they have taken, but even a low estimate of one hundred thousand dollars per person should be more than enough to bring about an end to this madness. Sooner or later the public will deal with those who are responsible, but as I have stated, it would be better if this were to be accomplished without the use of violence. Our goal should be to make them openly admit what they have taken part in and demand their resignations. Considering the crimes they have committed against us all, I think it could only be said that they would be getting off easy.

I have no idea what those who are presently in authority may try to do next. Since none of them seem to have the ability to think rationally, it makes it almost impossible to even speculate. If their plan is to continue killing those who have elected them by simply doing nothing, then drastic measures may be required. In a situation like this, a line from an old song that I heard years ago which stated, "Do unto others before they do it unto you" might apply. I believe those who have been in charge are finally starting to realize the situation they are in and should now know that nothing is to be gained by resisting.

If they do not have the common sense to react properly, there is a good possibility that the public could lash out at them with more than just words and protests. When the police and military are there to protect them, those in authority seem to think they can get away with whatever they like. But, obviously, the police and military are waking up to the injustices that have been done to them and their families also. So who can they now trust to protect them from those they have been harming? Over the past few decades, fear on the public's part has allowed them to remain in control. With the attitudes of the public changing rapidly in regard to this medicine's use, I hope this same fear will be what causes those who are currently in charge to do what is right.

To those who have been following my work and all the efforts of people who are doing similar things, I wish to thank you for your support. Without your help, it would be very hard to get the attention of the public and our quest would be futile. The role we all play, no matter how small, is of the greatest importance. We are on the threshold of a new day for mankind and with your help I know we can bring this about. I have written this book to educate people about the reality of the world in which we live in the hope that we can provide all forms of life with a future. If life as we know it on this planet is to continue, we must all act together to bring this about and if we do not, our earth and everything we know and hold dear will be destroyed.

We do not always choose our destiny. Instead, quite often it is something that is thrust upon us. In my case, that is exactly what happened. I am just a very ordinary man who was put in extraordinary circumstances, but at least I had the common decency to do what was right. That is much more than I can say for many among us and what they have done in the past. At least for once in our lives, we should all strive to achieve something better. We don't all have to perform miracles but we must start using the common sense and reasoning abilities we were given to improve what is going on in this world.

Long life, good health, and happiness are something we all deserve. If we work toward that end it can now easily be obtained. Would it really be too much to ask from those with vast amounts of money and power that they should work with us to achieve a better world in which we all can dwell? I hope, for the sake of us all, it is not, for at the present time our entire future hangs in the balance. If things are done properly, the situation we are in could have a happy ending, but if not, all hell could break loose. Personally, I hope rational thinking will prevail and catastrophe can be avoided.

The bodies of all living species can only tolerate toxins in their environment to a certain degree and if they continue to build up unchecked, the result will be the demise of these creatures. We have watched other forms of life become extinct at an alarming rate, yet we ourselves seem oblivious to the danger. Why can we not seem to understand that we are a great deal more fragile than Superman, whose existence can only be threatened with Kryptonite? Through our own lack of concern and reasoning, we have allowed what can only be considered lunatics to do whatever they wished to our planet while we have passively gone along.

Now our species and many others are on the brink of extinction and if we do not rectify the situation, this will become a reality. Our whole way of life has been based on deceptions and lies, which were put in place by power hungry individuals that seem to have no understanding of right and wrong. If we respond improperly to those who have caused this with their misguided schemes to enrich themselves, we will prove ourselves to be little different than the very people who have caused this all to come about. We must cast off violence and the use of weapons against each other, then work together in peace and harmony. If, by chance, we can achieve this goal and not bring harm to those who have oppressed us, perhaps indeed one day soon we truly will become the brotherhood of man.

Rick Simpson, June 2012

P.S. Tommy Chong recently announced on CNN that he has prostate cancer, which he intends to treat with the RSO. If he were really taking oil that was produced using our methods and if he followed my instructions, I would have little concern. But from what I have learned, he only took the medicine once a day at night and it seems he is using some type of full plant extraction to treat his cancer. I would use an extraction of this nature to treat skin conditions, but I feel the resins in their purest form should be used to treat those with internal cancer. As stated in this book, our method has been proven, but processes used by others can often produce oils that are much weaker medicinally. From what I have been told, Tommy has stage 1 prostate cancer and his life is not in danger at the moment, so even a weakened form of hemp medicine might be able to heal him. Tommy was given my contact information and he is now aware of the difference, so all I can do is wish him the best of luck with his treatment.

In late June 2012, I did return to Canada for six weeks and no one from the police or legal system came near me. Just as my son had stated, things there really have gone downhill since my departure and the Canadian government seem even more intent on locking everyone up for using cannabis. Back home those I came into contact with all seemed to know that this medication really does work, but they obviously lacked the resolve as yet to do anything about it. While I was in Nova Scotia, I received a report from some supporters, stating that Tommy Chong was now 99% cancer free.

APPENDIX I

THE RICK SIMPSON PROTOCOL

Start people with minuscule doses, the size of half a grain of dry short-grained rice. Although the oil is harmless, less is better than more for those starting treatment. In the beginning take just a tiny speck of this amazing substance every eight hours, then increase your dosage every four days on a regular basis and soon your tolerance will increase. If the person says he or she did not feel its effects or that they only felt them slightly, I would consider this a good dosage for a beginner. You just want to get a little bit of the medicine in their system so they can start getting used to it.

You never know exactly how the person will respond, so proceed slowly, and increase their dosage every four days, until the patient can ingest a total of one gram every 24 hours. The best way to accomplish this is to have them take doses that equal about a third of a gram every eight hours, once they are accustomed to its use. Still, I would like to remind those who experience difficulties that their dosage can be raised more slowly, but for best results, it should be ingested as rapidly as possible.

These are the dosage instructions that I recommend, if the patient can build up their tolerance quickly enough. If this protocol is followed, many patients can work their way up to the point in three weeks that they can ingest one third of a gram every 8 hours. But on average it usually takes most patients four to five weeks before they can ingest this amount per dose, after which they can continue taking one gram a day until they are cured or their condition is brought under control. I like to supply this medication in plastic syringes, which do not have needles, instead there is just a small opening that the oil can be squeezed through. Providing the oil in this manner makes it easier for the patient to measure their doses and it stops foreign substances from contaminating the medication.

The easiest way for most to understand the amount they should be ingesting is to compare it to something like short-grained dry rice. A beginner's dose should be about half the size of one of these grains of rice or about one eighth of an inch long, this amount would be equal to about one quarter of a drop. In some cases, those with a very low tolerance may even find that this may be too much for them to handle comfortably in the beginning, so, if need be, they could start with even less. Doses of this size should be ingested three times a day, early in the morning, in mid-afternoon, and about an hour before the patient goes to bed. All a beginner has to do is squeeze the equivalent of one half grain of dry rice from the plastic syringe and that is their dose. Even though we are talking about a very small amount and it will do no harm to the patient, due to its potency, this substance must be used with respect.

After four days at this dosage, it is then doubled to doses, which equal the size of a rice grain, or doses, which are about one quarter of an inch long when squeezed from the syringe. Then, four days later, the dosage is doubled again and this continues every four days until the patient can ingest the equivalent of about sixteen grains of rice per dose. This amount equals about eight to nine drops of oil per dose, which is roughly one third of a gram.

One ml is just slightly more than one gram by weight, so if patients wish, they can use this measurement to determine their dosage, at that point, patients usually continue at this dosage until they have achieved the desired effect with their medical condition. There will be patients who will not be able to increase their dosage so rapidly but I urge them to take it as quickly as they possibly can, so the oil can relieve their suffering. In addition, there will be those who can take this medication more quickly and I have no problem with that, as long as the patient is comfortable in taking it more rapidly, it simply means they will be healed much faster. In reality, I feel that the patients should remain in their own comfort zone when it comes to the use of this medicine. But I still think that anyone with a serious condition should not play games with this substance, since if it is not taken properly it may not be able to overcome the condition it was intended to treat.

When you can get high-grade strains of indica bud to work with, the oil that is produced will be extremely sedative. This is the effect the oil will have if you have produced the real "Rick Simpson Oil" and there is little to worry about. Patients simply fall asleep and eventually they will wake up. Some may feel a little stoned in the beginning but they will be unharmed, and usually within an hour after they get up, that sleepy feeling goes away. If the oil is produced from sativa varieties of hemp, expect trouble and a long-lasting energizing sativa high. You do not want people with serious conditions like cancer to be trying to take oil with these effects and the patient will not receive the medicinal benefits a good indica can provide. Not everyone likes being high and it is not the point medicinally to become overly stoned on this substance. But in some instances when the patients' life is in danger, giving them larger doses may be the only thing that can save their life.

The point is to get the medicine into the patient three times a day. The patient can simply put it on their finger and then scrape it off on their teeth. Then, take a drink of cold water or tea and they should find it quite easy to swallow. Some strains produce an extract that does not have a pleasant taste but this is easy to deal with. Simply put the patients' dose on a small piece of bread and fold it over, then pop it into their mouth and give them a drink of water. The same can also be done with the use of bananas or other types of fruit. The idea is to get the oil into the patient as quickly as possible but I still like to see that they remain in their comfort zone.

Everyone is different and our tolerance for this medication will vary from person to person, so be sure the patient is comfortable with the amount they are ingesting. With many serious conditions, it is important for the patients to ingest this medication quickly, so they might have a better chance to survive. As I have mentioned already, even though the oil is harmless, if too much is taken, often patients do not like the experience. So work up their dosage slowly; that way they will become comfortable with its use. Still, as we like to say, aggressive illnesses should be treated aggressively, so if I had something that was life-threatening, I would ingest as much extract as I could take in the shortest time period possible.

The standard treatment to reset your body to a good state of health is 60 grams of high-quality oil ingested over a three-month period. For those who have taken chemo and radiation, it is a good idea to ingest 120 to 180 grams of the oil as soon as possible. Usually, 60 g can cure a serious cancer, but for those who have been damaged by the medical system, often more is required to prevent the cancer from returning and to undo the damage these treatments have left behind.

Once the patient is healthy again, you can drop the dosage back to one or two grams a month or as much as the patient likes to ingest; from our perspective, the more the better. Do not skip the maintenance doses, as they are important to maintain good health. A gram or two a month or a drop a day after work in the evening does not sound like much, but it should be enough to keep your body healthy.

In addition, I like patients to use other natural things like apple seeds and wheat grass in conjunction with the oil treatment. From my experience, I would also have patients eat hemp seeds, since the oil they contain is so nutritious and good for the body. I also believe patients should try to get their bodies' pH up as quickly as possible by ingesting such things as watermelon, baking soda or lemon juice etc. I feel this is of the greatest importance and doing so can give the patient a much better chance to survive. Patients should also start eating more raw fruits and vegetables and eat less meat, especially the processed varieties, which contains more toxins. I am a strong believer in the use of juicing machines and I think that large doses of vitamin C can also be of great benefit. In addition, I feel that the use of sugar should be avoided since sugar actually helps to fuel the cancers growth, so I advise patients to use natural sweeteners like raw honey instead of sugar. But, I also believe in the use of natural substances like B17 which can be taken along with the oil, and it may indeed improve their chance of survival.

APPENDIX II

THE RICK SIMPSON PROCESS OF PRODUCING HEMP OIL

I usually work with a pound or more of bud from very potent high quality indica or indica dominant sativa crosses. An ounce of good bud will usually produce 3 to 4 grams of high-grade oil and the amount of oil produced will vary from strain to strain. You are never really sure how much oil you will get until you have processed the material you are working with. On average, a pound of good bud will usually produce about 60 grams of high-grade oil and sometimes you may even get substantially more from some varieties.

Many seem to believe the oil must be amber and that you should be able to see through it. Often the oils I produced did exhibit these traits but not always. The color and texture of the oil you are producing depends a great deal on the strain, method, and solvent that you are using to produce the oil. Don't be concerned if the oil you produce happens to be darker in color, this does not mean that such an oil is not a potent medicine. Indeed some of the strongest oils I have ever produced were dark in color, but they still had the desired medicinal effects.

I think these instructions should make producing this oil quite easy for anyone, but before you start, make sure that you have everything you will need to do it properly. All one requires is the starting material, solvent, a length of wood, two plastic buckets, a few small containers with funnels and coffee filters, an electric rice cooker, a fan, a stainless steel measuring cup, a coffee warmer and syringes.

The process I am about to describe involves washing the starting material twice with a good solvent such as pure naphtha or 99% isopropyl alcohol to remove the available resin from the plant material. Naphtha has proven itself to be a very good solvent to produce the oil, it is also quite cheap to purchase when compared to the cost of other solvents. It comes in different forms and under different names but the solvent I used is called light naphtha in Canada and in Europe it is often called benzin(e). If you go to a fuel supplier, you should not have too much trouble tracking some down. Naphtha has many industrial uses, and is often used to degrease engine parts etc., so I'm sure you should have little trouble finding what you need. Just to give you an idea of its many uses, it is the same substance used to fuel Coleman lamps and stoves. But, unfortunately, rust inhibitors are added to Coleman fuel, so I do not recommend that this fuel be used to produce oil. There is also medical-grade naphtha available in many countries in the world, but it is a bit more expensive and usually harder to get and I have not found any significant difference between pure light naphtha and the medical-grade version of it.

Butane can produce oil but I do not recommend its use as a solvent to produce this medication, since it is very volatile and would require the use of expensive equipment to neutralize the danger. In addition, using butane to produce the oil does not decarboxylate the finished product, so oils produced in this manner would be less effective for medicinal use, unless the extra time is taken to decarboxylate them properly.

The only solvents that I have direct experience with so far are ether, naphtha, and 99% isopropyl alcohol. Ether is my personal favorite and it is a very effective solvent but it is expensive and can be quite hard to get. I think the use of ether is better suited for closed distilling devices, since it is very volatile and its fumes make it dangerous to work with. Both ether and naphtha are more selective solvents in nature, which means alcohol is not quite as effective as a solvent but still it does work well. Alcohol will dissolve more chlorophyll from the starting material and due to this, oils produced with alcohol will usually be more noticeably dark in color. For a solvent to be effective, it should be 100% pure and 100% pure alcohol is expensive and can be quite hard to find. Naphtha on the other hand is quite cheap to acquire and is usually not too hard to locate. Next to the use of ether, naphtha is my solvent of choice.

All these solvents including alcohol are poisonous in nature but if you follow these instructions, solvent residue in the finished oil is not a concern. After the finished product cools to room temperature, it is a thick grease-like substance rather than an oil and it is about as anti-poisonous as you can get. Even if there was a slight trace of solvent residue remaining, the oil itself would act upon it to neutralize any harmful poisonous effect. In essence, all you are doing is washing the medicinal resins off the bud material. Then, after the solvent oil mix has been filtered and the solvent has been boiled off, you are left with the resins in their most medicinal form.

For best results, the starting material must be as dry as possible. Be sure where you are working is well ventilated and there are no sparks, open flames, or red-hot elements in the area. Place the starting material in a container of good depth to prevent the oil solvent mix from splashing out during the washing process. Then, dampen the bud with the solvent being used and the bud material is then crushed using a length of wood such as a piece of 2×2. After it has been crushed, add more solvent until the material is completely immersed in the solvent. Work the bud material for about three minutes with the length of wood you used to crush it. Then slowly pour the solvent oil mix off into another clean container, leaving the starting material in the original container, so it can be washed for the second time.

Again add fresh solvent to the starting material until it is once more immersed in the solvent, and then work it for three more minutes with the length of wood you have been using. Then, pour the solvent oil mix into the same container that is holding the solvent oil mix from the first wash you did. Trying to do a third wash on the plant material produces very little oil and it would be of little or no benefit as a medicine. The first wash dissolves 70 to 80% of the available resin off the starting material; the second wash then removes whatever resin that is of benefit, which remains.

Oils produced from the first wash are the most potent medicinally but if high-grade starting material is used, oil from the second wash also has benefits. If, for some reason, you have to work with material that is not as potent as it should be, it is best to use the oil from the first wash only for internal use and then start to grow or look for starting material that is of better quality. Remember, quality is more important than quantity and the better the starting material, the better the medicine.

Use something such as clean water containers with a small opening at the top and insert funnels into the openings, then put large coffee filters in the funnels. Pour the solvent oil mix from the first and second washes into the coffee filters and allow the solvent oil mix to drain through the filters to remove any unwanted plant material. The more funnels and containers you use, the faster it will be filtered. Once the solvent oil mix has been filtered, it is now ready to have the solvent boiled off.

If you do not already own one, you can purchase an inexpensive larger rice cooker with an open top that has both high and low heat settings to boil the solvent off the oil. Make sure that the rice cooker is set up in a well-ventilated area and place a fan nearby to blow away the fumes as the solvent boils off. This will prevent the fumes from condensing and posing a danger. Rice cookers are designed not to burn the rice as it cooks. The temperature sensors that are built in will automatically switch the cooker back on the low heat setting if the temperature within the cooker begins to get too high.

When producing oil, if the temperature gets a little over 300°F (148°C), it will begin to vaporize the cannabinoids off the oil and, of course, you do not want this to occur. If a rice cooker is working properly, it will automatically come off the high heat setting at roughly 230°F (110°C), which is above the temperature where decarboxylation is said to occur and is still well below the point that THC and other cannabinoids will vaporize. This is why I strongly recommend the use of a rice cooker to those who have never produced oil before, since it eliminates any danger of harming the oil in question. Plus the resulting oil is decarboxylated, which is also important, so it can achieve its full medicinal effects.

I suggest that people should not try to use crock-pots and similar appliances to produce oil. When I first tried to produce the oil, I used a crock-pot and since I did not know how much heat these devices can generate, the oil overheated and was ruined. So I think it's only sensible that a beginner should start out by using a rice cooker and follow our instructions carefully. Doing so could save them a lot of grief and money.

A distilling device can also be used to produce this medication and reclaim the solvent that is being used. This method really does make more sense than using a rice cooker, but stills that are designed to boil off solvents safely are expensive and most people do not know how to operate one of these devices properly. If one is available, I prefer to use a still myself, but, in some countries, owning a still is against the law. If one is serious and wants to produce large amounts of oil, look into distilling and educate yourself in the proper use of this equipment.

Always make sure there are no sparks, open flames, or red-hot elements in the area while you are filling the rice cooker or boiling the solvent off because the fumes produced from solvents are very flammable and toxic. I have used this same process thousands of times and have never had a mishap, but for your own safety, please follow the instructions and make sure the area is well ventilated. I also caution you to avoid breathing in the fumes that solvents produce since they can have unpleasant effects on anyone nearby.

Make sure that the fan is running and produces enough airflow to blow away the fumes, then fill the rice cooker until it is about three quarters full. This allows room for the solvent oil mix to boil off without spilling over. Put the rice cooker on its high heat setting and begin boiling the solvent off. Never attempt to do this without the use of a fan, since the fumes could condense and if they come in contact with the heating element, it might cause a fire.

As the level in the rice cooker drops, continue to carefully add the solvent oil mix you have remaining, until you have nothing left. When the level in the rice cooker comes down for the last time and has been reduced to about two inches of solvent oil mix remaining, add about 10 to 12 drops of water to the solvent oil mix that remains. This small amount of water allows the remaining solvent to boil off the oil that remains in the cooker more readily.

When there is very little remaining in the cooker, I usually put on a pair of gloves and then pick up the cooker and begin swirling its contents. This is done with the airflow from the fan still taking the fumes away and it can speed up the finishing process slightly. In a short time, the cooker automatically kicks off its high heat setting and then goes to low heat. As the last of the solvent is being boiled off, you will hear a crackling sound from the oil that is left in the cooker and you will see quite a bit of bubbling taking place in the oil that remains. Also, you will notice what looks like a small amount of smoke or steam coming off the oil in the rice cooker, but don't be concerned, as this is mostly just steam produced from the few drops of water that you added. After the rice cooker has automatically switched to its low heat setting, I usually let it cool until it can be switched to the high heat setting again. After the cooker has automatically switched itself to the low heat setting for the second time, I then take the inner pot out of the cooker and pour its contents into a stainless steel measuring cup.

There will be a small amount of oil remaining in the pot that you will find almost impossible to get out, unless you use something like dry bread to absorb the oil, while it is still warm. Then, small amounts of this bread can be eaten as a medicine, but remember it can sometimes take an hour or more before you feel its effects. So be careful how much bread like this you consume, because even a very small amount may put you to sleep for quite a few hours just the same as the raw oil will do itself. Another good way to clean up whatever oil remains in the pot is to wash the pot out with a small amount of alcohol to produce a hemp oil tincture.

A tincture such as this can be very effective in the treatment of skin conditions and just a little can go a long way, which can save you money. Since I often like to mix oil from several strains anyway, I usually simply leave the remaining oil in the pot until next time. By mixing oils from different strains, you receive the medicinal benefits from all these different types of oil and I have found such oils to be effective in the treatment of practically everything. If you have many different varieties of good hemp at your disposal, I think mixing the oils is a good idea, but if you do not, I believe the oil from just one strain will probably satisfy your needs.

Take the oil that you poured into the stainless steel measuring cup and put it on a gentle heating device such as a coffee warmer to evaporate off whatever water remains in the oil. Quite often, it only takes a short time to evaporate the remaining water off, but also some strains produce more natural terpenes than others. These terpenes can cause the oil you now have on the coffee warmer to bubble for quite some time and it may take a while for such oils to cease this activity. When the oil on the coffee warmer has stopped bubbling and there is little or no activity visible, take the oil off the coffee warmer and allow it to cool a bit. Another way to finish the oil without the use of a coffee warmer is to put the oil in an oven set at 120°C for about an hour. Both of these methods will decarboxylate the finished oil and solvent residue should not be an issue.

Then, using plastic applicators or syringes with no needles that are available in your local drug store, use the plunger to slowly draw the warm oil up into the syringes and allow it to cool. In a short time, the resin will become a thick grease-like substance.

Sometimes the resin is so thick that it can be hard to force it out of the syringes when cooled. If such a thing happens, simply put the syringe in a cup of hot water, then in a short time you will be able to squeeze your dosage out more easily. Sometimes a patient will force out too much oil, but if this happens, just pull back on the plunger of the syringe and the excess oil can usually be drawn back into the syringe without too much difficulty.

On average, a dry pound of material will require about 2 gallons (8-9 liters) of solvent to do the two washes that are required. If you plan to produce the oil from more or less starting material, simply do the math to determine roughly how much solvent you will require. From start to finish, it usually takes three to four hours to accomplish the whole process, and then the medicine is sitting there ready to be used.

It should also be mentioned that this oil has an extremely long shelf life. But for long-term storage, I would put it in a dark bottle with a tight lid or a stainless steel container. If kept in a cool dark place when stored, it can maintain its medicinal potency for years.

At first, it may seem daunting for some to try to produce their own medicine but in reality, this process is extremely simple. All you have to do is carefully follow the instructions and after you produce this medication a couple of times, you will find that it is not much harder to make than a cup of coffee. Once you have produced your own medication, it takes all the mystery out of medicine and you no longer have to rely on doctors in most cases, for now you have become your own doctor.

Have you found any other ways of making the oil?
There are many ways to produce the oil and I do not claim that my method is necessarily the best, but to my knowledge it is the only one that has proven successful in thousands of cases.

Indeed the method that we have shown the world would be considered crude at best, but a very pure form of this medication can be produced in this manner. My intention was to present a method of producing the oil with equipment that is readily available, so if need be almost everyone could produce their own medicine in a simple manner.

Up until I was raided in 2005, I had used distilling processes to produce the medicine and reclaim the solvents. This method is much less dangerous and is more 'earth-friendly', since the solvent is not wasted. But the police confiscated my equipment, which forced me to start using rice cookers to accomplish the task.

What other forms of extraction can be used then?
Again, there are a number of extraction methods and I do not profess to be an expert in such things. The problem with scientific methods like noble gas extractions etc. is that most people lack the equipment and knowledge to perform such extractions. That is why we showed the public the simplest possible way to produce this medication themselves.

There are also cold-water extraction methods that can be used to extract the resins. I have only tried to do this type of extraction a couple of times and the results were not as good as expected. Still, I know of people who say that they have produced high quality oil in this manner. Obviously, cold water cannot catch fire or explode, so cold-water extraction methods might certainly be an option, but one must make sure that the oil is decarboxylated before it is given to the patient.

What is decarboxylation?
Decarboxylation occurs when the molecules within the oil have been rotated to the delta 9 position with the use of heat so they become more medicinally active. The temperature at which this occurs is debatable, since many reports I have viewed on the subject do not agree. By doing what I have suggested, the oil is heated to temperatures well above that at which decarboxylation is said to occur. The carboxyl group is removed, which then allows the cannabinoids to fit into the CB1 and CB2 receptors of our endocannabinoid system and allows them to pass through the blood brain barrier.

Is there a way to make the oil more potent?
There are several ways of increasing the oil's potency, but again, many of these methods require specialized equipment and knowledge that the average person does not have. In the past, I have produced such oils and I do consider them to be more powerful and

medicinal, but with the laws that are in place and the equipment that is needed, it was impossible for me to produce any amount.

Is there anything I can do when the oil I produced or purchased is not potent enough? If good starting material is used to produce the oil, this problem should not be encountered, but I'm sure there will be those who will. When treating a serious illness, only the best will do, so if the oil you have does not measure up to the task at hand, I would get some more bud material and produce it properly. With someone's life hanging in the balance, this is no time to be playing with low quality oil. If you were the one suffering, wouldn't you want the best medication possible? So please try to provide the same for others.

More information about this medicine can be found in the other book that Rick has put out: "Phoenix Tears, Rick Simpson Oil – Nature's Answer for Cancer", and it is available on Rick's website: www.phoenixtears.ca.